The Heretic's Guide to Global Finance

The Heretic's Guide to Global Finance

Hacking the Future of Money

Brett Scott

PlutoPress
www.plutobooks.com

First published 2013 by Pluto Press
345 Archway Road, London N6 5AA

www.plutobooks.com

Copyright © Brett Scott 2013

The right of Brett Scott to be identified as the author of this work has
been asserted by him in accordance with the Copyright, Designs and
Patents Act 1988.

British Library Cataloguing in Publication Data
A catalogue record for this book is available from the British Library

ISBN	978 0 7453 3351 9	Hardback
ISBN	978 0 7453 3350 2	Paperback
ISBN	978 1 8496 4879 0	PDF eBook
ISBN	978 1 8496 4881 3	Kindle eBook
ISBN	978 1 8496 4880 6	EPUB eBook

Library of Congress Cataloging in Publication Data applied for

This book is printed on paper suitable for recycling and made from fully
managed and sustained forest sources. Logging, pulping and manufacturing
processes are expected to conform to the environmental standards of the
country of origin.

10   9   8   7   6   5   4   3   2

Typeset from disk by Stanford DTP Services, Northampton, England
Simultaneously printed digitally by CPI Antony Rowe, Chippenham, UK and
Edwards Bros in the United States of America

Contents

Contents

For Horatio, Teo and Djembe
Thanks for all the food and love

Acknowledgements

Thanks to mum, dad, and my brother Craig for everything. Sorry I haven't been home for so long. Thanks to Uncle Ant and Aunt Penny for political, musical and anthropological insights. Thanks to my grans. Thanks to Charlie, Harry, James, Hawkeye and Peter. I owe you guys a year's worth of beers. Thanks to Ziv, David, Tony and my other old shipmates for great times on the high seas. Thanks to Ilana and Leo for your comments, suggestions and great conversations. Thanks to the angels who lent me money, including Matt, Petia, Clare, Louis, Dom, Kirsty, Teddie, Danni, Richard, Paul and Ed. Thanks to my friend Mr Tuffin, for guaranteeing my rent in uncertain times. Thanks to Adam Stoff at Foyles café, for the great service. Thanks to Karl, for helping me with the name for the book. Thanks to my friend Craig Bailie, and sorry for missing your wedding. Thanks to the Fellows at the Finance Innovation Lab, for friendship and ideas. Thanks to Prof. Julian Cobbing for setting the initial spark, and to Prof. Ha-Joon Chang for encouragement. Thanks to the crew at MoveYourMoney UK, Joris Luyendijk, Daniel Balint-Kurti, James Marriot, Charlie Kronick, Ian Fraser, Louise Rouse, Seb Paquet, Kyra Maya Phillips, Will Davies, Tan Copsey, Josh Ryan Collins and Eli Gothill for cool ideas and guidance. Thanks to Andy for musings on economics, and to Eve, Jess, Natasha and Chris for kitchen-table philosophy and toleration of my freeform rants. Thanks to Tom Waits and Bob Dylan for keeping me going, and to Tess Riley, Rachel Bruce, Ben Paarman, Tor Krever, Kate Tissington, Cessi Hessler, Jessi Baker, Bethan Lloyd, Lucy O'Keeffe, Miriam Burton, JP Crowe, Mutesa Sithole and Rosee Howell for great conversations. Thanks to Sue Abrahams, for helping with graphics. Thanks to the team at Pluto Press, especially David Castle, for giving me the opportunity. Thanks to my computer, for being so understanding. Thanks to all the good-hearted rogues from the markets, and finally, thanks to Hoare Capital LLP, rest in peace.

Introduction

The financial system interconnects industries, governments and individuals around the globe. It steers money to them, diverts money away from them, intermediates between transactions, redistributes risk, and creates risk. This is a book about personal empowerment in the face of that system, providing a gateway through which a single person may gain access to it, combat the power asymmetries built into it, and use it for positive, heretical, ends.

RADICALISING REFORM AND REFORMING RADICALS

At any one point, there are always two sets of debates concerning the financial system. Occupying centre stage is the mainstream debate on financial reform. It drones on in the press, with obscure discussions on the capital requirements of banks amid extensive navel-gazing about the causes of the 2008 financial crisis. Politicians, pundits and think-tanks fret over central banking policy, or the problems created by the implicit government guarantees for the banks. These may be highly important discussions, but they are alienating for many people, often merely exclusive talkshops for political elites and economic experts. They are heavily weighted towards older men, and leave many deeper assumptions about finance unchallenged.

Against this backdrop, there is the radical debate within social, environmental and economic justice circles. These include a wide variety of civil society groups, direct action groups, humanitarian NGOs, student campaigners, human rights activists, trade unions, socialist movements, environmentalists, critical academics and journalists. Strains of radical debate are heard in many marginal 'speakeasies', from seminar-room discussions on critical theory, to literature found in anarcho-syndicalist squats, to informal pub conversations about 'the banks screwing the common people'. They are often strongly influenced by alternative schools of thought, such as Marxist and heterodox (non-mainstream) economics, deep ecology environmentalism, underdog identity politics, spiritual philosophies, anarchist and socialist theories, and even forms of defensive localism. Radical movements often perceive themselves as contesting *neoliberalism*, a term referring to political positions loosely based on a collection of neoclassical economic theories, favouring privatisation and deregulated global markets. Within this framework, financial intermediaries – such as banks – are targeted for financing unproductive speculation, a culture of disconnected treadmill consumerism, and corporations with atrocious environmental and labour standards.

I've always held a strong affinity for the radical debate. It's fiery and demanding, in contrast to the bland and technocratic mainstream discussions which often ignore the deeply unequal power relations within society. At many radical campaign events, the spirit is high, the ideas are exciting, and a captivating sense of community exists. The Occupy movements, for example, provided a forum for many individuals with insightful macro-level critiques of the structural flaws in our economic and social systems. The centrality of the financial sector, as a powerful repository for capital, is readily recognised by such activists. Many feel an intuitive concern that more and more aspects of society are becoming rapidly 'financialised', or dominated by the interests of financial intermediaries.

London and New York are the world's two largest financial centres, hosting a dense conglomeration of financial intermediaries. They are also two of the largest global hubs for social, environmental and economic justice movements, and for internationally focused NGOs, providing a perfect opportunity for such organisations to affect global capital movements. And yet radical access to major financial intermediaries remains very limited. This, in part, is due to radical groups being hugely underfunded, leaving them long on passion, but frequently short on technical expertise and staff. In the UK, there are an inadequate number of dedicated campaigns targeting the financial system, often consisting of only a handful of people.

Examples include the Robin Hood Tax campaign's efforts to implement a tax on financial speculation, the World Development Movement's campaign on food speculation, the Tax Justice Network's campaign on tax havens, and Platform London's campaigns against fossil fuel finance. MoveYourMoneyUK promotes bank consumer boycotts and FairPensions promotes shareholder activism. Watchdogs like Global Witness, Sandbag and Finance Watch undertake various financial investigations and policy campaigns, and larger NGOs like Oxfam, ActionAid and Greenpeace have small teams focused on financial issues too.

Other financial campaign groups operate in Europe, the USA and in other major financial centres across the world. Nevertheless, while such groups have opened important channels for radical perspectives on finance to be more widely heard, they tend to be subsumed within a broader justice movement that remains very much on the outside of the financial sector. Many activists still attempt to impact financial intermediaries indirectly, utilising media outlets, celebrity champions, petitions and demonstrations to create political pressure. In technical finance matters they often remain reliant on intellectual support from scattered critical academics, many of whom provide high-level analyses rather than more nitty-gritty practical information.

Thus, when pushed, many activists struggle to articulate what the ground-level processes of financialisation entail, or what goes on within a bank. Indeed, for most people, just looking at the websites of investment banks can be confusing. Goldman Sachs touts seemingly unrelated services like 'Sales and Trading', 'Corporate Finance Advisory', and 'Asset Management'. Where does the 'bank' part even come in? How is 'investment management' different from 'investment banking'? How does a hedge fund operate? What exactly is private equity?

This knowledge deficit is entirely understandable. Looking into the system of financial intermediaries from an external position is like looking under a car's bonnet with little knowledge of mechanics. Everything might appear as a unified metallic confusion of pipes and wires and cylinders. In the heat of argument, it's easy for the passionate social justice advocate to misunderstand or misrepresent a particular financial concept.

The conservative press readily jumps on such slip-ups to write protestors off as out-of-touch utopians peddling unrealistic pipe-dreams. The impulse for change is deep though, and people are learning. There is a new world of financial activism waiting to come to life, right on the doorstep of the world's largest financial centres. This book aims to help it take shape.

WHO AM I?

I have sometimes been characterised as a left-wing activist who 'went native' in the financial sector. Labels like 'left-wing activist', though, carry multiple interpretations, so it is important to briefly clarify my background. I grew up in South Africa, in an outdoorsy and artistic family who provided me with a strong ecological outlook. My understanding of the financial system was further influenced by my studies in critical Marxist history and anthropology of development at Rhodes University in South Africa, and by my studies with the fantastic, irreverent economist Ha-Joon Chang in Cambridge.

I consider myself to be an urban deep ecologist who undertakes anthropological explorations of finance, and other aspects of economic systems, in an ongoing attempt to test various approaches to change. Such explorations included spending two years helping to start a new financial brokerage in the midst of the financial crisis, an experience which will be described in this book. It is interesting to note that this experience in mainstream finance often gets me classified as an 'ex-financial insider', now 'out' of the sector. While it is true that since 2010 I've worked on financial activism campaigns, and have become closely involved with London's alternative finance innovation community, I do not see this as being work outside the financial sector. Above all, I seek to defy the pervasive insider-outsider dichotomy that is itself a major source of power for an entrenched mainstream financial regime. My aim is to help people reclaim a sense of broader ownership of finance. I am thus keenly interested in questions of how individuals and groups can 'hack' powerful financial structures, how they can subvert the power within those structures, and how they might create positive hybrids in the process.

WHAT TO EXPECT FROM THE BOOK

A third of the book seeks to help readers explore the ground-level processes of the financial sector. The remaining two thirds explore unusual ways in which that knowledge can be used in campaigns, and how one might build alternative do-it-yourself models of finance.

It is important to make clear that I am not an academic researcher in the traditional sense, and don't spend much time reading academic literature or journal articles. This book is not presented in the form of methodically researched and documented statements. Indeed, many books that do that leave a reader's existing thought structures intact. This book is less concerned with being correct in its assessments than it is with providing useful approaches to shake up thought in productive ways.

For example, the book offers only a limited analysis of what is wrong with the financial sector. The 'what is wrong and what to do about it' structure is a very common approach – perhaps reflecting our desire for clear answers to clear problems – but seldom works. I've often been at a dinner table where someone tells me 'why the financial crisis occurred', reciting sequential narratives they've learned but do not intuitively understand. My belief is that people should seek to speak from the heart rather than from the intellect. Mechanically reciting the reasons for the financial crisis is a lot less powerful than talking about your own experience with banks and debt, and indeed, it is generally only through our own experiences that we gain an intuitive sense of the broader system. Thus, rather than providing crib-sheets on how to argue against the financial sector, the book has a distinct bias towards anthropological approaches, gonzo journalism perspectives,[1] and experiential learning techniques that encourage the reader to seek access to experience.

Many of the book's technical descriptions may thus be at odds with more academic accounts, but they have nevertheless proven useful to me in the context of immersion in the financial sector. For example, my use of mobile phone contracts to illustrate the nature of financial swaps is intended to convey an intuitive sense of derivatives, not a pedantically accurate description. There is also no systematic attempt to provide references, but if I feel a particular book captures an issue especially well, I'll reference it. Drawing extensively on my subjective personal experience, many of my examples are focused on London as a financial centre, the UK economic justice community, and the European/ UK alternative finance community. The principles though, apply far beyond this. Indeed, alongside New York, London is a global financial centre from which many other financial centres take their lead.

Definitions: Financial Activism, Subversion, Heresy and Hacking

The words 'activist' and 'campaigner' are used throughout the book to refer not only to people who explicitly label themselves as such, but also more generally to individuals who focus their energy on contesting perceived power inequalities in society. By 'power', I mean the ability to get stuff done, to feel in control, and to have a sense of freedom from constraint. In this book, the term 'financial activism' means three things:

1. Engaging in campaigns against perceived injustice in the financial system.
2. Using financial techniques and technologies as campaign tools; for example, by targeting the War and Defence industry via a financial instrument.
3. The act of building alternative models to mainstream finance. This can involve people outside the explicit activist scene, including entrepreneurs, inventors and artists.

---

1. Reporting in which the journalist deliberately seeks to place themselves within the action.

I generally refer to the target of activism as 'financial regimes'. The focal point of financial regimes are 'financial intermediaries' – commercial banks, investment banks and investment funds of various sorts. In popular discourse, such intermediaries are often called the 'financial sector', or financial institutions, or the financial industry. Financial regimes though, extend beyond these intermediaries and refer more generally to arrangements of people, laws and norms that concentrate power in such intermediaries.

In such a situation of *asymmetric power*, activists or campaigners who challenge dominant financial regimes are engaging in 'subversion'. Subversives often have minimal resources at their disposal and seek leverage points for maximum disruption. In many people's minds, a subversive might be a Che Guevara-style guerrilla fighter or a direct action activist. This book though, explores areas that are often not recognised as forms of subversive activism. For example, the alternative financial innovation community engages in a creative form of Buckminster Fuller-style[2] subversion that seeks to bypass dominant systems. Anthropological approaches are subversive in their attempt to break down the 'self vs. other' divide between financial insiders and outsiders, thereby spreading *access*.

Subversion of entrenched financial regimes, in my vision, encompasses the process of openly exploring the financial system, using financial tools in ways they're not 'supposed' to be used, and by developing alternative modes of finance that challenge mainstream assumptions. This is quite different to a view of subversion as the process of outwitting, fighting, beating, spying or destroying. Simple curiosity can be a powerful tool.

I argue that the most disconcerting figure to financial regimes is not the eloquent but marginalised fighter of economic injustice outside the structures of power. Nor is it the reformist who tinkers on the margins, making changes within the intellectual confines of the mainstream. Rather, it is a figure who has access to financial regimes while being able to bend them in *heretical*

---

2. Buckminster Fuller was an inventor and 'renaissance man' who devoted his life to designing innovative ways to solve global problems.

ways. Thomas Aquinas described heresy as 'a species of infidelity in [people], who, having professed the faith of Christ, corrupt its dogmas'. To thirteenth-century Christian regimes, rogue strands of Christian thought were deeply disturbing, often a lot more so than different religions. In our case, a heretical figure might be comfortable in the micro-level practicalities of finance, but be driven by the rebellious spirit of radical theory, and possessing a creative flair for alternatives.

The outlook which, I believe, most approximates this, is that of the hacker. The term 'hacking' is frequently presented in the public domain as a form of malicious disruption, normally involving computers.[3] I do not use the term in that sense. The Hacker Ethos is something found all around us in everyday life, incorporating a lot more than computer disruption. A 'hack' is an action that combines an act of rebellion with an act of creative re-wiring. The term is the basis of the word 'hackathon', referring to an on-the-fly challenge in which people collaborate to create something new from something old. In this sense, one can hack a door by kicking it down (rebellion) and then using it to build a table (creation). The idealised hacker combines rebellion and creation into a seamless disruptive act, using each to power the other.

The Hacker Ethos often entails using things in ways they're not supposed to be used, thereby disrupting them through creativity. Hacker-style philosophies underpin the urban free-running (Parkour) movement, which hack the conventions of moving in physical space, avoiding pavements and instead running over things they're not supposed to run over. Slam poetry hacks a traditional art form by bending its traditional rules. DIY electronics enthusiasts hack electronic appliances, rearranging the work undertaken by apparent experts. Sarcasm, satire and puns are forms of linguistic hacking, as is 'black humour' that broaches serious subjects through humour. Capoeira is a form of movement hacking, a hybrid dance-fight that is neither pure fighting nor pure dance. Street artists hack walls and public

---

3. A Danish newspaper once mistranslated an article of mine to incorrectly suggest that I advocated hacking into the computers of financial institutions.

spaces by using them as canvases. Cross-dressers hack gender codes. The Hacker Ethos is embedded in many concepts of deviance and queerness – in the general sense of not abiding by 'normal' or established divisions.

Many hacker approaches attempt to blend three categories of action:

1. Exploring: *Empathetically* getting to know the nuances of systems, and gaining access.
2. Jamming: *Rebelliously* and *mischievously* seeking out the systems' vulnerabilities and exposing them.
3. Building: *Creatively* seeking to recombine the elements of systems to create something new.

Many individuals in society might focus predominantly on one of these. Adventurers may concentrate on the first, activists on the second, and entrepreneurs on the third. A campaigner might feel bewildered by finance if they throw themselves directly into the field of jamming without having the knowledge that comes from exploration, and without the pragmatic outlook that comes from building. The same could be said for groups that focus on merely exploring – for example, academics who engage in interesting but directionless study – and merely building – for example, entrepreneurs who create an uncritical myth of their own disruptive creativity. The mark of hacking is the attempt to power each of those impulses with the energy of the others. Exploring a beautiful beach is not subversive, but exploring an abandoned building where people are not supposed to go is. The impulse to explore the latter is driven by the desire to disrupt a conventional boundary, and do something creative with it.

THE BOOK'S STRUCTURE

The book is thus split into three parts, corresponding with the hacker categories – Exploring, Jamming, Building – identified above. Each part has two chapters.

Part 1: Exploring

To many people, the financial system often appears as a 'black box'. Financial knowledge is unequally distributed and frequently perceived as inaccessible. Chapter 1 seeks to help individuals orientate themselves in relation to the system. It provides an overview of the sector, puts it in geographic context, and sketches out zones of finance that feel intuitively wrong to many people, including financialisation, excessive complexity, and unethical investment. It then sketches out exploration principles to use when approaching this system, and three habits that you can integrate into daily life that can help you connect into the financial matrix.

Chapter 2 looks under the hood at the components of the financial operating system or, more accurately, ecosystem. It is not an in-depth manual covering every element, but a primer that builds up a stylised schematic of the major players, instruments and processes. It considers the two major financial intermediaries that we personally support – commercial banks and investment funds – and then moves on to describe investment banks. Particular attention is given to the secondary markets, home to financial traders and to derivatives. The chapter then describes the hedge fund ecosystem and how it interacts with other funds such as pension funds, before considering private equity. Care is taken throughout to provide accessible examples and experiential learning activities to help the reader develop an intuitive sense for these areas.

Part 2: Jamming

My view is that the first step to deeper financial activism is to engage in various forms of 'culture-hacking' that open up information flows, and that allow one to *feel* finance. Anthropology and 'gonzo' journalism, for example, are useful tools for gaining greater access to the financial system. They subvert the traditional insider vs. outsider dynamic that is upheld by both financial professionals and by many activists, many of whom all too frequently fetishise the external barriers to accessing and impacting the sector. Financial stereotypes – such as that of free-wheeling trader cowboys recklessly shooting from the hip – actually serve the interests of entrenched financial regimes, and breaking those stereotypes down is an act of empowerment. Chapter 3 thus explores the controversial notion of 'going native' in the financial sector, while sketching out some of the cultural dynamics such an explorer might encounter and study.

Chapter 4 considers how exploration and culture-hacking in turn open up useful new strategies of contestation, and opportunities to target the financial sector directly, rather than through indirect campaigns. Intuitive knowledge about the aims and constraints of investors, for example, can be used by activists to design campaigns on the frontlines of financialisation, aimed at disrupting capital flows into tar sands or into food speculation. The chapter also discusses some highly unorthodox uses of trading – through drag-queen hedge funds – and how one might seek to demonstrate the vulnerabilities of financial regimes in the same way a computer hacker demonstrates the vulnerabilities of IT systems.

Part 3: Building

The current financial system is chronically unable to steer money in positive ways. Many campaigns focus heavily on attempting to contain the negative aspects of the sector through regulations and policies, which are often capricious. The system is stuck in stagnant patterns, just like European art was constrained to scenes of devotional iconography in the pre-Renaissance era. Reformists struggle to think beyond immediate pragmatic 'realism', and radicals often struggle to engage with innovation processes that seem steeped in mainstream assumptions. Areas like environmental markets, for example, are seen by mainstream institutions as an exciting area of acceptable innovation, as are various forms of socially responsible investment. Environmentalists, on the other hand, view environmental markets with deep suspicion, and social justice campaigners see hidden agendas as Goldman Sachs invests tiny amounts in social projects. Chapter 5 though, argues that radicals need to participate in all areas of financial innovation, in order to balance the more moderate forces of 'reformed bankers'.

We often struggle with the concept of building 'alternatives', straining our minds trying to project what that means in real terms. Chapter 6 considers how radicals might rally around a vision of artistic finance that pushes the boundaries of what is considered realistic. The chapter builds a framework for approaching financial system change, one that doesn't seek to define a specific solution from the outset, but rather focuses on establishing desirable financial design principles – such as openness and diversity – from which experiments in financial fusion can be undertaken, including decentralised crowd-funding and peer-to-peer finance models, alternative currency systems, and co-operative risk-sharing systems. Vitally important though, is to create a feedback and testing system. On the one hand this means creating networks of collaborators who can build on each other's work. On the other hand, it means setting up communities of beta-testers who – as with the original Facebook and Twitter communities – can give alternative platforms the critical mass needed to kick-start viral network effects.

Hacking the Future of Money

In the conclusion I propose that we should devote less energy to fighting the immediate problems of finance while on the back foot. Rather, we should focus on building an extensive community of confident financial heretics capable of emerging on the front foot within a few years, ready to respond to the inevitable financial crises of the future. Throughout the book there are suggestions for projects in exciting areas that are waiting to be developed – so please get stuck in. I hope you find the book useful.

Part 1
Exploring

1
Putting on Financial Goggles

In a poem in *The Lord of the Rings*, Tolkien writes, 'All that is gold does not glitter, not all those who wander are lost.' It refers to the drifting, scruffy Rangers who patrol Middle Earth, moving openly in the face of power, understanding the signs and signals of the wild, and *watching* things. Financial rangers need to sketch some basic stylised maps, and to develop some exploration principles, so let's go straight in.

A FIFTEEN-MINUTE MAP OF FINANCE

The British £5 note is inscribed with the words 'I promise to pay the bearer on demand the sum of five pounds.' Money is so culturally engrained in us that we tend to not notice how mysterious that statement is. When asked what a pound is, we might resort to a form of circular reasoning, explaining that it is worth something because other people accept it for payments. In other words, it is simply a *claim on goods and services* from other people within a certain geographic area. A Brazilian Real has little value to a French shopkeeper. These currencies form the basis of local financial systems, and thus, within the overall global financial system, there is a Russian ruble financial sub-system which can be quite different from the Indian rupee financial sub-system.

Our relationship with money leads us into a relationship with financial intermediaries – such as banks and funds – that offer us services in dealing with it. A typical middle-class individual in a Western country might have access to the following financial services:

- *Current account for bank deposits*: When she's a teenager, she opens a current account at a high street bank, depositing money that her grandparents have given her.
- *Payments services*: She uses her bank to transfer money to others with bank accounts. She pays concert organisers for concert tickets. Other people pay her for music tutorials via their banks.
- *Foreign exchange services*: She takes a gap-year and purchases Mexican pesos from her bank with British pounds.
- *Insurance*: She buys travel insurance for her trip by paying a premium to an insurance company.
- *Unsecured long-term credit*: She returns from abroad, and decides to study, obtaining a student loan to pay for the tuition. She doesn't own much, so can't pledge collateral to secure the loan.[1]
- *Unsecured short-term credit*: She starts working full time, and upgrades her account to include an overdraft facility. She also gets a credit card. Both of these are short-term loan facilities, allowing her to buy things she doesn't have immediate money for.
- *Savings and investment*: In her late 20s she has extra cash. She wishes to invest it, putting some into a mutual fund that invests in company shares. Her employer also offers her a pension plan, paying part of her salary into a pension fund.
- *Secured long-term credit*: In her early 30s she borrows money to buy a house, obtaining a mortgage loan from a bank, which is secured on the house.

This is where many younger individuals' association with the financial sector stops, give or take a few more bank accounts, loans and insurance products. The overriding impression is of a one-way relationship with bland retail branches advertising apparently great financial deals, behind which exists an opaque

---

1. Collateral is any property that is used to guarantee a loan – if you don't repay, the lender seizes the property.

world. To this day, a surprising number of people still believe their money is stored in vaults in banks, waiting to be collected. Few who deposit money in a bank think of themselves as lending the bank money. This pervasive information asymmetry is one reason why banks are able to sell the inappropriate financial products that occasionally lead to mis-selling scandals.

Our personal dealings with 'small finance', though, do provide us with a vital stepping stone to understanding high finance. A huge company uses financial intermediaries for the same things we do, only they do it on a much greater scale.

Financial Sector Meets Real Economy: The First-hand, or Primary, Markets

There is a common distinction made between the financial sector and 'the real economy'. The real economy comprises individuals and companies within industries that produce things like cars, oil, soap and guns, or that offer non-financial services like advertising and entertainment. The textbook view presents the financial sector as a neutral intermediary between such firms or individuals, acting to facilitate *investment* flows between them.

Investors are people or institutions that have built up excess money they have no immediate use for, and who are looking to put it into economic ventures in exchange for a cut of what those ventures produce over time. They include:

- Individuals with savings: Often called 'retail investors'.
- Companies with savings: Perhaps they've had a good year and have built up cash.
- Governments with savings: For example, Gulf states with large excess oil revenues.
- Institutional investors: Huge funds – such as pension funds and sovereign wealth funds – that collect and pool these savings in order to invest them on behalf of individuals, companies and governments, often by parcelling the money out to the fund management industry (which includes, for example, mutual funds, hedge funds and private equity funds).

Our society is also full of 'investment opportunities' created by individuals or institutions that need money in order to engage in production, exchange or consumption. They include, for example:

- Small businesses that need start-up capital.
- Large companies that need money to expand operations, or to ship goods abroad.
- Multinational corporations that need money to acquire a competitor.
- Governments that need money to build a high speed railway, or to fight a war.
- Individuals who need money to buy a house, or to study at university.

Investors with savings invest in such investment opportunities. If an investor exchanges money in return for an ownership claim on a venture, they are engaging in *equity investment* – for example, your friend is trying to start a design company, so you invest in it and become a co-owner. If an investor exchanges money in return for a debt claim that entitles them to interest repayments, they are engaging in *debt investment* – for example, you lend a local farmer in your village some money, thereby *indirectly* investing in their productive activities.

Much investment though, takes place via intermediaries, and this is where banks fit in. *Commercial banks*, for example, facilitate debt investment by taking money from individuals and institutions, and using that as the basis from which to extend credit to borrowers in the form of loans. Commercial banks are connected together via a central bank, which attempts to influence their debt investment activities. *Investment banks* also facilitate debt investment, but they do it by arranging for investors to lend to companies and governments via 'bonds'. Investment banks also facilitate equity investment, whereby they arrange for investors to transfer money to companies in exchange for stakes of ownership called shares. Investment banking culture is thus one of corralling investors into actively investing via bonds and shares, whereas commercial banking culture is one of providing a more passive interface between investors and investment opportunities.

A debt claim like a bond or an ownership claim like a share are financial instruments or 'securities'. They entitle me to future returns stemming from economic ventures. Future perceptions of the real economy are thus a vital element of investment. Investment is unlikely to be steered into a factory producing chocolate-coated potatoes in Afghanistan, but it may be steered into Arctic oil exploration if there is perceived to be a future demand for that. In facilitating such investment, financial intermediaries run ahead of the real economy, activating industries by guiding money into them via financial instruments, or deactivating them by redeploying money away as circumstances change.

The Second-hand, or Secondary, Markets

Once financial instruments have been created, investment bank traders and specialist brokers help to redistribute them by pushing them around in second-hand markets. Many popular images of finance – for example, those of red-faced men standing in a pit shouting or holding two phones to their head – are drawn from secondary markets. A vast amount has been written about these markets; in the end though, they are just a redistribution system for investments that have already been made. A 'structured credit trader', for example, might buy up pre-existing bonds from original investors, in order to resell them in the form of a structured package to new investors.

Risk Management ... and Risk Amplification

Investment in ventures comes with many uncertainties, or risks. Insurance companies thus offer insurance for the purposes of protecting against that risk. Investment banks, on the other hand, deal in derivatives, which are effectively bets on things like bonds, shares and commodities, and which can be used for risk management, or 'hedging'. They are, however, equally used for risk amplification and speculation, as will be discussed in Chapter 2.

Cross-cutting Services: Advisory and Auxiliary

All of the above services are underpinned by professional advisors. Investment banks, for example, have whole divisions devoted to offering advisory services for mergers and acquisitions (M&A), helping companies to buy each other or rip each other apart. Ratings agencies like Moody's provide quality assessments of financial instruments, and data providers like Bloomberg and Reuters provide raw information on market prices for such instruments. The system is underpinned by laws and regulations, calling for accountants, lawyers, regulatory advisors and back office administration staff. The system is also underpinned by a huge technological infrastructure, manned by large cadres of IT, hardware and software professionals.

That's Financial Sector 101. Now let's problematise it.

DECONSTRUCTING THE FERAL FORCE OF FINANCE

In the framework presented above, the financial sector is rooted in the existence of all the other industries and economic activities. However, the view that financial intermediaries are *merely* the grease that makes other aspects of the economy work is the view most readily embraced by apologists for the financial sector. In contrast, many outsiders to mainstream thought argue that the system is not neutral at all. Those coming from Marxist traditions, for example, may argue that financial intermediaries extract rents from the real economy and gradually usurp it via 'financialisation'. During the 2008 financial crisis it emerged that much financing had been steered into an artificial bubble with little or no connection to the real economy at all, creating credit with no corresponding creation of goods and services. Much financing goes towards other financial intermediaries rather than non-financial firms, like banks lending to hedge funds to buy bank shares.

There are many more critiques coming from heterodox economic schools, such as followers of Hyman Minsky, ecological economics, or Austrian economics. These feed into the mainstream policy battles around changes to the system of rules that underpin financial activities. The political process sets out what the system 'should do', and the web of regulation is supposed to guide financial institutions towards that politically defined vision. Policy debates are thus another area in which ordinary individuals can interact with finance, perhaps via campaigns asserting that 'the banking sector has failed us' and calling on the public to pressure MPs to support a regulatory bill. Such initiatives butt up against financial lobbyists, who push back with dire warnings about the effects of new regulations on competitiveness, liquidity (ease of undertaking financial transactions), or credit availability (ease of borrowing).

Many mainstream financial sector workers are captured by the internal pseudo-scientific discourse of finance, failing to recognise the politicised nature of apparently pure economic rationality. They frequently brush off public concerns about finance, claiming that outsiders don't understand how the system actually works. Indeed, it can be the case that outsiders to mainstream finance are often captured by their own systems of thought. They might reveal a lack of holistic perspective when they criticise the sector without being aware that their own bank deposits support it. Public reactions against the financial sector may stem from deep intuitive concerns, but frequently take the form of loosely expressed condemnations that fail to really deliver a point to a professional who doesn't perceive the sector through an outsider's eyes.

Part of the problem is that many of us are often trying to imagine global finance as one component of a broader global economy. At such levels, it appears abstract. We bend our minds trying to understand hyperbolic statements like 'trillions of dollars slosh back and forth in global currency markets every day'. In the course of working on ethical banking, food speculation, and climate change campaigns, I have run workshops attended by members of the public. Many perceived the financial sector as something 'out there', out-of-kilter with their sense of what is normal. It may appear as a complex of intangible concepts, numbers, impersonal glass buildings, and people in suits, often tinged with an atmosphere of alienating 'wrongness'. To begin to break this down requires bringing one's view of finance back down to earth. This entails:

1. Putting finance into geographical context.
2. Identifying intuitive areas of concern.
3. Connecting personally to the system.

Grounding Finance 1: Geographical Context

Global finance is more like a collection of financial city-states. Financial intermediaries based in London, New York, Frankfurt, Zurich, Tokyo, Hong Kong and Singapore steer money around the world, but remain bounded within local and regional political systems that have different regulations, tax laws and business environments. Their activities are supplemented by offshore financial centres, such as the Cayman Islands, that make money by selling access to their sovereignty to multinational firms. The system works, via interlocking geographies and subsidiaries, to facilitate the flow of money within and across national borders, into diverse economic situations that play out over time.

London is arguably the world's most important financial centre. It is a giant market for hired financial guns spread over three financial districts – Canary Wharf, Mayfair and the City of London (referring to an independent borough within central London, often called the 'Square Mile'). The physical clustering of financial firms within these districts creates economies of agglomeration, stimulating information flow and personal relationships. London straddles three global time-zones – Asia and Australia in the morning, Europe, the Middle East and Africa (EMEA) during the day, and the USA, Canada and South America during the night.

New York is the other top contender for world's most powerful financial centre, hosting a cadre of Wall Street banks like Goldman Sachs, J.P. Morgan and Morgan Stanley. Chicago is a powerful commodity trading centre, and Connecticut hosts many hedge funds. The USA and UK are sometimes portrayed as close financial relatives, specialising in red-blooded 'Anglo-Saxon capitalism' with a focus on capital markets (stock markets and bond markets), while 'continental capitalism' in Europe leans more towards traditional bank lending. The financial culture of Japan is even more conservative than Europe, and the focus of countless Western business books puzzling over its traditional norms.

Some financial centres are the historical result of a national policy, or a side-effect of other economic activities. Swiss banking, for example, came to prominence through the country's bank secrecy policies. Hong Kong and Singapore developed from trade ports into powerful financial centres for Asian clients, such as Chinese companies that raise money via them. Emerging market countries – such as India, China, Brazil, Mexico and Russia – all have important financial sectors with unique characteristics, often focused on national economic activities. The financial community in Johannesburg has a focus on the financing required by South Africa's natural resources sector.

In less wealthy countries the financial sectors are often very inward-looking and offer more basic services. Uganda, for example, has a very rudimentary stock market, with less than 20 listed companies and no electronic trading. Such countries often host networks of informal financial services that are 'invisible' – such as family members giving each other loans, and loan sharks who lend money at exorbitant interest rates. One niche area of international development efforts is financial inclusion, aimed at widening and deepening access to formal financial services. Even in a country with a very advanced financial sector, like the UK, there are still poorer adults with no bank accounts.

Grounding Finance 2: Identifying Areas of Concern

Putting intellectual reasoning aside, what is it that *intuitively* or *emotionally* concerns you about the financial system? It is important to bring these underlying concerns to the surface and explore them. In my experience, the following four concerns are particularly common:

- Financialisation: A sense that the financial system is 'taking over', becoming increasingly disconnected from real economic activity, and creating ever larger economic bubbles that inevitably burst.

- Complexity: A sense that the financial system is 'out of control'.
- Unethical investment: A sense that the financial sector is amoral, or immoral.
- The culture of finance: A sense that the financial system encourages a toxic, menacing culture within financial institutions.

The Frontiers of Financialisation

There are many academic theories about financialisation. Initially though, it's useful to think about it simply as a broad term to describe processes in which *ownability, investability* and *tradeability* are extended. Something becomes financialised by becoming ownable, followed by becoming more widely investable via financial instruments, which in turn eventually become widely tradeable. Businesses, for example, are partially financialised as soon as you can own them and lend to them. The advent of stock markets and bond markets though, offered greater access to investors with little emotional connection to particular businesses. The advent of high-frequency electronic trading – in which the same shares might be traded thousands of times a day – has in turn extended the tradability of shares on stock markets to new extremes. The tradability aspect is important, because the ability to pass something on is a psychological *disconnector* distancing people from the underlying reality of the businesses owned and invested in.

The recent financial crisis stemmed in part from the increased financialisation of mortgages. Commercial banks have long been debt investors in mortgages, but the scale of investability was extended greatly by 'securitisation', whereby unique single mortgages were combined together to form homogeneous packages of mortgages (mortgage-backed securities) that investors other than banks could invest in too, and that could also be traded in secondary markets. One area of financialisation that is covered in this book is commodity financialisation

– the ability to 'invest' long-term in the short-term prices of perishable food commodities, rather than investing in actual food production. Another area I look at is carbon markets, where private ownership rights for pollution sinks are parcelled out, opening up deep fears among environmentalists that the use of such market systems to trade such rights will disconnect people from any communal ecological responsibility.

Opacity, Complexity and Systemic Risk

The financial system seems, at least at first sight, very complex and outside of anybody's control. Mainstream debates often focus on this, perhaps because politicians wish to show they are in fact in control. One major area of concern is the opacity of the system. The huge expansion of securitisation that led to the 2008 financial crisis was enabled by the poorly understood *shadow-banking* sector – a vast network of 'special purpose vehicles' (SPVs) registered in offshore tax havens or 'secrecy jurisdictions'. The offshore financial sector actively facilitates opacity, allowing companies owned by unknown people to hold unknown assets, thereby facilitating financial crime, money laundering and tax avoidance.

The other major concern is the interconnectedness of the system. Combined with opacity, interconnectedness creates *systemic risks* that cannot be adequately understood, and that therefore cannot be controlled. Could a rogue high-frequency trading algorithm cause a systemic meltdown of global stock markets? What are the systemic consequences of one big bank going bust? What if foreign investors flood into a country, only to stampede for the door, causing currencies to collapse in value, as they did during the Asian financial crisis? This book offers some unique ways to approach such opacity and interconnectedness.

Good Old-fashioned Unethical or Damaging Investment

Every damaging industry in the world is financed by investors. A major concern of justice movements is the seeming inability of the mainstream financial sector to pay heed to the environmental and social costs of the enterprises it supports. Climate justice movements have to grapple with the dynamics of tar sands financing. Human rights advocates have to grapple with those funding chemical weapons and dictators. International development professionals need to grapple with vulture funds that prey on vulnerable countries by buying up their old debt and forcing repayment. Much of the concern is around *accountability*. For example, huge physical commodity trading companies, banks and private equity firms often operate in vulnerable countries with unstable political situations, poor environmental regulations and exploitative labour conditions. This book looks at some novel means available for investigating such activities, and at methods for disrupting investment flows into damaging projects.

Grounding Finance 3: Getting Personal

Underlying all the other concerns, there is often an implicit or explicit concern about the 'culture of finance'. In mainstream circles this may manifest itself in discussions about how to 'rebuild trust' in the financial sector, and how to 'reform the values of finance'. This deep human level of finance intermingles with other deep zones of concern, such as the *unsustainability* in the sector – the fact that it facilitates an economic system geared towards short-term profit maximisation rather than long-term societal and environmental balance – and the visceral *inequality* of the sector, exemplified by huge bonuses.

Perhaps a key difference between the mainstream and radical debates on these issues though, is the depth of concern. Many mainstream commentators, for example, worry about increasing complexity, but believe that it can be controlled by appropriate regulation. Radicals are more likely to feel that such complexity is deeply embedded in capitalist modes of production, almost like a DNA code that you cannot escape from. Indeed, for many campaigners, global finance appears as a deep feral force with enormous resources at its disposal. In the face of such a force, justice movements often struggle with a sense of powerlessness, especially as they are often dependent on unpaid internships, the generosity of squeezed donors, and sympathetic but isolated departments in universities.

It's little wonder that direct action movements such as Occupy attempt to engage in creative guerrilla tactics, perhaps imagining themselves as a type of vanguard paving the way for a populist uprising similar to the Arab Spring. Such campaigners often present themselves as 'fighting finance', 'containing finance', or 'weakening finance', in order to regain ground lost to it, to protect the commons from enclosure, and to strengthen civil society. The problem, however, is that the financial system bears no resemblance to a dictator with a face, who can be deposed from power and replaced. Barring a few prominent CEOs, the concept of a financial 'ruling class' appears abstract. I can understand how Mubarak was overthrown, but what does it even *mean* to 'bring down financial capitalism'? The imagery of revolution frequently just leaves individuals feeling confused.

A Personal Story

This was the situation I found myself in during early 2008, when I was working at a South African left-wing socio-economic policy institute. Since the early 2000s I had been guided by a deep sense that economic systems were skewed in favour of unaccountable power structures. I'd devoted much energy to researching a host of global justice issues, focusing on understanding critical political economy and environmentalist theories. In the process though, I didn't focus on the messier ground-level interactions the theories were constructed from. I could critique the World Bank, but couldn't understand a World Bank loan document. I could talk about 'global financial capital flows', but when faced with people who had practical experience in the business world, couldn't adequately explain what they were. Since I rarely spent any time with such people, however, I was seldom challenged. My beliefs felt untested, and it was this feeling of disconnection from the gritty processes of finance which led me to a controversial adventure.

I decided to throw myself into the financial jungle and explore it first-hand. I had an undergraduate degree in anthropology, and was interested in experimenting with the concept of using an anthropological outlook within an activist programme. Activist anthropology, in my conception of it, is a process of actively *buying into* something perceived to be negative, whether it be the financial sector or any other industry. It is superficially similar to the concept of 'selling out' – where an individual passively allows themselves to be drawn into a system of power – but is starkly different in the sense that it is undertaken deliberately and unapologetically. In my case, I moved to London and found work at a start-up derivatives brokerage firm in September 2008, the same month that the investment bank Lehman Brothers collapsed. I suspended my countercultural identity, and opened myself up to a foreign world in order to gain access.

A start-up company affords one unique experiences not available to juniors within the graduate programmes at major banks. My young colleagues and I were loosely guided by a gung-ho management team of ex-traders and brokers who had split off from major financial institutions to start the company. After less than three months of training, our colourful boss walked in and told us to 'get on the fucking phones!' We were attempting to specialise in three of the world's most exotic derivatives markets (inflation, property and longevity swaps), and I entered a surreal world of pitching such instruments to fund managers, traders and corporations as the financial sector descended into turmoil. In so doing, we had to compete against huge established firms with far greater resources at their disposal. Much of the time we were required to direct our own endeavours with little oversight. Many of our efforts were ultimately failures. I was ejected after almost two years as the firm slowly fell apart. It was a deeply draining experience that challenged many complacent assumptions I had previously been happy to hold, both about myself and about financial institutions. It was, however, also a very empowering experience, and one in which I developed deep emotional ties. It gave me new tools with which to begin to understand the processes at work within the system.

The Importance of Denying Experts

My experiences in mainstream finance made me aware of the need to challenge the concept of 'financial experts'. The apparent financial expert on TV maintains the appearance of being in confident control of a wide array of information, but for the most part they have a highly specialised knowledge. The expert on the current intricacies of the commodity markets, for instance, may have limited knowledge about the current dynamics of the stock market. An algorithmic trader may be very poor at analysing long-term macroeconomics. The average financial worker will not understand the deep structures of the system they work within, but collectively they give the impression that the sector 'knows itself'.

Like professionals in any industry, a key advantage financial professionals have is their anecdotal practical experience. This gives them the conviction to say casually, 'let me tell you how derivatives work'. They believe that knowledge is within their grasp, and know how to go about finding it. They also speak the *language*. When one picks up a copy of the *Financial Times* and reads 'The Eurozone spreads are widening', the words can seem entirely alien. If Latin was a language of power in medieval times, held by small cliques of priests, then financial terminology is the language of power nowadays. Textbooks using such language to present the current incarnation of the financial sector appear almost as scientific manuals, readable only to insiders. Even in its most mathematical and abstract incarnations, however, finance is just a set of techniques forged amid the changing power dynamics of human relations. Over time it has developed a jargon that alienates outsiders, consisting largely of intuitive concepts phrased in an unintuitive way – verbal complexity, not actual complexity. 'Interest rate', for example, could be rephrased as 'the price of renting money'.

Financial professionals are protected by these perceptions of finance as a hard science. Every time the term 'complex derivatives' is used in the media or elsewhere, it further reinforces and implicitly endorses the power of those who present themselves as a financial elite. You may not feel comfortable challenging them, in the way you may not feel comfortable challenging a NASA scientist on jet propulsion dynamics. This is a major barrier to people engaging with, and truly challenging, the sector. Anyone seeking to grapple with finance thus needs to suspend belief in the established dualism between those who know and those who don't.

Re-orientating Towards a Network Approach

To complement this, however, a deep personal question needs to be asked. Do you see yourself as separate from the financial system, or as a part of it? In my experience, many justice campaigners often hold four, perhaps subconscious, mental positions:

1. Perceiving the financial system to be something external to themselves.
2. Related to that, perceiving problems of the system to be signs of this external system's strength.
3. Following from that, believing that the aim of activism is to weaken the system, or constrain it.
4. In turn implying that the system will view campaigns as malicious attacks, setting up an insider vs. outsider and us vs. them dynamic.

The financial system is, though, embedded deep within our social structures – in the very words we use, the legal rights we hold, and the philosophical concepts we subscribe to. It has feedback loops and trade-offs, and unexpected reactions to attempts to alter it. A better starting point – which can later be challenged – is as follows: *Money* is, in large part, a social construct existing in peoples' minds. Our use of it supports, and thereby implicitly helps construct, financial intermediaries such as banks and pension funds. Everyone in society is thus part of the financial system, forming an interconnected network. It is however, a network that concentrates power in profoundly unsustainable ways, both socially and environmentally. The problems of finance stem from blockages of power – entrenched financial regimes – which weaken the system to the detriment of others. These stagnant regimes – exemplified in the actions of mainstream investment banks and funds – are sources of *vulnerabilities*. Such regimes appear coherent in the short-term, but threaten longer-term system resilience. Financial activists apply themselves to exploring these regimes to locate and expose vulnerabilities, thereby seeking to strengthen the financial system for the benefit of broader society.

An analogy can be drawn with the computer hacking community, and the related Open Source movement. One task by which that community defines itself is that of maintaining the openness of networked systems, so that those systems don't concentrate power. Which party best serves the internet: Creative Commons groups, which seek to hold it open, or Microsoft? The analogy with the financial system needn't hold in its entirety, but it provides a compelling way for the financial activist to think of themselves initially. When interacting with a networked system of power – and one that is embedded in our own actions – the language of hacking and network disruption is more intuitive and empowering than the linear (before vs. after) and dualistic (us vs. them) language of revolution. It encourages us to see the financial system as a series of interacting ecosystems of which we are a part, a system with design flaws at different levels. One can take part in an ongoing 'shit-stirring' adventure, akin to a financial Wiki project, in which we target stagnant financial regimes while simultaneously seeking to maintain system openness and resilience.

CONNECTING TO THE FINANCIAL MATRIX: BECOMING A HACKER

Urbex – or Urban Exploration – movements are groups of individuals who engage in seemingly random explorations of train tunnels, sewerage systems and derelict buildings. There is no 'point' to the exploration. It's open-ended, driven by a rebellious curiosity, the search for novelty, and the desire to uncover that which is not supposed to be seen.

Open-ended exploration of the financial system can have a similarly rebellious spirit. Walking calmly into an investment bank to look at the artwork in the reception area when you're not supposed to be there can feel liberating. This explorer ethic is intrinsically empowering, but it's also very useful for uncovering the nuances of systems. A computer hacker, for example, will spend hours simply looking at code, openly exploring how it's constructed, formulating and deconstructing hypotheses. The process will culminate in an ability to recognise opportunities for creative mischief, or reconstruction. As the journalist Steven Levy wrote in his book *Hackers: Heroes of the Computer Revolution* (1984): 'Hackers believe that essential lessons can be learned about the systems – about the world – from taking things apart, seeing how they work, and using this knowledge to create new and more interesting things.'

To continue the hacker analogy, we often initially think of the financial sector in a similar way to how we initially think of high-tech products such as computers – *like a black box that we interact with without knowing how it actually works*. These days, technological literacy may be taught in schools, or picked up by experimentation, and younger people often criticise their grandparents or parents for being fearful of technology. Financial literacy though, remains poor at all ages. If I were trying to encourage someone approaching any apparently complex system I would recommend five basic exploration principles:

- *Principle 1: Push away fear.* Fear of systems hampers the desire to explore them. It creates defensive preconceptions, making institutions and individuals appear aggressive and menacing, which shuts down opportunities for understanding.
- *Principle 2: Suspend preconceived beliefs.* We often interpret data within the parameters of what we're looking for. If I'm hypersensitive in looking for greed, I'm likely to find it. Such expectations hamper insight, but they're also subtly disempowering. You're in the bank lobby, and you're seeing greed everywhere, feeling *out of place*. That outlook reduces access, and with it increases the

power of the institution which appears subtly arranged to repel outsiders. Many people say 'I'm not good at maths' when asked about finance, perhaps imagining financial professionals as mathematical virtuosos in command of dark financial arts. In many areas of finance though, ordinary personal relations are far more fundamental than mathematics. The financial worker's skills are often straightforward, and their apparent personal characteristics are often projections of the people doing the observing.

- *Principle 3: Embrace the complexity.* The belief that the financial sector is incredibly complex is a pervasive preconception. While it may be well founded, it can also form a layer of protection for entrenched financial regimes. Instead of embracing the complexity, we have a tendency towards implicitly or explicitly imagining the system in the abstract as an external monolith, diminishing our belief that we can access 'it'. We may also imbue the system with agency or intent ('the system seeks to exploit'). What appear as immutable structures from afar, however, are often highly permeable structures when viewed up close. Suspending the natural impulse to unify an otherwise chaotic view of the financial system is how we discover the cracks.
- *Principle 4: Forget theories.* People often say 'I don't know anything about economics' when explaining their confusion about finance. Finance is not academia, and most people within it don't have a deep understanding of economic theory. It's a practically orientated industry, and like any other industry, it provides the raw information from which economic or other theories may be created. Overtly viewing it through the eyes of Keynes, Marx or Smith misses the point of exploration, which is to construct one's own hypotheses about the system.
- *Principle 5: Embrace the mundane.* Some people imagine that finance is boring, and switch off when hearing terms like 'balance sheet' and 'equity investment'. Finance though, like electronics, ecology and computer coding, ceases to be boring when one realises how understanding

it can give one the ability to see things that many people cannot see. It unlocks a capacity to act that far outweighs any initial dullness.

A hacker outlook inclines us towards seeing beyond face-value structures, and towards seeing the interplay between different human players with partial perspectives. It also involves examining all received wisdom or beliefs about the system. For example, even the apparently simple idea that finance has a 'function' or 'purpose' in the macro-economy can diminish our ability to view it around us. It is useful to keep in mind the acronym POSIWID – *the purpose of a system is what it does*. It was coined by cybernetic theorist Stafford Beer, who explained that 'According to the cybernetician the purpose of a system is what it does ... which makes a better starting point in seeking understanding than the familiar attributions of good intention, prejudices about expectations, moral judgment or sheer ignorance of circumstances.'[2] Theorists like Beer explicitly seek to understand circuit-like interconnections in society, rather than building pictures of standalone structures.

Let's sketch a basic model of some components of a possible financial circuit. Consider which of the sections in brackets you have the best understanding of:

(Financial intermediaries), staffed by (financial professionals), offer (financial services) to (clients in the broader economy) and to (other financial institutions), in order to (achieve certain outcomes), using (financial instruments), (financial theories), and (technology), within a (social/cultural/political/legal context), with (consequences for broader society) and (the environment), all of which we interact with via (personal relationships), (our use of money), and via the (political process).

That may seem slightly daunting, but a holistic picture of the system can gradually be built up by becoming aware of the interplay between these various components. Luckily, this can

---

2. Stafford Beer, 'What is Cybernetics?', *Kybernetes*, Vol. 31, No. 2, 2002.

be done in your spare time, by picking up the three useful habits described below.

Habit 1: Reading the Financial Papers

When I first started learning the language of finance, I used a simple yet incredibly effective technique. I began to read the *Financial Times* each day. The point is not to understand the language, but merely to let it flow over you. Within a few weeks, you will begin to recognise the terms and put them together. Within a few months, you'll notice trends, and sense the interconnections between financial players and instruments. You'll see examples of current deals, trading conditions and investor sentiment, which will take the obscure edge off more theoretical analyses.

Most stories can be categorised into a handful of areas. There are stories about people raising money from investors. There are stories about 'the markets' and current prices for financial instruments. There are stories about derivatives and their regulation, and about 'mergers and acquisitions'. More marginal stories might concern technology systems. By reading all these, you can begin to sense the basic features of different areas. See if you can categorise the stories you read within the following areas:

Broad category	More specific area
CENTRAL BANKING	The Central Bank of a country, such as the Bank of England, or the Federal Reserve
COMMERCIAL BANKING	Retail banking, for individuals and SMEs
	Corporate banking, for big companies
INVESTMENT BANKING	Primary Capital Markets, where shares and bonds are created
	Secondary Markets or 'Sales and Trading', where those, and other, financial instruments are pushed around
	Mergers and Acquisitions advice, and other forms of advisory services
PURE BROKERAGE	Interdealer brokers and other specialist brokers that intermediate among traders

INVESTMENT MANAGEMENT	*Real money funds*, including pension funds, sovereign wealth funds, insurance funds, and endowments
	Fund Management Houses (e.g. BlackRock) that offer mutual funds and other investment funds to real money funds and to individual people
	Alternative Investment Managers that offer Hedge Funds and Private Equity Funds to real money funds, and to wealthy individuals
	Wealth Management (Private banking), for uber-rich people
INSURANCE	Insurance, for individuals and companies
	Reinsurance, for insurance companies
AUXILIARY SERVICES	Investment Consulting
	Compliance, Risk Management and Operations
	Data Providers and Ratings Agencies
	Accounting and legal services
	Information Technology

Habit 2: Seeing the World in Interconnected Balance Sheets

A capitalist economy might be thought of as an expansive collection of 'assets' that are owned by people, and which are used to produce goods and services for exchange. All of these assets were financed, in the sense that someone had to exchange money to acquire them. How was your local corner store financed? Did the owner obtain a formal loan from the financial sector, or was the money an informal loan from a relative? Or did he self-finance it by saving up money? The local geography of finance can be directly experienced, breaking down inorganic, ahistorical viewpoints by helping one sense how its abstract global flows are rooted in societies, times and places. Past financial decisions are embodied in the current economic structures we see all around us. Derelict buildings signal abandonment by finance. Perhaps they were brought to life in an era when liquid money flowed lava-like into real estate, solidifying into structures that no one ended up having a demand for. They are monuments to failed investment decisions.

We can see finance on the streets. For example, perhaps we see a van used by a local builder named Seb. There are really only two ways for him to have financed that asset. He either used his own money to buy it outright, or he borrowed money. In the former case, we say the asset is financed using *equity*. In the latter case, we say the van is jointly financed between Seb and a bank using a combination of equity and debt. This principle applies, in a fractal[3] fashion, from Seb's van all the way up to a giant global corporation.

We're used to the concept of borrower vs. lender, but this dualism is often false. The relationship is either *mutualistic*, or it is *parasitic*. They are both *investors*, and they both invest in the same venture, only the debt investor (lender/creditor) does so indirectly by riding[4] on the equity investor (borrower/debtor). The key difference is legal. An equity investor technically owns an asset, and is entitled to gains that come from owning it, but a debt investor owns a contract that says they're entitled to be repaid by the equity investor with interest. In the breach of that contract they will take the equity investor to court and seize the asset, thereby 'converting' the debt claim into an equity claim. Thus, in our second scenario, Seb doesn't unconditionally own the van. He will slowly pay the bank their debt claim, to the point where they have *no claim* any more, at which point the car will no longer be financed by any debt, but will be wholly financed by his equity.

Imagine Seb is working on a house owned by the Habib family. A house is the biggest asset that the average person might co-invest in with a bank. The Habibs are the equity investors in the house, and the bank is the debt investor. If the Habibs fail to make repayments on the house, their ownership claim lapses, and the bank will become the equity investor through foreclosure proceedings.

This principle that assets need financing by either equity or debt investors can be visually expressed in a balance sheet. This shows the monetary value of an asset (shown on the left-hand *asset side*), relative to the claims against that value (shown on the right-hand *liabilities* side). The value of both sides must be

---

3. A pattern that re-occurs at different scales.
4. Hence the concept of being 'saddled by debt'.

the same: If the house is worth £250,000, there is only £250,000 worth to claim. Claims in this case include the debt claims of the bank, and the equity claims of the Habibs.[5]

Habib's House Value: £250,000	Barclays debt claim £200,000 ('Thanks for partnering with Barclays')
	Habib's equity claim £50,000 ('Any time')

A crucial difference between debt and equity claims is that the value of the debt claim remains relatively *fixed*, but the value of the equity claim *fluctuates* as the value of the house goes up and down. If a house price plummets, the bank retains the same debt claim, and the owners are left with a much smaller piece of the pie. Thus, it is generally less risky to be a debt investor than it is to be an equity investor. Insolvency occurs when the value of an asset dips below the value of the fixed claims against it. That might be the point where the bank forecloses, and tries to wrench the house away from you.

Habib's House Value: £201,000	Barclays debt claim £200,000 ('Start foreclosure proceedings')
	Habib's equity claim £1,000 ('Oh crap')

Finance is crucially underpinned, therefore, by very old philosophical and political concepts of *claims on things*, and how you obtain those claims. Most things in the world have claims against them. If you paid for this book using your own money, you have an equity claim. On a balance sheet, the asset

---

5. There can be other claims too, such as tax claims and claims from suppliers who are waiting to be paid.

side would say '*The Heretic's Guide to Global Finance*' and state how much it's worth. The liability side would say 'my equity', showing your claim, mirroring the value of the book. In the (unlikely) event that the book goes up in value in the future, you reap that gain. If it gets damaged, you'll probably not. With most 'consumption goods', the value goes down fairly rapidly: The value of a toilet roll gradually depreciates to zero. 'Investment assets', on the other hand, are supposed to maintain, or increase their value (exhibiting growth). A business is an investment asset. Imagine them as balance sheets as you walk past them.

Note though, the subtle psychological message imparted by the hard-lined balance sheets I drew above – two columns joined together, with rigid boundaries, standing up vertically. In reality, balance sheets are permeable and imprecise conduits, spread horizontally across the surface of the earth, interlocking with other balance sheets. Their hard central lines represent political interfaces, with people making claims on assets, and others making claims on those people. The money flows to the shop owner from his corner store, but where does it go from there?

Habit 3: Plugging Your Everyday Actions into Corporations

Financing a corporation is not that different to financing a house. A housing corporation, for example, is like a large-scale version of an individual owning a house. Instead of one person being the equity investor, an army of shareholders take that role. Instead of one bank providing a single mortgage, numerous banks provide huge loans, and other debt investors lend via bonds arranged by investment banks. It's the same principle, just with a lot more players and much larger sums. The assets of a corporation might be worth £10 billion, and it's likely that financial intermediaries were involved in sourcing both the debt and equity investment for those, helping to 'fill up' the right-hand side of the balance sheet with claims.

A corporation is thus an investment vehicle, jointly co-financed by debt and equity investors, and operated by professional managers on behalf of the equity investors. Put slightly differently, a corporation is a collection of income-producing assets ring-fenced under a common name, acting as a conduit by which equity investors (shareholders) and debt investors (banks, and bondholders) can obtain claims on those.

Shares are little slices of ownership. With this in my hand, I can claim ownership returns in the form of *dividends*. If four people put equal amounts of money together to buy a basil plant, there are four shares each representing a quarter of the ownership, and they all get to draw on the leaves as dividends. Chevron corporation, on the other hand, has almost two billion shares, which many thousands of investors will buy in exchange for tiny percentages of ownership in Chevron, which in turn is a conduit for ownership stakes in subsidiaries, which in turn have ownership stakes in specific assets like pipelines, oil concessions and refineries. As a shareholder, I am one of five interest groups that extract value from those productive assets: Labour contracts entitle employees and managers to a cut. Suppliers take a cut. Debt investors extract interest payments. The government extracts taxes. The rest goes to me.

It's useful to browse the annual report of your favourite global corporation. Their balance sheet represents their accountant's estimation of all the things the investment vehicle owns, and who gets to claim them. Some will be financing their assets with much higher proportions of debt than others. The amount that's financed by debt relative to the amount financed by equity creates a property known as 'leverage', representing a *power dynamic* between debt and equity investors. Debt investors use equity investors to protect themselves. Equity investors use debt investors to boost their returns. It's a potentially mutualistic relationship, but, dependent on circumstance, one party can come off better than the other. The deep politics of finance largely revolves around this interplay between debt and equity investors making claims on assets. There's an entire academic discipline called Corporate Finance devoted to how to combine these two forms of investment, while simultaneously aligning the interests of the managers of these companies – such as CEOs – with the interests of the investors.

How do we experience this in everyday life though? Every time you purchase something from a corporation, you are exchanging money for a good or service. That money is being captured by an asset on the asset side of the corporation's balance sheet, and subsequently flows to those with claims on the corporation. What fragment of my purchase of Old Spice is being captured via labour contracts to employees of its parent company Procter & Gamble? How much to suppliers of the plastic? How much is flowing via financial conduits to Procter & Gamble debt investors and equity investors? How much of those equity returns flow to the shareholder Blackrock Asset Management, and from there to my pension fund? If you begin to ask these questions, you will over time be able to perceive yourself within a system of money flowing in 'cybernetic circuits', a feedback system with no explicit beginning, or end ... other than in the extraction of natural resources.

2
Getting Technical

FINANCIAL INTERMEDIARIES:
THE HIGH PRIESTS OF FINANCIAL INSTRUMENTS

There is no intrinsic reason why I'd have to use formal financial institutions to engage in investment. For example, I could arrive with a lump sum of money in Kenya and invest it directly in an ownership stake in a local farm, thereby becoming a shareholder in the productivity of soil, earthworms, seeds and labour. My legal shareholding certificate would be a financial instrument, or security, entitling me to future returns from the farm. If I wanted a debt claim on the farm instead, I could lend money to the owners. The loan agreement would also be a financial instrument, entitling me to interest returns.

In general though, we seldom obtain financial instruments directly, because financial intermediaries insert themselves into the process. I might, for example, deposit my money in a bank, which may be lending to Kenyan farms. I may have money in a mutual fund which is putting a percentage of that into buying up Kenyan farms. I might contribute to a pension plan which allocates a small amount of its overall portfolio to a private equity fund which is buying a Kenyan farming conglomerate. Perhaps my bank is lending to that private equity fund too. In the end, I am buying up Kenyan farms (equity investing), or lending to them (debt investing), without knowing it. Financial intermediaries make the claim on those assets, and then you make the claim on the financial intermediaries.

Literature about markets focuses on the titanic banks and funds, but big finance gets most of its money from little people. It's ironic that retail investors like us are the most important constituent of the financial system, but are also the most ignored and inert, and constantly patronised by the entrenched financial establishment. In some countries, especially the USA, there are significant numbers of 'day traders' and small-scale investors encouraged by investment gurus to ignore funds or banks and to take control. Most of us though, contribute our money towards creating centralised financial beasts that battle it out with each other in the financial markets.

In this section we'll first look at two sets of intermediaries that we directly support: Commercial banks and investment funds. We'll then move on to consider investment banks, hedge funds and private equity funds.

The Old Guard: Commercial Banking

The first group of financial intermediaries we directly support are commercial banks like HSBC and Lloyds that have ATMs on street corners. They are generally split into retail banking divisions for individual people and small businesses, and corporate banking divisions for larger companies and corporations.

Commercial banks obtain money from people and institutions in the form of:

1. Deposits: People and companies depositing money into them.
2. Debt from the wholesale markets (big funds that lend them money).
3. Equity investment: People and institutions who buy shares in the bank.

That money forms a backdrop against which they extend loans, or credit, which is the right to use money for a certain amount of time.[1] The cost of buying that right is known as the interest rate: A 4% interest rate means, for example, 'I'll pay £40 to rent £1,000 for a year'. One conventional way of portraying a commercial bank is as a *buyer and seller of credit* – they 'buy credit' from depositors and institutions by paying them an

---

1. Much like a rental lease is the right to use a property for a certain amount of time.

interest rate, and 'sell credit' to borrowers by lending to them in exchange for an interest rate. They make their money off the difference: If they buy £1,000 at a 1% interest rate (£10), and sell it at 4% interest rate (£40), they take the £30 in the middle.

This conventional description, however, is somewhat misleading. A commercial bank does not lend the money you deposit *directly* to others. Rather, they work with a fractional-reserve system, lending out more than what they take in deposits. In other words, they lend cash which mostly doesn't exist in their 'vault', which is another way of saying that they create new money when they lend. Thus, if I obtain a loan of $5,000, I'll suddenly see $5,000 in my bank account, which I can theoretically draw out, but in reality only a small percentage of that $5,000 previously existed in the bank, the rest being new electronic money which never previously existed.

Many people express incredulity or shock at this idea, and monetary reformists (for example, the UK pressure group Positive Money) attack fractional-reserve banking as an unstable form of legal counterfeiting.[2] While these are very important critiques, it's also important to resist the impulse to jump to an immediate judgement. Finance is a cultural system, and so is money. Many people believe actual coins and notes are more 'real' than electronic money, but money is money if people accept it. When you accept an electronic payment from someone who has received a loan, you are expressing confidence in the overall monetary system. It's thus a system which crucially rests on social confidence: Commercial banks have to be able to convince people that they have sufficient reserves[3] of 'real' money (from the original deposits and from its equity investors), and good loans that will come due, such that they will be able to cover short-term claims against the bank. This underpins the debates on banks' 'liquidity ratios' (cash buffer) and 'capital ratios' (equity buffer) – the smaller their cash buffer and equity buffer,

---

2. A good book to read on this is J. Ryan-Collins et al., *Where Does Money Come From? A Guide to the UK Monetary and Banking System* (2011).
3. Held at an account the bank has at the Central Bank.

the more profits they can make, but at greater risk. If people suspect banks have lent in an imprudent fashion, and that they will not be able to pay depositors back, *bank runs* can occur, during which everyone tries to extract cash from the bank at once.

Retail Banking vs. Corporate Banking

When we deposit money in a bank, we are selling them short-term credit, and when we borrow from a bank, we are buying credit which is often comparatively long-term. We are seldom sure whether we are receiving or paying a fair price (interest rate). This information asymmetry plays to the banks' advantage. Retail banks are often glossy facades consisting of a marketing department that convinces people to deposit and an IT service feeding loan applications into spreadsheets for statistical assessment. There are very few actual 'bankers' who assess loans. The laminated brochures in their branches are like funnels guiding you onto various parts of their balance sheet. Current account advertisements lead you to the liabilities side (they owe you something), and car loan deals lead you their asset side (you owe them something). Many retail banks offer *insurance* services too, normally via a separate insurance subsidiary.

Corporate banks offer similar services, but they actually hire true bankers to assess loans, to build relationships with large clients, and to develop packages of bespoke services to attract them. HSBC's corporate banking division will have individual bankers who specialise in, for instance, deciding whether to lend a property company £80 million to build a new retail warehouse development on the outskirts of London. They will be guided by senior managers who set lending and risk targets for different sectors. Loans above certain sizes will be escalated up the ranks for credit and risk committees to check. Those teams theoretically keep an eye on the big picture and can shoot down deals brought to them by their corporate loan bankers if, for example, they think they have too many construction loans, or are too exposed to Asia.

Here's a simplified example of a deal:

Global commodity company Glencore wants to raise $250 million for a mining development in Angola. The Glencore financial director and treasury team approach Citibank's corporate banking division and explain the terms they'd like. The Citibank team, in this case led by a senior banker with expertise in mining, wants to lend, but they have credit restrictions per company, per region and per sector. They pass the deal by the bank's risk management teams, who give it the go-ahead. The actual job of ensuring Citibank can finance the loan is left to the Citibank treasury, which manages all the requests for money from the lending teams. They have to make sure Citibank stays within certain capital and liquidity ratios. If necessary they will enter the wholesale money market to borrow money from institutional investors, while in the background salespeople and adverts are convincing retail investors to deposit money.

The essence of commercial banks therefore, is that they engage in debt investment against the backdrop of money put into them. There are many complexities to the process that this book cannot cover in detail, but financial explorers who wish to delve deeper into their operations should consider the following four areas:

1. *Syndicated loans and project financing*: Citibank may not feel comfortable lending the whole $250 million to Glencore, but might take the lead in arranging a *syndicated loan* in which they contribute $150 million, and get Washington Mutual and Bank of America to lend $50 million each. The project will be jointly financed between three banks as debt investors and Glencore as the equity investor. In *project financing* deals – often used in big infrastructure projects – large consortiums of players, including banks and funds, take equity stakes and debt stakes in a single project.
2. *The Black Ops of bank treasuries*: We often think of banks as taking deposits and then lending the money out, but much banking works in the opposite direction. Lending deals are arranged, and the money to fund them is 'filled in' by the bank's treasury. Bank treasuries have a bird's-eye view of all the money flows in a bank, and engage in a dark art called 'asset-liability management' (ALM) to keep the bank afloat. Banks with poor ALM can get into serious trouble.

3. *Central banks and the payments system*: A country's central bank is the bank for banks. Commercial banks are required to have 'reserve accounts' at the central bank, which is where most transactions in the economy end up getting settled. When I make a payment with my debit card to someone who banks at the same bank as me, the bank just settles it internally, moving money from my account to theirs. If, on the other hand, I'm paying someone at another bank, it leads to a tiny shift from the central bank reserve account of my bank (Co-operative Bank UK) into the central bank reserve account of another bank (perhaps HSBC UK). By altering its policies, the central bank can affect the operations of all its bank clients, and this makes central banks highly politicised entities, leading to heated debates on whether they should be independent of government or controlled by government.

4. *Multilateral financial institutions*: The system becomes more complex for international payments, which involve taking money out of one bank, converting it into a different currency, and then depositing it into a bank in a different country, all of which entails movements between central banks. At a global level, the Bank for International Settlements (BIS) and the IMF exert an important influence on central banks, and are at the forefront of global-level financial politics.

Brontosaurs: The Slow-moving Firepower of Institutional Investors

The second group of financial institutions we often directly support are *institutional investors*, the huge funds that pool people's money together and invest it on their behalf. CalPERS, the California Public Employees Retirement System, for example, manages around $180 billion on behalf of Californian public sector workers. In financial slang, these organisations are sometimes referred to as 'real money' funds, because the money they manage is not borrowed, making their ownership of the assets they invest in entirely 'real'.[4] Big sources of real money,

---

4. They're entirely equity financed by, for example, pensioners.

other than pensions funds, are *insurance funds* (managing large pools of insurance contributions), *sovereign wealth funds* (managing money from states like Qatar), and *endowments and foundations* (managing bequests to, for example, universities).

Imagine you found yourself in charge of a teachers' pension fund, required to look after a modest £25 billion for your members' retirement. Where would you invest it? Would you be happy making those decisions yourself, in-house? In reality, you're likely to draw up a broad investment strategy with the help of investment advisors, and to then outsource the actual management to various *fund managers*, parcelling the money out to them in chunks.

This is the world of Fund Management, also called Asset Management or Investment Management. The *Financial Times* has a section in the middle full of listings of specific funds, each with their own specialisation, focused on particular 'asset classes' such as shares, bonds, commodities and property. The Horizon Access Vietnam Fund, for example, specialises in buying shares in Vietnamese companies listed on the Ho-Chi Minh stock market. That's not likely to be something you'll feel qualified to do if you're running a UK teacher's pension fund, but you might throw £10 million to the Horizon Fund to do it for you, especially if your investment advisor suggested Vietnam was a hot emerging market worth gaining exposure to.

Famous fund management houses include BlackRock and Fidelity. In addition to offering funds for institutional investors, they offer *mutual funds* (or unit trusts) that small investors like us can pool money into, and exchange traded funds (ETFs), a type of mutual fund listed on a stock market. I too, as a lowly retail investor, can buy into the Vietnamese miracle via a mutual fund advertised on the side of a London taxi.

A special sub-section of the fund management industry is called alternative investment management. It hosts two notorious players known for their high-risk strategies: Hedge funds and private equity funds. Hedge funds engage in a wide variety of creative investment strategies, all the way from high-speed algorithmic trading to such things as bankrolling poker players to play online poker. Private equity funds, on the other hand, specialise in one strategy: Buying and selling entire companies, generally while using large amounts of debt. Both are only open to investment from 'accredited investors' thought to be big enough to handle the risk. As a lowly retail investor, I cannot invest in these, but my pension fund can. Indeed, hedge funds and private equity funds are crucially reliant on contributions from large institutional investors (see page 79 for a description of this).

To grasp how the fund management industry operates though, we need to fill in the final piece of the puzzle: The investment banks, which create many of the financial instruments that funds invest in.

Tyrannosaurs: What the Hell is an Investment Bank?

Barclays Group has a commercial bank called Barclays, which you see on the high street. It also has an investment bank called *Barclays Capital* (or BarCap), which you don't see on the high street. BNP Paribas has a large commercial bank in France, but also a significant investment banking operation in the UK, USA and Asia. These are examples of hybrid, 'universal banks'. Goldman Sachs and Morgan Stanley are examples of (relatively) pure investment banks.[5]

If you go onto an investment bank website, you'll tend to find three main services:

- *Primary Capital Markets*: A division that helps companies to raise money, either by helping them to sell shares of ownership to equity investors via initial public offerings (IPOs), or by facilitating bond offerings, where debt investors lend companies money.
- *Secondary capital markets* (Sales and Trading): A division that facilitates second-hand markets in the shares and bonds that have already been created, by buying them

---

5. Technically speaking, this changed during the financial crisis when they converted into bank holding companies in order to gain access to emergency funding. They don't have substantive commercial banking operations though.

from initial investors and reselling them to new investors (market-making). They also package combinations of financial instruments for resale (structuring), and engage in derivatives trading (see page 63).

- *Corporate finance advisory, and mergers and acquisitions* (M&A): A consultancy division that advises big companies on how to raise money or how to swallow each other up.

These are effectively three separate 'personas' with the same brand name, and there is nothing inevitable in having them under the same roof. To confuse matters, many investment banks have *fund management* and *private wealth management* divisions too. Fund managers are normally *clients* of an investment bank, rather than part of an investment bank, but this is a form of vertical integration: The fund manager Goldman Sachs Asset Management (GSAM) might be a client of the Goldman Sachs trading division. Private wealth management, sometimes called private banking, is the art of helping extremely rich individuals to invest their money, a service that Swiss banks like UBS and Credit Suisse are famous for.

The Underwriters: Herding the Capital Markets

Investment banks are creatures of appearance, using their reputation to insert themselves between investors and real opportunities. The Primary Capital Markets division of an investment bank specialises in the art of *underwriting*, a process of coaxing groups of investors into putting money into a venture that's sponsored – vouched for – by an investment bank. They give groups of debt or equity investors the *confidence* to invest in an enterprise, by vouching for its investment worthiness.

Bond: A Big Fragmented Loan

A company that wants to borrow money can either borrow from a commercial bank, or it can issue a bond. A bond is just a very large loan, but instead of there being just one lender, it is split into pieces that can be 'bought' by the people doing the lending.

Let's hypothetically imagine that in 2014 the weapons manufacturer BAE Systems wishes to raise $2 billion for the acquisition of a company, and wishes to raise the money via debt investors through a bond. BAE's treasury team approaches Deutsche Bank and asks them to arrange a bond offering. Deutsche agrees to be the 'lead bookrunner' on the deal in exchange for a fee. They deploy a team of analysts to draw up all the details, while another team scouts for potential buyers of the bond. These buyers are most likely to be big funds, or high-net worth individuals (the super-rich). The analysts 'price' the deal, finding out what interest rate (also called the 'coupon') the investors are prepared to accept. Once Deutsche lines up enough institutional investors to buy the bond offering, the deal is 'fully subscribed' and is completed. BAE receives a $2 billion loan from the investors (now called bondholders), of which several million goes in fees to Deutsche. This bond is named BAE 6% 2034, referring to the interest rate and the year in which the bond matures.

Common types of bonds include *sovereign bonds* issued by governments, *investment grade corporate bonds,* issued by stable, low-risk companies, and *high yield corporate bonds (junk bonds)* issued by risky companies. *Asset-backed securities* – which came to prominence during the financial crisis – are often treated as being part of the bond family. These are like bonds backed by a package of other bonds. For example, a collateralised loan obligation (CLO), is a group of junk bonds packaged together. Anyone who lends via such a CLO is, technically speaking, lending to a whole group of high-risk companies.

An experiential learning technique is to borrow £100 by issuing your own bond. Get a friend to be your investment bank. They write a one-pager on why people should invest, and produce 20 pieces of paper with '£5 bond' written on it. They pitch the deal to investors (other friends of yours), and get friends to buy the bonds (aka. lend) by paying £5 each. They transfer the money to you, minus a £5 arrangement fee. This isn't so far from the reality of a bond deal. Indeed, 'buying paper' is financial slang for lending money via bonds.

Shares: All in it Together

The stock market – such as the London Stock Exchange – is a market for ownership stakes. A company that 'lists' on the stock market is raising money by selling ownership stakes (shares) in itself to equity investors (shareholders). A company doing this for the first time does so through an initial public offering (IPO), facilitated by an investment bank.

Let's imagine a deal involving Trafigura, which is a privately owned commodity company. They decide that they need to expand, and will do so by opening their ownership up to a wider pool of investors in exchange for cash. They approach J.P. Morgan, which puts together a team to work out the details, including doing valuations of what Trafigura is worth so that the shares can be priced for sale. J.P. Morgan co-ordinates efforts to line up big investors, including going on a 'road show' to convince investors to subscribe to purchase shares. If all is successful, the deal is closed, the money is transferred to Trafigura, and the new shares are transferred to the investors. The shares are simultaneously listed on the London Stock Exchange, which provides assurance of their quality, and which acts as a central market for secondary transactions in the shares. In the next section, we'll look at how these secondary markets work.

IN THE PITS, ON THE PHONES, THROUGH THE WIRES: SECONDARY MARKETS

Above we saw how financial instruments or securities are created. Many financial instruments though, are transferable, meaning that if I hold a bond or a share I can sell it to someone else. In doing that, someone else is taking the place of me lending, or taking my ownership stake. I'm handing over the investment baton, as it were. Thus, if *primary markets* are where financial hot potatoes get baked, *secondary markets* are where they get thrown around. This concept of primary and secondary markets is not unique to finance. For example:

- The primary car market involves car manufacturers distributing cars through primary car dealerships, such as the Bentley showroom in Mayfair where cars are sold first-hand. Separately from that, there is a market in second-hand cars, including classic Bentleys.
- You might have bought this book first-hand in the primary market from a distributor who is working in conjunction with the publisher. On the other hand, you may have bought it at a second-hand book store from a book dealer.
- Outside many popular concerts there are 'ticket touts' who buy tickets and then try to re-sell them for a profit. They're creating a secondary market; eBay also hosts an electronic secondary ticket market.

Second-hand car dealers, book dealers and ticket touts are all *traders*. They buy and sell things, attempting to make a profit in the process. The first trader I met was in Zimbabwe. He'd drive a truck to South Africa, stock it up with kerosene stoves, and then drive back to sell them in rural Zimbabwe, hoping that the kerosene stove market hadn't been flooded in the interim. If he was successful, he'd make a profit. If not, he'd make a loss. Investment bank 'sales and trading' divisions host the financial version of such traders, facilitating secondary transactions in shares,[6] bonds, currencies and instruments such as derivatives. While it is fine to call them 'traders', it's actually more precise to refer to them as 'dealers', to capture their middleman status. The terminology of secondary markets gets confusing, so let's quickly clarify a few terms:

- Trader: Someone who buys and sells things.
- Dealer (also called flow-trader or market-maker): A trader who buys and sells things by explicitly setting themselves up as a middleman.
- Broker: Someone who helps others buy and sell things by introducing buyers to sellers.

6. There are also niche 'stock-brokerages' and trading houses that do this too.

Thus, I could be a currency trader buying and selling currencies online in my pyjamas, but to be a dealer I would have to have clients calling me up asking for quotes on what they could buy from me and sell to me. Dealers deliberately advertise themselves as being prepared to buy and sell from 'end-users' of products: They walk into the proverbial village square and shout 'I will buy and sell!' They thereby create a market around themselves, facilitating trade flow and helping to ascertain market prices for products. Investment bank trading divisions, however, sometimes get called 'broker-dealers', because sometimes they're just introducing buyers to sellers (broking), and sometimes they're buying from sellers in order to sell to buyers (dealing).

Dealers and End-users

For any market transaction to get completed four factors need to be in place: A buyer, a seller, an agreement on quantity, and an agreement on price. At any one point in a market, there are people who want to buy and people who want to sell, but they may not agree on quantities or prices. There is thus a constant process of *stand-off*. It's also possible that such buyers and sellers are wandering around not knowing where to find each other. In the past, for example, people would sometimes use newspaper classifieds to buy and sell securities: 'Seeking 20 shares in British East India Company. Prepared to pay 3 shillings.' The person seeking shares in the British East India Company appears to want the shares for *intrinsic* reasons, and is seeking them out. Perhaps they've done their analysis and believe it's a good investment opportunity. We refer to them as an 'end-user'. They have an actual vision behind their decision to buy or sell. In modern-day financial markets such players might include, for example, mutual funds, hedge funds, corporations, institutional investors and high-net worth individuals.

The role of dealers is to position themselves to help these end-users transact. Dealers have no intrinsic desire to hold financial instruments. Rather, they're seeking to grease the cogs, and take a cut in the process. In other words, end-users make money off *things* while dealers make money off *making things happen.* An investment bank dealing desk combines three roles to achieve this:

1. *Salespeople*: Salespeople attempt to make friends with end-users to find out what they might want to buy or sell. They phone these clients, take them out for drinks, share ideas and give price quotes, attempting to induce them to transact.
2. *Dealers*: The salespeople provide a friendly interface between the end-user and the desk's dealers (market-makers, flow traders), who are the ones that actually do the buying and selling with that end-user client. Salespeople, in a sense, work for the dealers.
3. *Analysts*: In the background, analysts produce research for the salespeople to give to end-user clients, aimed at inducing those clients to trade. Quantitative analysts, or 'quants', help the dealers price financial instruments and manage the risk they take on in the process of dealing.

Sometimes these roles can get blurred into one, especially in electronic markets where intermediation is easier. Whatever the case, the relationship between end-users and dealing teams often gets abstracted into the jargon terms 'buy side' vs. 'sell side'. To outsiders, this is confusing, seeming to suggest one side buying financial instruments and the other selling them. The terms though, actually refer to end-users 'buying' intermediation services from dealing teams. An analogy is as follows: When I buy a tin of Heinz baked beans off the shelf at Sainsbury's, I am buying a *product* from Heinz and simultaneously buying an *intermediation service* from Sainsbury's. Heinz too is buying an intermediation service from Sainsbury's. Sainsbury's is joining us up, and taking a cut in the middle, like an investment bank for baked beans. In the world of consumer goods therefore, both I and Heinz are buy side, and Sainsbury's is sell side.

A market made up purely of sell-side intermediaries would be like ticket touts endlessly buying and selling tickets to each other rather than to concert goers. Admittedly, that happens fairly extensively in financial markets, but initially at least, let's work on building up an idealised model. Consider the diagram in Figure 2.1.

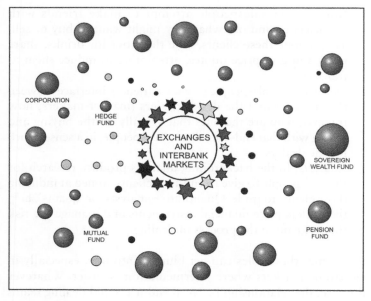

Figure 2.1

1. The circles represent end-users. On the far boundaries are big funds and corporations that do comparatively few, but comparatively large, transactions. In the closer rings are speculators, such as hedge funds, that do far more transactions.
2. The inner ring of stars represents the sell-side investment banks and brokerages that offer end-users access to central exchanges (see below), or that engage in 'over the counter' (OTC) dealing transactions with them (see page 59).
3. In the middle is a special section called the interbank market, hosted by 'interdealer brokers' who create a market for dealers within the market for end-users (see page 62).

'The markets' often referred to in the financial press are thus constituted by a core of dealers and brokers operating in central exchanges and via interbank markets, servicing various rings of short-term speculators, long-term investors and corporations. Let's break these parts down.

Sell-Side Ecosystem 1: The Liquid Electronic Pits

Exchanges are centralised and formalised marketplaces for financial instruments. In the past they used to consist of trading pits, but most exchanges nowadays are *electronic*. Imagine them as being a bit like financial versions of eBay, except an eBay that you have to be a qualified member to use. They are attached to clearing houses – such as London Clearing House (LCH. Clearnet) – which process the trades, much like Paypal processes trades for eBay.

Merrill Lynch, for example, is a member of the New York Stock Exchange. They act as a conduit via which their clients, such as hedge funds, can gain access to the exchange in return for a commission fee. As such, a stockbroker at an equities desk at Merrill Lynch is a bit like an order processor. They might give trading ideas to clients – for example, calling a hedge fund client to suggest they buy General Motors shares – and if the client agrees then the stockbroker just fills out their order on an electronic form and submits it to the exchange. The exchange attempts automatically to match the order with an opposite order submitted via another broker, dealing with a different client.

Merrill Lynch will also offer services to allow its clients to 'short' shares, which is a way of betting against a company in an attempt to profit from a fall in the price of its shares. An analogy for this is borrowing a book from a friend, selling it on eBay for £10, then attempting to buy it back later at a lower price (perhaps £7), then returning it to your friend, and keeping the £3 difference. Merrill might offer a seamless service helping a client to borrow shares, sell them and later to re-buy them. They may also offer *margin accounts*, where they lend money to clients to help them engage in speculation.

Long vs. Short, Bull vs. Bear

In financial markets, the slang for wanting to buy is 'going long' – 'I want to go long Chevron shares' – while the slang for selling is 'going short'. People who are going long are 'bullish'. People who want to go short are 'bearish'. In the final analysis, a Merrill stockbroker, along with all the other exchange members, is submitting orders for clients buying or selling to bet on company share prices (entering into a position) or to shut down a bet against a company share price (closing a position). The resultant streams of orders being submitted creates a centralised 'order book' listing all pending orders.

One way to visualise this is to imagine a room hosting a type of moving auction. On one side is a bullish crowd *bidding* for things from a bearish crowd on the other side who are *offering* things. People are occasionally switching allegiance from one side to the other. If we had to freeze that scene at any one point, we'd see a bid price – the highest current price that someone is prepared to buy, or go long, at – and we'd see an offer price – the lowest current price that someone is prepared to sell, or go short, at. Those bid and offer prices are statements of intent to transact, or orders. If they weren't there, it wouldn't be a market. By definition, the bid price must be lower than the offer price, because if it wasn't, a trade would have already been done. Thus, *there are always two prices*. The single price one sees on a business TV news report is an imaginary price in the no-man's-land between the bid price and the offer price.

The Black Art of Reading Markets

The distance between buyers and sellers – called the *bid-offer spread* – represents the extent of their stand-off. A tight bid-offer spread, where bid prices are very close to offer prices, suggests a highly charged and very 'liquid' market, where trades are always on the verge of happening. A market with lots of closely bunched orders is one with a big jostling crowd as it were. Those orders are 'liquidity' waiting to be soaked up. If you arrived at that market, and wanted to transact immediately, you could quickly soak up an order (in financial jargon, you would be called a 'price taker', someone who just accepts the best available price, rather than attempting to specify a price they'll transact at – like when you arrive in a shop and just accept their offer price rather than trying to haggle). In currency markets and major stock markets the crowd of participants at any point can number thousands, and it can take milliseconds to complete a trade.

In addition to the explicit orders, there are potential or *implicit* orders. A shift downwards in the price of Chevron shares might induce some sellers to become buyers, changing the stand-off dynamic and causing the price to go upwards again. It's emotional. The inflection point may be a substrate of positive sentiment (buy orders) that cannot be broken through. If people get panicked though, prices can go into freefall as the buy orders dry up and such substrates disappear. Alternatively, in the face of euphoric expectations, ceilings of negative sentiment (sell orders) might evaporate, sending prices soaring.

High-frequency Traders in the Emotional Substrates

Many people looking at a market only see the surface – the best bid and best offer – but in any market there are deep layers of buy and sell orders beyond those, waiting for counterparts. Algorithmic traders, and particularly high-frequency algorithmic traders, believe they can 'read' patterns in these orders, or in micro price movements, and design programmes intended to rapidly buy and sell to exploit those. Investment banks and specialist brokers (such as Interactive Brokers) are happy to indulge them, racing to offer services allowing them to submit orders microseconds faster. The May 2010 'Flash Crash' – where the US stock market imploded and then quickly righted itself as if nothing had happened – has been linked to such activities. The intuitive fear around this, and a source of much regulatory debate, is of an uncontrollable 'rise of the computers' going haywire. Indeed, in August 2012, Knight Capital lost $440 million thanks to a rogue algorithm.

Sell-Side Ecosystem 2: The OTC Swamps

Highly liquid markets – like currency trading on electronic platforms – almost allow end-users to forget that there is an intermediary. Not all financial markets are like this though. Many financial markets are actually *illiquid*, characterised by financial instruments that are non-standardised, harder to price and harder to find. This includes the securitised products of the financial crisis, and derivatives such as swaps. Many of these instruments are traded in *over-the-counter* (OTC) markets.

OTC markets, unlike centralised electronic exchanges that have visible order books, cannot be 'seen' in a central location. The global market in second-hand Bentley cars, for example, is OTC, because there is no obvious visible marketplace where it exists. Financial OTC markets are fragmented, created via telephone calls and private trades that are recorded in the IT systems of separate investment bank dealing desks, each of which is like a mini-exchange that doesn't communicate much with the others. OTC markets are perfectly legal, but together they appear like a global black market in financial instruments. The only way one builds up a picture of the collective 'order book' of, for example, bonds of the Russian gas company Gazprom, is by guessing it or asking people in the know. These markets thus have a very different feel to electronic markets, requiring much more personal interaction. They are often slower. For example, arranging to transact in a securitised product (such as a mortgage-backed security) can take days or even weeks, as buyers and sellers take a while to agree on prices and other details. OTC markets are also much larger than exchange traded markets, and a major regulatory debate revolves around the systemic risks they pose. The US Dodd-Frank Act, for example, is pushing to have these activities centralised via newly created exchanges and central clearing platforms.

A Story of OTC Dealing

Illiquid markets are often more interesting than liquid markets, but they can be very frustrating for the people involved. Physical property, for example, is not something you can actively 'trade', because buildings are non-standardised and the transaction costs associated with buying and selling them are high. Conceptually speaking, illiquid markets can resemble awkward social gatherings, where participants stand around trying to guess what the others want. They can easily seize up due to too few players (perhaps there's only 20 participants), a lack of diversity (perhaps they all want the same thing, and so don't have opposite orders to match), or the participants' unwillingness to provide orders due to a lack of information and confidence. Or perhaps there's simply not enough of something to be traded, or the product is obscure, making it hard to assess. They often have wide bid-offer spreads, where buyers' ideas of good prices are far from sellers' ideas of good prices.

Dealers become very important in these markets to break the gridlock. Imagine a situation where a large mutual fund specialising in emerging market bonds wants to buy bonds of Gazprom. Those bonds are probably held in chunks by all sorts of investors around the world, but attempting to locate them is difficult. The fund manager decides to phone Dimitri, a friendly salesperson at J.P. Morgan who is part of an emerging market bonds *dealing desk*. Dimitri's team make it their business to know where Russian bonds are, and what their price may be, such that they can quote prices for them. Dimitri relays the fund manager's request for a quote to his desk's dealer, a surly guy called Hendrik.

Dealers will sometimes maintain an inventory of products to sell. Perhaps Hendrik bought some Gazprom bonds from another fund earlier in the week and is now *warehousing* them, almost like he's got them 'stocked on the shelf'. If so, he can immediately attempt to sell that inventory at a marked up price to the fund manager, making money off the 'spread' between what he bought the bonds at, and what he sells them at.

On the other hand, Hendrik has to be careful about warehousing too many Gazprom bonds. He may struggle to sell them, *running risk* and perhaps losing money, like Sainsbury's overstocking on Heinz baked beans and then having to sell them at a discount. Hendrik likes to pride himself on the artfulness of his dealing, strategically building up an inventory, holding it and managing the risk while attempting to offload it onto others. This is important, because dealing desks occasionally 'blow up' when they finding themselves sitting on a large risky position they cannot offload.[7]

Dimitri needs a quote to pass on to the mutual fund manager. It turns out in this case that Hendrik doesn't actually have the bonds available. Hendrik nevertheless decides to quote a price, believing he'll be able to find them if necessary. The sales team has relationships with other clients who may be induced to *sell* to Hendrik, but he also has another option: He can source the bonds from *other dealers* in the 'interbank markets'.

Interbank markets are a market for dealers within the broader market for end-users. They are like an uneasy neutral ground in the midst of a war. The salespeople at J.P. Morgan and at Goldman Sachs are relentlessly chasing after the same clients, but in the background a bond dealer at J.P. Morgan may cautiously agree to do business with a bond dealer at Goldman Sachs, like soldiers on opposite sides agreeing to exchange rations, because each has something tasty the other wants: *'I'll fling you some bully beef if you can fling me some canned peaches.'*

A less warlike analogy is to think of interbank markets as a wholesale warehouse where the dealers trade with each other at wholesale prices to restock themselves. In the derivatives markets (discussed below), the interbank markets provide a way for dealers to enter into bets with each other to *lay off* their risk against each other. There is no physical location for this market. It is created over phone lines, emails and Bloomberg chat messages (like a financial Gmail chat). Very importantly, these markets are facilitated by a special class of financial player almost completely unknown to the public: The *interdealer brokers*, or IDBs.[8]

IDBs are brokers who intermediate among those who intermediate. They bring the interbank markets to life by acting as conduits by which dealers can do business with each other. A J.P. Morgan dealer like Hendrik might need something from other dealers, but he's nervous of calling them directly to

---

7. In markets I was involved in, Goldman Sachs fired an entire eight-member dealing team after a position they had warehoused blew up.
8. Big IDBs include ICAP, Tullet Prebon, BGC, Tradition and GFI.

probe for prices. After all, they're technically his competitors. Interdealer brokers though, provide him with an anonymous mask, so he can do back-alley deals with other dealers who also don't want to reveal themselves.

Hendrik phones up a rough but amiable Yorkshireman called Bill at a huge IDB called ICAP and says, 'Bill, I'm looking to buy £25 million in Gazprom 4.95 2022 bonds at $105. You have 30 minutes.' Bill's team sets out like a pack of stealthy hyenas, getting on the phones to *other dealers*, searching for the bonds. They negotiate back and forth, finding a dealer at the French bank SocGen who's prepared to sell to Hendrik. Bill takes a commission, Hendrik buys the bonds, and then sells them to the fund manager. Dimitri gives Hendrik a high-five and everyone is happy.

These interbank markets thus create much of the liquidity (ability to trade) that exists in the broader market. They allow dealers to (uneasily) pool together their resources in a virtual central repository, which in turn emanates outwards to end-users. If those interbank markets seize up, as in the financial crisis, the rest of the system can seize up too.

Shadowlands: The Murky World of Derivatives

OTC markets have become somewhat notorious, and the focus of much regulatory attention, because of their association with *OTC derivatives*. Derivatives are, in effect, bets that can either be used to speculate on something (to take on risk), or to 'hedge' against something (to protect against risk). During the financial crisis, a particular type of OTC derivative known as credit default swaps (CDS) caused great instability because they allowed people to bet on the likelihood of bonds defaulting (not being paid back), and thus when bonds did default, huge organisations that had taken these bets on, such as AIG, were severely impacted.

Not all derivatives are OTC though – futures, for example, are traded on central exchanges – and many of them are relatively straightforward. In this section, we'll go through the three main classes:

- *Futures and forward contracts*: A contract to buy or sell something at a price set now, for delivery at a specific point in the future.
- *Options*: A contract giving the option to buy or sell something in the future at a set price.
- *Swaps*: A series of forward contracts linked together.

Risk and Risk Management

The economic system is characterised by risk. Risk is basically the inability to tell the future.[9] Should I buy a house now? Maybe house prices will go down within six months, in which case to buy now would be too hasty. Alternatively, they could go up. My lack of action is a risk in itself, but my lack of knowledge of the future affects my confidence in present decisions. The higher my *risk aversion*, the less I am willing to act in the face of the unknown future outcomes. Businesses have many risks too. A future spike in the price of electricity might make an aluminium smelter unprofitable. The investors in those businesses have risks. If an aluminium smelter goes bankrupt, the debt investors may lose their money. The American equity investors in a Russian aluminium smelter might lose if the value of the ruble declines relative to the dollar.

Risk management techniques seek to deal with risk. The most classic technique is called *diversification*, commonly known as 'don't put all your eggs in one basket'. Institutional investors use this principle extensively (see page 79). Another technique is to get insurance, paying someone else a fee (premium) to take the risk on. The higher the perceived risk, the higher the premium that will have to be paid. A Florida insurance company with excessive risk exposure to Florida hurricanes may, in turn, insure itself with a *reinsurance* company like Swiss RE. The insurance industry is immensely important, but people often tend to consider it rather run-of-the-mill. The public tends to be more darkly fascinated by derivatives.

---

9. There is a literature in finance debating whether risk is the same thing as uncertainty. The common argument is that risk is 'quantifiable uncertainty'.

The use of derivatives in risk management really entails *betting on the risk factor that could harm you*, such that if it actually occurs your loss is offset by a gain you make on the bet. They're just as likely to be used for pure betting though:

- *Scenario 1: Derivatives for speculation.* Imagine I enter into a bet on a horse race. The bet derives its value from the outcome of the race. It's a *horse-racing derivative*, which synthetically creates a situation in which the outcome of the horse race impacts on me, without me owning any horses. I am using it to speculate on the outcome of the race.
- *Scenario 2: Derivatives for hedging.* Now imagine that I actually own a horse that is competing in the horse race, and that I simultaneously enter into a bet that my horse won't win. If my horse wins, I'll make prize money, but I'll lose on the bet. If my horse doesn't win, I'll make money on the bet. The two situations offset each other. I have used a bet to hedge myself.

The financial sector deals in bets on financial instruments, commodities and economic conditions, but the horse racing example illustrates the ambiguous nature of such derivatives. Textbooks might state that derivatives exist to allow people to hedge themselves (as in Scenario 2 above), but that's a bit like arguing that the horse betting industry exists to help horse owners protect themselves from risk. It's partially true, but fails to capture the fact that horse bets mostly allow widespread speculation, amplifying the economic effects of a horse race far beyond the immediate participants. Horse bets allow 'horse racing risk' to be synthetically replicated and escalated.

A key nuance of financial derivatives is that unlike normal bets where the payoff is fixed, the payoff from a financial derivative often isn't. A normal bet on the weather might be 'I bet it will rain on Tuesday', with a defined payoff for the winner of the bet. A financial *weather derivative* though, might be 'I bet it will rain no more than 200mm between January and May. For every millimetre of rain over that amount I will pay $1,000 to you. For every millimetre under that you will pay me $1,000.'

A common feature to all bets though, is that they need *two sides* in order to exist. Someone has to enter into the bet *against* you, and if you win, the money flows to you from that other person.

Derivative Family 1: Futures and Forwards

Calling derivatives 'bets' needs to be taken with a pinch of salt. They're often structured as contracts that don't look exactly like bets, even if their economic effect is very similar to that of betting. Let's consider forwards and futures contracts to illustrate this.

Forward contracts occur in many industries. For example, BG Group might agree to supply a fertiliser manufacturer with a certain amount of gas in a *month's time*, at a price set *now*. An informal forward contract may be you agreeing now to pay £500 for a piece of artwork that will only be finished in six months. In the financial sector, a forward is an over-the-counter bilateral contract between, say, J.P. Morgan and British Steel, agreeing a rate at which British Steel can convert currency in 23 days' time.

A futures contract has the same basic structure, except it is much more standardised and is agreed upon via a derivatives exchange (such as Eurex) by parties that probably never meet each other. It specifies a price now for a standardised transaction that will take place at a standardised point, such as three months, six months, or a year in the future. You'd never find a futures contract for an artwork, because artworks look different to each other, and thus need to be negotiated on a case-by-case basis. You could find a futures contract for a specific grade of oil though, such as West Texas Intermediate oil, or Brent Crude oil.

An oil futures contract imports its value from the underlying oil. Imagine a futures contract to buy a unit of nothing, for nothing, to be delivered in one year. That contract would have no economic significance. Now replace the nothing with something like oil, or corn, or a share in BP. Suddenly you're locked into a future transaction with specific contractual terms, and in doing so, you're also locked into a bet on whether those contractual terms will turn out favourably or not. This in turn can become a bet on the underlying asset itself.

An oil future thus becomes a bet on oil. Right now, I agree to buy 1,000 barrels of oil from another person, via a futures contract, for $100 a barrel, to be delivered in three months' time. If the price of oil goes up over $100, the value of holding a contract which allows you to buy it for less also goes up. Price of oil goes up, value of contract goes up. Price of oil goes down, value of contract goes down. There are a few more technicalities, but the essence is that I've artificially synthesised a situation akin to holding virtual oil. On the other hand, the person on the other side of the contract is holding a type of *inverse virtual oil*, or anti-oil, which goes down in value as oil prices increase.

Imagine I am a hedge fund speculator who believes the price of oil is going to go up. If in three months the price in oil in the physical 'spot markets' (markets where actual physical barrels of oil can be bought immediately) is $109, I can buy it at $100 via my futures contract and then sell it in those spot markets at $109, making a $9 profit.[10]

Imagine, on the other hand, that I'm a physical oil trader at Trafigura, and that I've agreed to deliver real physical oil to a jet-fuel refinery in three months' time. I haven't yet sourced that physical oil, and I suspect that its price is going to go up in that time. I don't want to get caught in a situation where the price skyrockets, so I enter into a futures contract to buy oil at $100 in three months. Like the speculator, I'm entering into a bet that the price of oil will go up, but unlike a speculator, I'm using it to protect myself. Let's imagine though, that in three months' time the price of oil actually goes down to $89. I'm able to buy it in the spot markets for $89, and deliver it to the refinery, but I've simultaneously lost $11 on the futures contract, meaning I've paid $100 altogether. The future protected me from *upswings* in the price, but only at the expense of me forgoing any gains from a drop in price. It creates stability in my expectations. I know that, no matter what happens, I'll basically end up paying $100.

---

10. The example is stylised: In reality, speculation (and hedging) often won't involve people taking physical delivery of oil. Many futures are 'closed out' prior to delivery and settled in cash, which means that the speculator would simply be paid $9 by a counterparty.

There is an alternative strategy for both the speculator and the physical oil trader hedging their position: They could literally buy up physical oil and store it somewhere. Trafigura actually does have access to big oil liners to do that with, but for most people based in a plush office in the City, virtual oil is much simpler than getting their hands dirty with actual hydrocarbons.

Derivative Family 2: Options

Options are bought by one party and sold by another. Buying an option is akin to *paying to keep one's choices open* – either buying the right to do something, or buying a right to stop doing something. To sell an option is to sell the right to do something, or to sell the right to stop doing something. A *call* option is an option to do something. A *put* option is an option to stop doing something, like an escape clause. The price for either option is called the 'premium'.[11]

Call options and put options abound in everyday life, but we don't normally pay for them. An acceptance offer from a university which is valid for three months is like a free call option. A shop return policy that allows you to return clothing within a week if you're not happy with it is like a free put option. In the financial world though, I might pay someone $5 for a call option giving me the right to buy crude oil for a price of $75 in six months' time, or I may pay $3 for a put option giving me the right to sell it at $75 in six months' time. If I buy such a call option on oil, I am betting that the price of oil will rise above $75, and if I buy a put option, I am betting the price will fall below that.

Options, unlike futures, exhibit an *asymmetric payoff*. This is a fancy way of saying that the person buying them obtains unlimited potential for gain (upside), by accepting a limited loss

---

11. Options are the only derivative that can literally be 'bought' or 'sold'. You actually hand over a premium to buy a contract. Futures, like bets on horses, cannot really be 'bought' – you enter into them – but in financial slang, 'buying futures' refers to the counterparty who is contractually agreeing to buy something in the future.

(paying the set premium). The person selling them, on the other hand, accepts a limited gain (the premium), in exchange for exposing themselves to unlimited potential for loss (downside). Selling options is more daunting, therefore, than buying them. Like futures though, options can be used for both speculation and hedging. If I'm a physical oil trader at Trafigura who wants to protect against the price of oil going up, without losing gains from the price of oil going down, I can buy an oil call option. Paying the premium allows me to have my cake and eat it.

What should the premium be though? Or, put another way, what is the price of 'keeping one's options open'? For a long time no one really knew how to price option premiums. It's an abstract puzzle, but it was eventually (sort of) cracked in 1973 when the *Black-Scholes* option pricing model came out, a mammoth in financial history. There's no need to know the details of it, but the price of options is closely related to *volatility* – a chance of something happening is greater when there are wild swings in events – and *time* – a chance of something happening is greater the longer you give it. Buying long-term options for a volatile commodity, for example, could be prohibitively expensive. Cerebral traders though, often buy and sell options in interesting combinations for different effects, building up layered cocktails to make bets on both prices and levels of volatility. Mathematical types get very excited about this, giving the cocktails names like 'butterfly spreads'.

Derivative Family 3: Swaps

A forward contract locks in the terms of a single future transaction right now. A swap is just like that, except it does it for a *series* of future transactions. Consider the following three steps:

1. *Uncertainty*: Imagine an electricity bill you have to pay every three months for a year. You don't know precisely how much each bill will be. It's a series of unknown future transactions stretching out over time, like a dark highway that you only

see as you drive forward. Ring-fence those future transactions together in your mind.

2. *Imagining no uncertainty*: Now imagine you wanted to replace that ring-fenced unknown group with a known group, like a perfectly illuminated highway you can see from beginning to end. You look into the future and project that, *on average*, the bills will be £60 per quarter.

3. *Freezing that vision*: Now you attempt to actually replace the unknown group with the known group. You approach the electricity company and ask them if they can fix your quarterly electricity bill at £60. You are asking them to *swap* your unknown future electricity payments for known ones.

In order for this agreement to take place, it has to fit in with both counterparties' vision of the future. Perhaps the electricity company offers to fix it at £70 per quarter, and you counteroffer with £65. They agree, offering you a bilateral contract to pay £65 per month for electricity. They are implicitly thinking that you are going to use £65 or less worth of electricity, and you are implicitly thinking that you're going to use £65 or more, but on average, you've collectively fixed a vision of the future.

There are many real world examples of this type of implicit swapping, where one party replaces a floating variable transaction with a repeated fixed transaction. Mobile phone contracts allow you to pay a stream of fixed monthly payments regardless of how much you use. Week-long Oyster card deals on the London Underground enable you to travel as much as you want for a fixed cost. These are examples of swaps implicitly embedded in real world packaged deals, but most financial swaps are explicitly separated from real world situations: Imagine having a normal pay-as-you-go mobile phone, and entering into a bet on the side to offset it, such that the *net effect* ends up being like having a fixed phone contract. Now imagine you could enter into the bet without having the mobile phone. The former is a situation of hedging phone costs, the latter of speculating on phone costs.

In the financial world there are many floating variables. Interest rates, for example, fluctuate up and down. Virtually every major company in the world borrows money, and thus has exposure to *interest rate risk*. Perhaps this is why the interest rate derivatives market is the world's biggest derivative market. Anglo American might enter into a bilateral *interest rate swap* contract with Barclays Capital to replace a series of variable future interest rate payments with an equal number of fixed interest rate payments. A multinational UK company might sell a product through a subsidiary in Thailand, only to discover that the Thai currency depreciates and all the cash they've accumulated suddenly loses value relative to the pound. This is one reason why currency derivatives are the world's second biggest derivatives market. If you scour the annual reports of FTSE 100 companies you'll notice they all use some version of interest rate and currency derivatives, with names like FX swaps, cross-currency swaps, or forward rate agreements (FRAs). There are *commodity swaps* for commodity prices, and *equity swaps* for share prices, and *credit default swaps* for default risk. These are all classed as 'vanilla derivatives', because they're like plain vanilla ice-cream, industry-standard tools.

Other derivatives though, are classed as 'exotic', like swaps for the level of inflation, the amount of cargo on ships, the price of property, and weather conditions. Exotic derivatives tend to be more specialist and weird, like an olive-oil based ice-cream with capers and saffron. There are no limits as to how exotic they can get, but the more exotic they are, the harder it is for them to get widespread use and critical mass, meaning they remain comparatively niche. Swap markets I have experience of include inflation swaps, sub-sector property swaps (for example, bets on the changing level of an index of Central London property prices), and longevity swaps – bets on how long people will live for.

The (not so) Glorious Business of OTC Swaps Dealing

A longevity swap sounds rather abhorrent to most people, but their reality is much more mundane. The people most interested in them are actuaries at large pension funds or life insurance companies, who are tasked with calculating how much exposure their organisations have to changing life expectancies. A pension fund, for example, is in a tricky position if an average population keeps on getting older. They have to plan now for how to potentially pay out a lot more in the future. The arcane discussions around longevity swaps really concern whether it is possible to 'hedge' that situation, such that they don't get caught out in 20 years' time.

Pension funds also drive the inflation swap market. The *defined benefit pension fund* – now rapidly going out of fashion – promises to pay employees a certain pension for the rest of their lives once they retire. There are UK government regulations to protect pensioners under such schemes, stipulating that the amount paid out to pensioners must be indexed (pegged) to inflation[12] to prevent pensioners' buying power being whittled away. Thus, when inflation is expected to increase, a defined benefit pension scheme is exposed to a greater future liability. A pension fund manager has to design an investment portfolio right now that will be able to cover those future payments. This is one reason why they try to buy commodities and property, which are believed to track inflation, and why they buy inflation-linked bonds (index-linked gilts). Somewhere on the Morgan Stanley trading floor, though, lurks another solution. It's an exotic derivatives desk, with a couple of guys dealing in inflation derivatives. One's the salesperson, and the other is the actual dealer. The salesperson calls the pension fund up, and spins a story about how they should enter into a bet on increases in future inflation via an inflation swap, thereby increasing the fund's correlation with inflation and protecting them.

Derivatives dealing teams are the chief purveyors of such solutions, but their job is to make money dealing various contracts between end-users. They will offer prices to attract them in much the same way a sports-betting bookie quotes odds to attract people to enter into bets. Let's say that, after two weeks, the salesperson convinces the fund manager to enter into an inflation swap with them. The pension fund is now partially hedged against inflation, but the Morgan Stanley dealer, having entered into a bet which exposes him to an upswing in inflation,

---

12. As measured, in the UK, by the Retail Price Index (RPI), or Consumer Price Index (CPI).

now has to make a decision. He either 'runs the risk', hoping that he's on the winning side of the bet, or he needs to hedge himself too. Most derivatives dealers, like sports-betting bookies, aim to structure their 'trading book' to attract an equal weight of end-users on either side of a bet, so that no matter what actually happens, they'll make money.

The dealer gets his salesman on the phone to the water utility Thames Water. Thames Water is granted a monopoly to provide water for London, but in exchange for the monopoly they give up the right to decide on the price for that water. Rather, the regulator (Ofwat) calculates how much utilities are allowed to charge, based on a formula that takes into account increases in the level of inflation. Thus, the revenues a water company receives are, roughly speaking, *positively correlated* to inflation. This applies to many large regulated monopolies, such as the National Grid. These utilities though, like most large companies, operate as a dynamic system between the things they own and the things they owe, between their assets and liabilities. While their revenues from assets are correlated to inflation, the interest they may pay on their debt might not be. Perhaps their revenues stay fixed while their debt payments go up, squeezing them into unprofitability. The Morgan Stanley salesperson has a solution for them: 'Why not increase the correlation of your liabilities to inflation, by entering into a bet *against* inflation via a swap?'

The actual pitches are a lot more sophisticated than this, and the mechanics of a financial swap contract are fairly tricky, but this is the gist of it. At the end of the year, the Morgan Stanley desk has entered into various swaps with pension funds, while offsetting those with other swaps to utilities, plus a bunch more with speculators such as hedge funds. They also buy inflation-linked bonds here and there, and offset residual risk in the interbank markets via interdealer brokers. They end up with a balanced position, taking a little cut in the middle. Such swaps can be over £100 million in size, so a little cut might be significant.

Tailor-made Risk: Structured Transactions

I've had many bizarre experiences trying to sell derivatives to fund managers and financial directors of FTSE 100 companies.

They often just put the phone down, partly because they always have salespeople and brokers trying to flog them derivatives, but also because many companies have actually had bad experiences trying to use them. Derivatives, for example, are *inherently leveraged* – you can enter into a massive bet merely by placing a deposit down. If managed incorrectly, they can be very risky.

Big institutional investors may have conservative 'mandates' – legal charters – which do not allow them to use derivatives for pure speculation purposes. Derivatives dealing desks, however, will often have structuring teams that create 'structured products' that look like normal bonds, but that have embedded derivatives. A fund manager might phone the structuring desk and say 'I want a bond-like product that gives me exposure to broad commodity prices.' The desk designs a bespoke structured product for them, and the traders source the various components – such as commodity futures, or options – in the background. It's like paying a holiday company for a comfortable and balanced packaged tour of Egypt. The more structured the deals, the more fiddly they become, requiring cerebral modelling by the quants who specialise in pricing them.

Velociraptors: The Hedge Fund Ecosystem

Investment banks' attempts at innovation are often driven by an obsession with winning client business – luring an airline, say, with a bespoke jet-fuel hedging strategy, or luring fund managers with a new structured product. One of their prime targets though, are *hedge funds*. Many investment banks have a division called Prime Brokerage which specialises almost solely in trying to win business from hedge funds.

Hedge funds have a simple model. They convince accredited investors – super-rich individuals as well as institutional investors like pension funds – to invest money into them. They then complement that by borrowing lots of money from banks. They take a management fee, and then they trade, claiming a significant percentage of whatever they make.

Hedge funds, to some, are the quintessential financial market rock-stars. A hedge fund could be five people in a Mayfair office with a theory, who just trade all day. Theirs is a different mindset to that of an investment bank salesperson or dealer on a crowded trading floor, phoning clients each day. It's no secret that investment bank dealers often want to end up as traders for hedge funds. Perhaps Hendrik has been working for J.P. Morgan for several years, and is getting itchy feet. He wants to be let off the leash. He might find his way onto a *proprietary trading desk* within the bank, given free rein to speculate with the bank's own money, although regulatory efforts are underway to limit such activities within banks. Perhaps Hendrik decides instead to start up his own emerging market bonds hedge fund. Investment banks' trading divisions are like incubators nurturing the next generation of hedge fund employees.

The USA and London are the biggest hedge fund centres. The aristocratic old buildings around Berkeley Square in Mayfair are jam-packed with shiny plaques with names like 'Thames River Capital' engraved on them. If you hang out in Mayfair bars, the statistical chances of meeting a hedge fund manager are significant. They are often intriguing people. Bear in mind that to start a hedge fund, you have to be able to convince initial investors to entrust you with a lot of money. It could be a mere £10 million, or perhaps £3 billion. It's possible that I could start a hedge fund from my room, opening a spreadbetting account and issuing a prospectus explaining my vision, but it's highly unlikely that many investors would back me. If, on the other hand, you're a socially dysfunctional nerd spinning a creative megalomaniac vision and behaving like a temperamental prima donna, then ordinary investors might believe you have a key to financial alchemy.

The alchemy that investors are looking for, and the main way hedge funds sell themselves, is *absolute return*. A straightforward fund like a mutual fund tends to be judged according to how well it does *relative* to an overall market. If the FTSE 100 stock index goes down 10%, and a mutual fund's returns only go down 8%, it's thought to have done relatively well. That doesn't cut it for hedge funds. They're often out to defy economic gravity, to eke positive returns regardless of the external environment. They refer to this as the search for *alpha*, the art of finding gold in a tin-mine. In the search for gravity-defying alpha, hedge funds will engage in many unusual strategies, making them a great source of business for investment bank dealing desks.

Hedge funds are renowned for borrowing lots of money to *leverage* the returns of their club of equity investors. If I am able to borrow 90% of the money I use, I am ten times leveraged – for every 1% gain or loss the fund makes, there is a 10% gain or loss in the original equity stake. If I am able to borrow 99%, I am 100 times leveraged. Hedge funds like Long Term Capital Management (LTCM) reputedly needed almost no money of their own to put on enormous trades. They went bust spectacularly in 1998, contributing to the perception that hedge funds are 'spivs', flashy speculative chancers to be contrasted with more prudent long-term investors.

Design Your Own Hedge Fund: Spreadbetting

A powerful experiential learning technique is to run your own small hedge fund. Draw up an investment philosophy – lottery ticket hedge fund? – and pitch it to your friends, imagining them to be sceptical pension fund managers or wealthy barons. Get ten of them to give you £20 each and then execute your strategy. Perhaps open up a *spreadbetting account* with a company like IG Index. It's a bit like signing up to a small investment bank prime brokerage service. Spreadbets are highly leveraged derivatives. Entering into a spreadbet on BP shares essentially means you've borrowed money to buy BP shares via IG Index, though most amateur spreadbetters are not aware of this. With leverage, the £200 you've raised from your 'equity investors' could be used to speculate on thousands of pounds worth of shares (thanks to your 'debt investors'). You might end up with a gambling addition, but you'll also get a basic feel for the dynamics of being a hedge fund manager.

The DNA of Trading

Many people casually think hedge funds throw around large sums of money recklessly, which in many cases is untrue. Their survival requires high standards of risk management and their strategies can be very sophisticated. They employ a raft of trading strategies – with names like 'global macro' and 'convertible bond arbitrage' – some highly quantitative, others exclusively qualitative. When boiled down though, they all amount to the same thing: *Buy low and sell high*. That works either way around – you can also sell high and buy low and make money (shorting).

The eyes of a trader are keenly accustomed to spotting opportunities to buy low and sell high. Try walking through the streets with the eyes of a trader: Do you see something you could buy, and then sell again within a week for more than you bought it? Can you spot bargains in the Portobello road antique market? Are you confident that you can 'beat the market' by seeing value in a battered vintage hip-flask that is underpriced, or are the antique dealers smarter than you?

There are really only two types of trade: A trade that puts you into a speculative position, and a trade that tries to get you out of it. The first is a speculative trade, exposing you to risk. The second is a hedging trade that gets rid of that risk.[13] All speculators eventually have to hedge themselves out of a position to either claim their gains, or to cut their losses. There is a trading spectrum based on how long the trader is prepared to keep a speculative position open for. Scalpers enter into a speculative position and then immediately try to close it out via a hedging trade. Swing traders enter into a speculative position and ride with it in search of bigger gains. An arbitrage trader enters a speculative position and *simultaneously* hedges it somewhere else – that's a sign of inefficiency between markets, like being able to buy a book on eBay and simultaneously sell it on Amazon for a higher price.

The biggest schism in speculation styles is that of fundamental vs. technical trading. Speculators using *fundamental analysis* try to analyse the underlying reality of a market. A commodities hedge fund might study reports on corn supplies and corn demand to inform their trading of corn futures. Speculators

---

13. This even applies, in a more abstract sense, to corporations: They might enter into a risky 'position' by building a factory, which they may then hedge with an offsetting derivative.

using *technical analysis* make a science of studying the price patterns created by other traders, abstracting them into technical indicators like 'Fibonacci retracements' and 'Eliot waves' that are supposed to reveal emotional or psychological trends in markets. They don't try to trade 'reality', they try to trade other people's perceptions of reality. If a market is dominated by enough technical traders, it could lapse into a 'postmodern' state, with traders trading perceptions of perceptions of reality.

There is much folklore about the supposed characteristics of traders, but in essence they have to be able to see information and react proactively with it. Many academics, for example, are good at analysing information, but how many have the decision-making power to do something with it? Traders might use psychological tools to control their responses to information. Much like poker players, their aim is not necessarily to win every single hand, but rather to win on average. Many trading techniques involve repeating a pattern over and over again, testing to see whether it wins on average. This is a highly imprecise science though, and many traders believe they've discovered some winning formula only to get wiped out by a statistically improbable 'tail risk'. This happened to the aforementioned LTCM hedge fund.

The Hedge Fund Ecosystem Within the Real Money Ecosystem

The main reason hedge funds exist, however, is that big investors hire them to manage money. They thus need to be seen within the broader framework of those investors. All investors express views on the future by deploying money via financial instruments, but a large pension fund or university endowment fund, for example, has a particularly long-term view. It's very risky for them to make *singular bets* over a 30-year horizon. Imagine you're a fund manager 30 years ago, about to bet your entire portfolio on equity stakes in American record player companies. That's like putting your money into a time machine and setting it for a future that doesn't exist. The prudent fund-manager wants lots of time machines, hoping that through the haze of uncertainty they mostly won't lead to black voids, but rather to a collectively pleasant future.

Long-term investors thus do not merely look for high, absolute returns. They look for comparatively low risk and low volatility – fluctuations in returns – seeking to balance risk and return. To do this they'll draw up an 'asset allocation' strategy to diversify – spread the risk of – their portfolio. They may allocate their money as follows:

- 60% in shares: This in turn will be diversified into many smaller sections like UK shares, emerging market shares, etc.
- 20% in a 'fixed income' portfolio of bonds: This might be further diversified into government bonds, corporate bonds, higher risk junk bonds, and maybe some 'mortgage backed securities'.
- 10% in property: Most likely to be commercial property that provides rent.
- 5% in cash: Keep some cash on hand to actually pay your pensioners.
- 5% in 'alternative investments': Includes hedge funds, private equity funds, commodities and various exotica.

As discussed on page 48, the manager then parcels the money out to various specialist fund managers who will themselves be running more specific diversification strategies in order to extract the most return from any given sector relative to a level of risk. Perhaps the property section is entrusted to a medium-risk Aberdeen Asset Management property fund, which builds a portfolio of London offices, industrial warehouses and retail shopping centres.

Hedge funds slot into the high-risk end of this schema. A pension fund looking after $30 billion is not going to spend the day trading that, but they might dedicate 5% ($150 million) to higher risk endeavours, throwing $15 million apiece to five hedge funds and five private equity funds (see below). Perhaps they also allocate money to commodities, via a new 'commodities structured product' designed by an investment bank structuring desk (see the food speculation section on page 150).

The hedge fund ecosystem is thus a flashy enclave within the slower moving world of institutional investors. Hedge fund traders, in my anecdotal experience, often look down on large institutional fund managers as boring fat sheep, while seeing themselves as lean insightful panthers. In the minds of the institutional managers though, hedge funds may appear like feral cats chasing after imaginary balls of string, or their own tails, having duped investors into giving them money.

The investment banks court both with different strategies. Herding hyperactive cats is different to herding big indifferent sheep. The dealing desk salesperson must encourage the cat's overactive imagination ('yes, you are a powerful independent panther'), and they must encourage the sheep to not get left behind by the large flock ('you are prudent and wise among your peers'). The power dynamics run back and forth between the players, who will work with each other some of the time, but also turn on each other in times of crisis. These are 'the markets'.

THE DEAL-MAKING TRIBES

Secondary markets have a day-to-day quality to them. The trader gets up early in the morning. Financial instruments get bought and sold. Prices change. The markets close, and the traders go home. They repeat the same pattern again the next day. Outside the day-to-day markets though, is another world inhabited by the 'deal-makers' in investment bank Corporate Finance Advisory divisions, Mergers & Acquisitions (M&A) divisions, and in private equity funds.

M&A Bankers: Advisors to the Prince

The abiding irony of free-market systems is that the actors within them constantly attempt to short-circuit free markets by centralising economic activity within hierarchal corporations. Corporations are like non-national principalities spread out via networks of ownerships and obligations. The impulse to continually ring-fence more assets under the control of a corporate brand name is powerfully felt by senior corporate managers hired by corporate shareholders. CEOs sometimes appear almost pathologically bent on winning control of productive assets around the world, often regardless of whether it makes business sense. They're always on the lookout for the big move that could upset an existing balance of power.

In 1513 Niccolò Machiavelli wrote *The Prince*, a treatise on political deal-making and power-mongering. M&A bankers are the financial equivalent of advisors to the Prince, or to many corporate princes. They help facilitate the corporate equivalents of assassinations, coups, alliances and invasions. They spend much time whispering into the ears of CEOs, suggesting companies they may *acquire*, or *merge* with, pitching battle ideas in coded language like 'value creation', 'merger synergies' and 'vertical integration'. Perhaps they offer tax structuring advice, suggesting ways to split the company up via offshore subsidiaries to reduce the 'tax burden'. It all comes down to the same thing: Control more, make more, pay us fees.

Goldman Sach's M&A team might pitch an acquisition idea to Shell – 'have you considered buying this Canadian oil-drilling company?' – and then pass Shell to the bank's primary capital market bond issuance teams to raise money for that endeavour. M&A bankers are actually like consultants, but together with primary capital markets teams they're often referred to as 'investment bankers', and contrasted to traders. Consider the following excerpt from the book *Barbarians at the Gate* (1990), by Bryan Burrough and John Heylar:

> Wall Street had always been split into two, sometimes warring camps: Investment bankers – smooth, dapper, trained at Andover and Harvard – and traders – red-faced Jewish and Irish kids who went to City College and made their living hollering at each other on the trading floor.

Nowadays the distinction isn't as clear as it used to be – trading has got a lot more cerebral – but the quintessential image of the investment banker is really that of the M&A professional greasing up vain CEOs with their hot ideas.

Shadow Tycoons: Private Equity

In much the same way that trading floor dealers rely on hedge funds to drive much of their trade flow, M&A teams rely on *private equity funds* to drive much of their 'deal flow'. M&A bankers charge fees for advising people on buying and selling companies, and as it so happens, private equity funds exist solely to buy and sell companies. While dealers aspire to end up in hedge funds, M&A bankers often aspire to end up in private equity funds.

Private equity funds, like hedge funds, rely on investment from institutional investors and very rich people, and like hedge funds, they use large amounts of leverage. Unlike hedge funds though, their outlook is comparatively long-term. If an investor puts money into a private equity fund, they may not be able to take it out for eight years. This is because buying and selling whole companies is more time consuming than buying and selling currencies or small chunks of shares. Much like property development, private equity comes in seven to ten year waves or 'vintages' of different character. At any one point there are maturing vintages – funds that started investing several years ago – and new vintages being started based on the fashion of the day. Perhaps one focus of the 2013 vintage of funds will be African agriculture. Perhaps a wave of brochures will be produced for institutional investors, promising them great untapped opportunities in Kenyan commercial farming operations. Once a private equity fund is up and running, they're under pressure to search for deals, buying up a portfolio of businesses and seeking to 'improve' them in order to raise their value. They need to do this within the limited life of the fund, and then need to exit the investments by re-selling them, after which money is returned to investors.

Barbarians at the Gate was famous for painting a notorious picture of private equity groups like Kohlberg Kravis Roberts (KKR), working in tandem with M&A bankers to play on, and prey on, corporate executives. Critics argue that private equity funds destroy jobs, egotistically believing they can improve companies, but really just using leverage to artificially extract gains out of companies that would have been better off without them. Others argue they bring new life to moribund enterprises, creating more jobs in the long term. The truth is probably a mix of the two, but the 2012 American presidential candidate Mitt Romney faced a hammering for his role in Bain Capital, a private equity house that managed to botch a few deals.

Start Your Own Private Equity Fund!

Combine £10 pounds of your own money with £10 from four of your friends. Issue a bond (see page 51) for £100. Now you have £150. Use that to buy an object at a second hand store, one you believe you can restore within three months, after which you need to sell it to pay back the debt and equity investors. Let's imagine that you buy an old gramophone record player.

Scenario 1: You insert new electronics into it, creating a retro DJ deck that you're able to sell on eBay for £250. You pay the bond back with interest, leaving your fund with around £145, up from an initial £50. That's a 190% return, but it's split unevenly: You return £25 to each of your friends, taking £45 for yourself as a reward for performance.

Scenario 2: You do a terrible retrofitting job, and could only sell it for £130 pounds. Once you've paid back the bond, you've got £25. That's a 50% loss, showing the double-sided nature of leverage.

Scenario 3: You also buy an old school desk with a lid, and create a cool integrated DJ deck that opens and closes. You're able to resell them at a much higher price than their two independent values. Well done, you created a 'synergy', the M&A holy grail. On the other hand, perhaps the DJ who buys the combined setup realises after a while that it's just too heavy to lug around. They're forced to sell both to a scrap dealer at a third of their original value. That's a failed synergy.

The Visionaries: Venture Capital

Venture capital (VC) funds are related to private equity, but instead of buying existing companies, they invest in new start-up companies. They spend their time meeting entrepreneurs, trying to decide if they're about to build the next Twitter. Studying where venture capital firms invest is interesting, because it signals where investors believe the next big thing will come from. Popular VC areas include internet companies, medical companies and technology companies, including cleantech renewable energy companies. The VC industry is closely integrated with the 'cool' world of start-ups, and venture capitalists are often ex-entrepreneurs. It thus has a very different feel to the investment banking and trading arena.

To get a good feel for the VC industry, listen to podcasts like *This Week in Venture Capital* or *This Week in Startups*. Take a look at the websites of venture capital firms like Sequoia Capital. They offer various funds, and each fund will have a portfolio of companies they've backed. They don't expect that every deal will work. Like record labels and book publishers, they're hoping to hit a few big home runs from several swings of the bat.

A more informal version of venture capital comes from angel investors, very rich people who put money into start-up companies, much like the investors on the popular *Dragons Den* television show in the UK. *Angel-List* is a website that has become a very important classifieds list for start-ups and angel investors wishing to meet each other.

CHINESE WALLS AND HIDDEN INFRASTRUCTURE

The world of the deal-makers is built around corporate politics. An M&A banker at Credit Suisse can find themselves in possession of very sensitive information – perhaps they know a company is about to launch a takeover bid – that people on the Credit Suisse trading floors would *love* to know about. Investment banks, therefore, are required by law to keep the two quarantined from each other via 'Chinese walls', in order to prevent insider trading, which is the use of confidential information while trading.

There are many other regulations and reporting requirements financial institutions have to keep track of. Large numbers of back office and middle office operations staff are supposed to monitor what's going on among front office bankers, keeping records of all transactions, and keeping the huge IT systems working. There are Compliance and Risk Management teams that are supposed to be internal watchdogs stopping stupid or criminal behaviour among traders, a bit like military police trying to keep control of soldiers.

Over the years a giant auxiliary support industry has built up to help banks and funds go about their business. There are specialist custodian banks like 'BonyM' – Bank of New York Mellon – that specialise in holding everyone else's assets. There are financial PR companies, financial recruitment companies and financial lobbyists. A huge financial intelligence industry includes data providers like Bloomberg and Reuters that pump out raw information, and thousands of firms that attempt to interpret it. The three rubber-stamp industries include ratings agencies that make quality-assessments of financial instruments, accounting firms (such as KPMG, PWC and Deloittes) that sign off deals and audit accounts, and corporate lawyers (in London dominated by 'the Magic Circle' firms) providing the legal sinew that underlies all transactions.

TRACING INTERCONNECTIVITY

That's the basics of the financial system. It shapes the economic landscape, steering claims on the productive economy via financial instruments, redistributing those claims in secondary markets, and helping corporate behemoths to usurp each other, or to fragment. Its various ecosystems are interlinked. The corporate ecosystem relies on the banking ecosystem and the institutional investor ecosystem, and all of them, in the final analysis, rely on us.

Once one becomes aware of these interconnections, seeing past the face value of your everyday experience of finance is easier. What happens when I buy a storm insurance policy? Is the insurance company selling the risk to a reinsurance company?

Is the reinsurance company entering into derivatives contracts with an investment bank to repackage that risk in the form of catastrophe bonds that can be sold to my pension fund? Is my decision to buy a shirt manifested in a *Financial Times* article about stock market prices for retail store shares? As one part shifts, the rest shifts, perhaps in unpredictable butterfly effects. A great exercise is to read a financial newspaper and see if you can connect all the stories together. Is the story about China connected to the story about UK pensions, or are they isolated?

In Chapter 1 we began by describing how a typical person uses the financial sector. We left off with the person obtaining a mortgage. Let's imagine the story continuing:

> In her mid-30s she starts her own business. She struggles to get a small business loan from a bank, but gets money from angel investors by allowing them to take part ownership of the business. Within two years the business has taken off and she raises further money from a venture capital fund that helps her push it to the next level. After five years her company is doing extremely well. The VC and angel investors want her to raise even more money by listing the company on the stock market. An investment bank helps her sell shares to big investors in an IPO.
>
> It is three years later, and now she runs a corporation that needs to borrow more money to expand internationally. The corporate banking division of a commercial bank lends her company £180 million. Now though, her company has interest rate risk on those borrowings. An investment bank dealer enters into an interest rate swap with her company to offset that, and sells them currency options to protect against currency fluctuations. In the meantime, the M&A division of an investment bank suggests that she takes over a rival business. Her company will need to borrow £300 million to do so. The investment bank's primary capital markets division facilitates a bond issuance, getting large investors to pool money together to lend the money for the deal.
>
> It's four years later, and the merger has made her business sluggish and slow. An investment bank corporate finance team advises her on how to 'optimise' her tax to reduce costs, setting up an elaborate tax avoidance system hosted via offshore financial centres. It's going to take more than that to boost the company's flagging profits however. Hedge funds in the secondary markets are betting against the shares in her company, forcing

the value down. A private equity firm takes advantage of the low share price to launch a hostile takeover bid to buy her company.

Before the news of the takeover bid is made public, she uses a shell company registered in the Cayman Islands to buy a large block of shares in her own company, via the brokerage division of an investment bank. She thinks the shares will rise in price once the news is public. A week later, the private equity company succeeds in its takeover bid and fires her, breaking up her company into three parts and selling them off over six years to foreign investors.

The regulators suspect her of insider trading, but the charges cannot be proven, given that her Cayman Islands shell company has a private bank account in Switzerland which is invisible to the authorities. The charges fade away.

Part 2
Jamming

3
Financial Culture-Hacking

NETWORKS OF INFORMATION AND TRUST

The financial system is as much an intermediary system for information, and theories about that information, as it is about money. People make investment decisions based on information. Financial intermediaries deploy information to make money flow. Companies try to hide information to keep money flowing. Financial markets are like a huge social internet, constituted by information flows and webs of knowledge, some public, and some private. Tapping into those is a major aspect of understanding and accessing the system.

The Bloomberg Terminal, providing streaming financial data, is a source of raw, wild, information that is treated with almost religious reverence by financial professionals. Its design seems to be inspired by old *Star Trek* films, with a colour-coded keyboard and retro text set against a black backdrop like the old DOS systems. Instead of being navigable by a mouse, you actually have to type in codes and hit 'enter'. The code WEI unlocks information on world equity markets. BTMM accesses global bond markets. It has advanced calculators to work out values and crunch statistics. It has databases of company information and profiles of individuals. For all its low-fi chic, the Bloomberg Terminal is a crucial component in the functioning of the capitalist financial system.

In the end though, Bloomberg is a machine, just another source of information within the overall noise of public data and analysis. To navigate through the noise, people use human trust networks that hyperlink them to more valuable private knowledge. We all understand this every time we seek advice: For example, I can go onto ten websites that have flat information about a company, but I struggle to trust it amid the noise of advertisements and multiple opinions from faceless people. The information is hard to connect to, similar to listening to someone reading a prepared speech from a piece of paper. Thus, instead of relying on flat information, the trader phones up a broker and says 'What are other traders saying about this revenue figure I'm seeing?' They want *colour*. They want to hear the inflection of tone in your voice. Most of the information is between the lines, and what we all really want is advice from trusted contacts who can give quality, targeted analysis of information in context. Let's consider two financial examples:

1. Imagine you're a financial director at a water utility that wants to hedge inflation risk with an inflation swap. Derivatives are a bit like financial contraband. They're legal, but they're also perceived to be risky, giving them an illicit edge which inclines people towards seeking networks of trust. It's like someone looking to buy drugs for the first time. Dodgy 'boiler-room' operations are the financial equivalent of street dealers, likely to offload poor quality merchandise at a bad price. You don't want to randomly approach faceless dealers from a position of weakness. If you've never bought financial dope before, you might not know what it should cost.
2. Imagine you're at a bank that has found itself in possession of several shopping centres because you stupidly lent to a property developer that can't pay back. Your bosses tell you that you have to get rid of the properties – it's a bank after all, not a property manager. You don't want to widely publicise the fact that you're looking to sell though. Maybe potential buyers will be suspicious about what the true value of the properties are, and bid the price down. Discretion is advisable. What you may do is meet a trusted contact for coffee, and gently suggest to him that you have tricky assets that need to be quietly sold off.

Take a look in cafés in Mayfair, Canary Wharf and the City. There are always people in suits furtively meeting each other on neutral ground, away from the formal boardrooms. Social bonds make markets go around, whether they are old boys' networks, expat networks, ethnic networks, age-group networks or simply networks of people who like each other. Dealers and brokers put a *lot* of effort into establishing these networks of trust. Information differentials are power differentials, and intermediaries need to convince clients that they're not out to make them look like suckers. They want to appear approachable and trustworthy. In major financial centres, a simple beer can be behind a 300 million pound deal.

This principle applies far beyond financial markets. What shops do you repeatedly go to? Much of this book has been written in the Foyles café in London, largely because I've got to know the friendly staff. Getting to know them creates strands of familiarity and trust. Likewise, financial markets, especially those that require phone-based or face-to-face interaction, are vibrant precisely because the relationships formed create a richness of experience. The human connections become emotionally embedded, and people deal with each other simply because they know each other.

This helps to shed light on why banks and brokers spend so much on entertainment. I worked for a start-up company with a limited entertainment budget, but many of the senior managers who had come from large financial institutions were very used to spending a few thousand pounds on a dinner for clients. This extravagance – which is outrageous to most people – is enabled by an asymmetry between individuals and institutions. Certain *individuals* are gatekeepers to certain *institutions*. We're used to the concept of government corruption, where an official in charge of granting a multi-billion dollar oil concession receives a luxury car that is worth a lot to the individual official, but is small change to the institution. Likewise, if the decision of a senior manager at a mid-tier pharmaceutical company has the potential to earn a large investment bank £500,000 in profit, a £5,000 dinner is small change too.

Imagine you're that manager, feeling harassed and overworked by your CEO. A banker invites you to a Gordon Ramsay restaurant that you've always only walked past. You think, 'Why not, I might as well use them.' You go, and try to be pleasant. You notice he's bought you vintage single-malt whisky, and after a while you're getting a bit drunk. As both of you get progressively merrier, you begin sharing stories about your bosses, sympathising with each other's gripes. You're aware that there is a game being played, but you actually begin to like each other, giving each other secret knowledge and bonding on some basic level. He picks up the bill and you stagger home with a warm glow. The reason London and New York can sustain so many overpriced restaurants is that individuals don't pay, companies pay. I don't pay, the shareholders pay.

Information and trust work in positive feedback loops. You build trust by sharing information, but information flows when there is trust. This process gradually allows one to access deals – for example, the broker uncovers a large holding of distressed bonds that a fund manager is discreetly trying to get rid of – which, if executed well, builds *reputation*. Reputation then serves as an external signal that people can trust you, like the way you might trust M&S humus to be good quality. Reputation – also called 'goodwill', or 'brand' – is a hard-fought resource, and it is the financial intermediary's most important asset. Not many people remember Drexel Burnham Lambert: It was one of the largest global investment banks until it was dragged down by a handful of trading scandals in the 1980s. If Goldman Sachs takes advantage of its reputation to gouge customers – which it has been busted for on several occasions – it runs a serious risk. As my boss once said to me and my fellow brokers, 'Reputation, my boys, takes many deals to get, and one deal to lose.'

This dynamic plays out in actual physical space. Whether it's bankers hanging out in pubs in the City, or venture capitalists hanging out at Silicon Valley conferences, they're all there to build up trust, develop their local reputation, and to obtain information. Venture capitalists don't make investment decisions based on internet searches. They want inside information, and hunches from friends.

MOVING BEYOND STEREOTYPES

The vision of financial culture I presented above – involving networks of informal trust – is not one that is widely focused upon in the public domain. Financial culture, especially in the wake of the 2008 financial crisis, is a very emotive topic. The sector is often caricatured by pundits across the political spectrum as a Hobbesian landscape in which professionals lead 'nasty, brutish and short' lives, relentlessly attempting to capture the massive amounts of money up for grabs, gouging it from each other if necessary.

The quintessential image of the aggressive individual lacking any sense of responsibility or internal control is most exemplified by Gordon Gekko, the ruthless private equity warlord from the film *Wall Street*. He uses his arrogant assertiveness and high intelligence for self-serving purposes. Patrick Bateman from *American Psycho* is another great pop culture example, particularly in the infamous 'business card scene' where he and three other investment bankers compare cards in a state of macho, narcissistic paranoia. Such figures feed into more general public stereotypes about finance. A rough-and-ready way to identify these popular notions is to use the autocomplete function on Google search, which guesses your search query based on previous searches from others:

Search	Resultant autocomplete suggestions		
Why are bankers...	Hated	So greedy	So rich
Why aren't bankers...	In jail		
Why are banks so...	Powerful	Corrupt	Evil
Are traders...	Rich	Smart	Gamblers
Are investment bankers...	Rich	Smart	Evil
Why are investment bankers...	So arrogant	Paid so much	

While it's true that there is extensive obnoxious behaviour in the financial sector, with lavish spending sprees, use of prostitutes, and vulgar displays of power, many astute thinkers on political economy recognise that 'banker-bashing' – whereby the problems of finance are presented as stemming from people's character flaws – is not a very useful approach. The figures of Gordon Gekko and Patrick Bateman have some basis in reality, but mostly they are stylised predators, micro-level human abstractions used to represent the extremes of a destructive macro-level system. No actual human ecosystem would last more than a few weeks if it consisted solely of predators, and financial markets would quickly implode if Gordon Gekko was widely emulated. Financial markets, as alluded to earlier, run on a fine balance between competition and co-operation. This vision of 'co-opetition' contrasts with the vision of pure Darwinian struggle, which obsesses about the act of competition rather than the outcome of survival.

Regardless of accuracy though, public stereotypes serve a purpose. Joris Luyendijk, who interviews anonymous financial professionals on his *Guardian Banking Blog*, discovered first-hand the vehemence of the sentiment against bankers when his comment section was flooded with incendiary language like 'GO TO HELL GREEDY BANKSTERS!!!!!' The capital letters and exclamation marks are literary tools for shouting loudly as it were. Their use reveals the public phenomenon of 'banker-bashing' as an attempt to lash out at a system that one appears powerless to act against.

This keenly affects how financial insiders present themselves to the public. During the Occupy protests for instance, we saw financial professionals engage in different types of defence: There were those who attempted to argue 'we're not as bad as that', undertaking diplomatic missions to 'discuss differences'. There were ex-insiders who sheepishly or triumphantly presented themselves under the guise of 'reformed bankers', aligning themselves wholeheartedly with the critiques. Then there were those who unapologetically dismissed the movement, aggressively waving £50 notes from windows at them.

I've frequently been mistaken for a reformed banker, and often get asked for tales of corruption and skulduggery from 'the dark side'. I argue though, that the very concept of the dark side serves the interests of entrenched financial regimes, particularly because it reinforces a *self vs. other* divide, which in turn reinforces an existing power dynamic that merely reduces one's access to the sector. If we are interested in reducing a power asymmetry, then a more effective method is to break that divide down, rather than perpetuate it. In short, I believe in developing greater empathy towards the sector. The position can be summed up with the following analogy: *The person who dislikes computers will never be a computer hacker*. Likewise, curiosity and empathy for the diverse human components of financial systems is one of the most powerful tools of subversion.

FINANCIAL CULTURE-HACKING: ANTHROPOLOGY AS ACTIVISM

There are many interesting examples of financial anthropology. *Out of the Pits* (2006) by Caitlin Zaloom painted a very interesting picture of life in the Chicago commodity trading pits. *Liquidated: An Ethnography of Wall Street* (2009) is an excellent in-depth study by Karen Ho into the internal culture of investment banks. Academics like Donald McKenzie, Karin Knorr-Cetina, Vincent Lepinay, Horacio Ortiz, Karel Williams, Fabian Muniesa, Daniel Buenza, Yuval Millo, and many more, have done important work in the field of Social Studies of Finance. Most of these studies have remained within academic circles though, rather than being used in campaigns.

The term 'Culture-Hacking' – coined by the Canadian theorist Seb Paquet – can, on the other hand, be used to refer to forms of anthropology that have an explicit disruptive intent. I use it to refer to attempts to gain cultural access to a system in order to develop an internal sense for how to work it to your advantage, or to play with it. A culture-hacker aims to build intuitive, situated knowledge about what initially appear to be alienating cultural systems, enabling them to be themselves in a situation of 'otherness' that would otherwise repel them. Culture-hacking comes in different levels of intensity, from milder cultural explorations to gonzo journalism, forms of playful culture-jamming, and deep-level immersion. In the following sections we'll explore these, and simultaneously explore some of the dynamics of financial culture.

What We Can Learn From Louis Theroux

Louis Theroux is an amazing, and subversive, cultural adventurer who explores the most bizarre and dark areas of human experience. If you haven't watched his BBC shows, take a quick look on YouTube. He spends time with prisoners, hardcore racists, survivalists, gamblers, drug addicts, paedophiles, neo-Nazis, gangsters, porn stars, swingers and other extreme groups. Many people in society are intimidated, suspicious, disgusted, or secretly fascinated by such groups, but Louis' great talent is to join their inner circles and win trust. He doesn't disguise himself to sneak his way in. He's simply curious and open. He listens, and people open up to him.

An outlook like Louis Theroux's is useful because it seeks to increase awareness of commonality and reduce hypersensitivity to apparent difference, and thereby unlocks the ability to learn. He breaches a barrier that exists, weakening the traditional self vs. other divide that would normally sustain it. You can often sense him flinching inside – for example, as a rabid homophobic racist says something deeply offensive – but he holds himself open where most of us normally close up to protect ourselves or fight.

This 'quasi-Buddhist' – or perhaps Gandhi-style – approach can be controversial when applied to economic areas that activists are campaigning on. Some, especially in more hardcore activist movements, fear that if one is too concerned with cultural nuance, you open yourself up to 'cognitive capture' by an imagined 'enemy'. A well-known campaigner, for example, once aggressively challenged me, arguing that even learning about finance involves buying into the flawed assumptions of the system. His implicit argument was that a campaigner could protect themselves from the ideological viruses of capitalism by deliberately refusing any interaction with the system.

Here though, is one example where a Louis Theroux approach would have been useful: I once witnessed a tax justice campaigner amongst a group of corporate accountants, many of whom had years of experience with how corporations obfuscate tax structures via opaque 'transfer pricing' arrangements and tax havens. It was an informal setting, and it was a prime opportunity for him to obtain a deeper understanding of the issue. The way the accountants used language though, continually hit deep ideological pain-points in the campaigner, causing him to repeatedly react and argue his case. The result was an irritable clash between incompatible cognitive systems using the same concepts in different ways.

The main problem with this situation, however, was that it wasn't actually obvious that the accountants ever disagreed with him. It was more that he was hypersensitive to negative interpretations of what they were saying. As he repeatedly drew attention to division, he made it a reality, and was thus pushed away from information that was otherwise available. In so doing, he effectively left a subtle financial regime unbreached. A situation like this is likely, in turn, to reinforce his pre-existing perception of himself as part of a group of the outsiders who have no access – a self-perpetuating thought system that becomes hard to see beyond. The lack of access thereby became more entrenched.

Going Gonzo: Building an Inner Map of Financial Culture

Louis Theroux's approach is a light version of *gonzo journalism* – journalism in which the journalist explicitly attempts to reduce the distance between themselves and the 'object' of their investigation. It was made famous by Hunter S. Thompson in such books as *Fear and Loathing in Las Vegas: A Savage Journey Into the Heart of the American Dream*. Unlike the traditional investigative journalist who often accepts, and perhaps even defines themselves by, barriers to access, the gonzo journalist tries as far as possible not to believe in the barriers. In the case of the financial sector, such a journalist aims to personally explore the various economic power relations, psychological dynamics, peer effects, practical constraints and interests that create and lock in people's beliefs. They don't seek to 'report on the financial sector', they seek to experience it and come to grips with it intuitively. For example, if they're trying to learn about high-frequency trading, they may phone NinjaTrader – a high-frequency brokerage firm – and open an account. In this way, information is obtained – which can then potentially be presented to the outside world – but equally importantly, territory that is imagined to belong to insiders is taken over as boundaries are denied.

A great place to experiment with this is on financial forums. Check out the *Wall Street Oasis*, *Trade2Win* and the *Wilmott* forums. These are online equivalents of the coffee houses of days gone by where speculators might have gathered. They're often frequented by actual traders and bankers, so you can openly ask questions about how things work. They're great places to test out ideas and weaknesses in arguments, for example, by putting up contentious topics. Once one becomes attuned to the environment, the opportunities to learn begin to seem extensive. Listen to conversations on trading and investment podcasts from iTunes – such as *StockBroking101*, *The Disciplined Investor*, and *Trend Following with Michael Covel* – or watch *Financial Times* video interviews with fund managers while you do your ironing. You'll learn how different people think, and will learn about finance far quicker than by reading any book. Search for 'corn trader' on LinkedIn, and browse the profiles of the commodity speculators. One can trace whole swathes of the agricultural trading community in this way. Attend random financial conferences, and go to financial Meetup.com groups. Professionals openly talk about their operations in such settings.

If you're based near a financial centre, try spending time amongst the buildings. Watch the ebb and flow of financial professionals, and listen to conversations. The activist group Platform London designs free downloadable audio tours to guide one around the physical space of the oil financing complex. You can develop your own tours too. A corporation exists far beyond its immediate headquarters: Visit the offices of the major investors that fund it, the accountants and lawyers that sign off its accounts, the ratings agencies that assess its bonds, and the stock exchange where its shares are listed.

These explorations can actually be fun. You can put on a suit, carry a copy of the *Financial Times*, and hang out in the lobbies of the world's largest investment banks. Tell the receptionist you're just waiting for someone to come down. Feel like getting into the Bank of England? You can do so by buying a vintage £5 note on eBay and requesting to change it for a new note. Feel like watching metal traders in action? You can book to watch the trading pit sessions at the London Metal Exchange, the last open-outcry pit exchange in London. Hang around outside and speak to the traders on their smoking breaks between setting the global price of metal. It's incredible the information one picks up merely listening to people talking on phones in Canary Wharf.

Global financial centres, such as London, host a kaleidoscope of financial internationalism, lean, young and multi-ethnic. You'll notice that the shy and nerdy mix with the loud and abrasive. Reserved Oxbridge types mix with freewheeling libertarians. The deeply analytical mix with the highly impulsive. The sector is skewed towards men, those with higher education, and those with the social networks to enter it, but is also more diverse than many people imagine. Many old timers in London finance will frequently talk about the 'Big Bang' of financial liberalisation in 1986, and how it cracked the old boys' clubs that previously dominated, creating a class of *nouveau riche*. Sitting outside an investment bank for 30 minutes and watching the people going in and out will show you this. Keep a look out for the following four aspects:

1. *Nationalities and ethnicities*: Major investment banks are not nationalistic institutions. In some cases they may have a bias towards hiring citizens from the countries they operate in, in order to do business with local companies, but many roles are highly international. An investment bank has clients around the world, and has to cover all major global languages. It's often easier for them to run a few big offices in key financial centres than to try run lots of smaller operations everywhere, so many expats end up working in London, New York and Hong Kong banks, including large numbers of South Asians, East Asians, Eastern Europeans, Australians and South Africans. Banks are far more interested in hiring top international graduates and people with international exposure in other industries, than they are in hiring cosy local elites.

2. *Age groups*: Finance, unlike some industries, is a sector where youth can dominate over experience. Traders, for example, are often just a few years out of university. A person with a PhD in a new statistical concept may know it better

than anyone else, and banks may be eager to give them an opportunity to apply it. Indeed, much of the 'feral innovation' that sparked the financial crisis came from highly educated young people, with little reputation to protect, keen to apply their skills. The crisis consequently led to much discussion about whether older managers even understand what the juniors below them do. Senior managers are certainly not stupid, but older management layers of banks are heavily dominated by white males who rose up the ranks at a time when banking was less meritocratic and required different skills. In some areas of finance – such as boutique private wealth management – these old-school types still dominate.

3. *Gender imbalances*: Banking has traditionally been male-dominated, and this bias still exists, especially in the front-office ranks of traders and deal-makers. *Wall Street Women* (2012) by Melissa S. Fisher traces the hard road women have had in entering the industry since the 1960s, but over time women have come to play an increasingly prominent role. One common question in gender and finance literature is whether men behave differently, perhaps egotistically seeking out aggressive roles that allow them to take on risk. There is little scope to discuss this literature here, but it is an interesting, and challenging, area for feminist studies. Luyendijk's *Guardian Banking Blog* hosts various interviews with female professionals: Some interviewees cite feeling empowered by the sector; others though, suggest that they feel a need to appear 'more Catholic than the Pope', displaying hard-edged 'finance-like' behaviour in order to break through the glass ceilings that hamper upward mobility.

4. *Educational status and class*: The front end of banking is still weighted towards those from upper social classes, but much less so than several decades ago. There is a premium on university education, especially for those who study technical, mathematical and scientific subjects. Financial institutions develop strong relationships with universities, trawling them in the UK 'Milk Round' in search of high achievers. Many roles though, do not require a high-end elite education. For example, brokers and salespeople are often recruited for

being personable. The ranks of interdealer brokerages and certain types of trading (such as open outcry trading in pits) have a significant working-class element. These professionals are sometimes referred to as 'wide boys' or 'barrow boys', in reference to old market traders selling vegetables and illicit goods.

Becoming Attuned to Cracks

Financial institutions often portray themselves as serious places where serious people get serious things done using serious techniques. In reality though, financial professionals are often engaged with finance in non-serious ways, donkeying about, cutting corners, skiving off, mocking their superiors, and building models without knowing whether they'll work. Playfulness is a characteristic of ownership. If I own a house, I can walk around naked in it, paint pictures of Jimi Hendrix on the ceiling, and smoke a shisha pipe without asking a landlord's permission. Financial professionals will often slouch into work, maintaining an external appearance of properness, but feeling a basic sense of ease. To them, the suit, skyscraper and excel spreadsheet seem friendly, normal and often mundane.

Justice campaigners frequently imagine financial professionals in too serious a fashion, almost buying into the vision, perpetuated by the PR departments of the banks themselves, of a well-organised and co-ordinated world of elite professionals. Furthermore, many campaigners often band together on the basis of shared belief, and may project this when thinking about financial professionals, perhaps imagining them as ideologically united. Consider the following – particularly extreme – formulation of this view, from the far-left Whitechapel Anarchist Group (WAG), who I spent time with in 2010:

The City of London is perhaps the most highly concentrated manifestation of exploitation on the planet. Looming oppressive dehumanising ravines of glass and chrome in which each soulless tower represents a distilled accumulation of the blood, sweat, suffering and death of millions of impoverished people, as well as immense environmental devastation on a global scale. Intermittently populated by swarms of parasitical automatons who scurry to and from the multi-layered edifices of suffocating bureaucracy in which to conduct their odious practices.

WAG – which has since disbanded – is not representative of broader justice movements, but the perception of the financial sector presenting a unified oppositional force is seductively easy to accept, and readily used by many populist politicians. It is thus important to stress the point that financial institutions can operate without any unified foundation of belief. In the context of brutal overall competition between institutions, the industry is surprisingly non-judgemental, accommodating all manner of informal trust-building, co-operation, creativity and diversity. You may be gay and black, and immensely good at doing clean-energy deals. The wealth managers on the floor above you might, on the other hand, reflect the old-school conservatism of their old oil-baron clients. The emotions of the trading floor below you might coalesce into libertarian thought systems, or fragment into rebellious, even anarchic, thought.

In my experience, the culture of finance is a hybrid, spanning unlikely combinations between rarefied intellectualism and gregarious wheeler-dealing. At its best, there may be networks of people held together in easy, jostling, game-like behaviour, competitive but mutually respectful and collectively empowering. At its worst, that behaviour can degenerate into an unaccountable, disconnected and clawing individualism with no trust or mutual respect. While banks and other financial institutions might seem unified or daunting from a distance, when viewed up close they are often multi-layered mutating structures. Here are some of the fissures to consider:

Between Classes of Institution

There are clear hierarchies between classes of institutions. For example, investment banks trump commercial banks, but, as a collective, hedge funds and private equity firms generally trump them all. The different types of institutions have very different internal atmospheres too. The atmosphere on a brokerage desk is rowdy and vulgar, whereas the atmosphere in a large fund management company like BlackRock, or a private wealth management company, is often much quieter, refined and analytical. A cerebral fund manager is not likely to feel at home in a strip club with a group of ICAP brokers, and is more likely to prefer entertainments like wine-tasting or music concerts with other fund managers, or with more intellectual traders. In other words, there are much higher levels of elitism in certain types of institution.

Between Institutions Within the Same Class

Within the ranks of investment banks, J.P. Morgan trumps UBS, but Goldman Sachs trumps J.P. Morgan. Deutsche Bank, Barclays Capital and Credit Suisse battle for the position of top European investment bank. There are league tables produced to show which banks dominate at various activities: For example, Goldman Sachs routinely dominates M&A advisory activity, but Barclays Capital is dominant in interest rate swap trading. In the commodity derivatives trading arena, Goldman Sachs, Morgan Stanley, Barclays Capital and J.P. Morgan take the lead. French banks like BNP Paribas and Société Générale trail slightly behind the front pack, but are ahead of many others like RBC and HSBC's investment banking division. Japanese investment banks like Nomura and Daiwa are important in Asian markets, but lag behind in Europe.

Between Financial Instrument Classes

Many investment banks make a distinction between 'cash' and derivatives desks: A 'cash equities' desk, for example, will be staffed by people who literally trade actual blocks of shares. Next to them might be a 'delta one' derivatives desk, which trades equity derivatives based on shares. It's possible that they may be merged into one, such that they can present a united face to a client interested in equity markets. Alternatively, all the derivatives traders across asset classes could be put together on one part of a trading floor.

Derivatives traders may lord themselves over bond, equities and currency traders, due to the more complex nature of what they have to trade. Likewise, exotic structured derivatives traders may try to claim precedence over those who trade 'vanilla' derivatives like interest rate swaps. Prior to the financial crisis, structured credit traders, who packaged together mortgages and junk bonds to resell as securitised products, might have tried to claim precedence over the others – but this, understandably, is no longer the case.

Between Bank Divisions, and Between Individual Desks

The internal structure of an individual bank is a fragmented federation of teams competing with each other to gain support from the bank's central authorities. In the heat of activity, this can take a confrontational form. Trading divisions may battle the M&A divisions, and individual trading divisions can battle each other. A good book to read to get a feel for this is Michael Lewis' 1989 pop-finance classic *Liar's Poker*. It profiles Lewis Ranieri, a pioneer of mortgage-backed securities. He came from an Italian New York background, starting in the mailroom at the investment bank Salomon Brothers (now part of Citigroup) in 1968. By the early '80s he presided over a motley group of loud Italian New Yorkers and highly intellectual mathematics students, defending his crew from other teams that thought such mortgage securities were a waste of time.

In many cases though, inter-team and inter-division rivalry takes a lighter form, reflected in the use of internal stereotypes by different professionals to jibe each other based on their roles. The straightforward trader pokes fun at the highly intellectual quant who sits next to him. They both, in turn, poke fun at M&A investment bankers as wannabe politicians with slick suits and big smiles. The M&A teams, in turn, might lampoon traders as sloppy, moody layabouts who go home at 6 p.m., rather than working the long hours they do. Individual trading desks can be a site of subtle struggle. Traders may joust with their own salespeople in the way that chefs have friction with waiters. Younger salespeople attempt to subtly poach clients from older salespeople who have become too proud to cold-call, while attempting to fit within the inter-generational hierarchies.

Short-term Cohesion Amid Long-term Uncertainty

One very interesting aspect of financial culture is the acceptance of conflict as a fairly routine and non-distressing aspect of existence. For example, brokers are frequently on the receiving end of trading desk frustrations, as a trader caustically abuses them over the phone for messing up orders or not understanding the trader's vision. Brokers though, write this off, seeing traders as being temperamental drama-queens. As the frustration dissipates, the trader chats to the broker as if nothing happened. If you watch the activity at the London Metal Exchange, you'll see people literally screaming at each other, and then 30 minutes later they are in the pub together laughing. It's an 'all's fair in love and war' mentality, where individuals form loose, short-term bonds of trust against the backdrop of long-term uncertainty.

Outsiders witnessing aggressive behaviour on brokerage and trading floors are, however, prone to interpret it as reflecting a lack of trust among aggressive individuals. While some conflict is indeed the result of true aggression, I would argue that many brokers or traders do not feel that fighting affects the fabric of their relationship. A comparison can be made to military life, where soldiers' rough behaviour towards each other is often one aspect of a broader camaraderie. Another comparison is the way I might fight with my brother – I feel no need to apologise to him because we don't see our conflict as an aberration that has to be resolved. There can even be a certain liberating quality to a trading room for more reserved individuals who have grown up in cultural environments that have taboos on fighting, or where they've always been expected to be 'nice' to people.

Brokerage and trading floors do, however, have codes to mediate conflict, as well as certain internal norms that are supposed to be followed as loosely federated teams aim towards institutional goals. Many of these are fairly intuitive to most people: For example, if a salesperson from one team has made an effort to establish a potential client, another salesperson is expected to respect that relationship, and may be shunned if they don't. In an investment bank M&A division, the need for a team to display cohesion is particularly important, because sealing a large M&A deal is a process of gauntlet-running, requiring team members to juggle and co-ordinate several aspects of the project at once.

A Management Illusion?

The media often focuses on CEOs and the senior management of banks. These public figureheads are supposed to be responsible for bringing out the best qualities of those below them. They are also responsible for convincing bank shareholders and regulators that they are in control. Their ability to control though, is directly linked to their ability to monitor. Monitoring requires two things:

- Firstly, it requires structured hierarchies that link senior management via middle management to individual traders or bankers. Objectives, targets and orders from on high are supposed to be communicated down the chain and the results are supposed to be communicated up.
- Secondly, it requires robust IT systems that can collate information about what is occurring at all levels of the firm, so that the bank's central authorities can have oversight.

There are multiple weaknesses in this system however. The 'troops' on the frontlines can easily post dis-information to superiors who potentially don't understand the financial products, and who, in the context of the short-term targets they're trying to meet, may have little incentive to care. As for the IT systems of large financial institutions, they are chaotic layers of programs added over time, such that few people may actually know a bank's overall exposure. Financial IT professionals can tell all sorts of horror stories about bank systems that were designed in the 1980s and that cannot be tinkered with because the person who designed them has either left or died. A company like BP could be dealing with several different divisions at a single bank – for example, getting loans from one, derivatives from another, and insurance services from still another. It's highly unlikely that the bank's CEO could get a clear picture of exactly what dealings they have with BP, never mind the thousands of other clients, at the push of a button.

A recent addition to this mix is the concept of *systemic* risk. At any one point, a bank like Morgan Stanley will be borrowing from many different institutions, while warehousing extensive inventories of financial instruments and derivatives exposures from different trading desks. It may be the case that they feel in control of their own operations, but they cannot fully account for the operations of the other banks they are connected to via loan and derivative relationships. A good analogy for systemic risk is electricity systems: One power line might be in good working order, but if it is connected to other power lines in grid systems, a failure in one weak power line can cause an overload of electricity to be redirected towards others, overwhelming them all like a chain of dominos. An everyday example of systemic risk occurs when someone takes a calculated risk in running across a road in front of an oncoming truck, without realising that others are doing the same from the other side of the road, such that they crash into each other in the middle as they try to get out of the way of danger. Regulatory bodies, which used to be focused on checking that single banks were above board in their individual risk-taking, now have to take a systemic risk approach, looking at inter-bank connections.

Playing in the Cracks: Financial Culture-jamming

Once one gets past the initial appearance of flat uniformity in the financial sector, it becomes clear that there is great potential for outsiders to use it as a creative playground for cultural mash-ups. In the past, protest artists have attempted to do this. The subversive performance-art duo The Yes Men have mastered the art of mimicking professionals to break into conferences and dupe them. Groups like AdBusters have been pioneers in the field of 'guerrilla semiotics' or culture-jamming: One might transform a billboard advertisement, for example, so that J.P.

Morgan Asset Management and Barclays Capital cunningly shift to J.P. Morgan Ass Management and Barclays Crapital. The joker is a powerful subversive figure, pricking bubbles of exclusivity and power by mocking apparently serious authority figures and traditional symbols.

There are not nearly enough jokers though, and much protest art still struggles to break down barriers. The exploits of The Yes Men live on in YouTube videos, but the breaches they open quickly close up. They temporarily embarrass corporate culture in a very entertaining way, but they don't actually confuse anyone for long, or maintain the breach. The much more difficult task is to create permanent or self-reinforcing hacks, viral memes that embed themselves into a system, and that actually change thought patterns. Which image, for example, is more subversive: A graphic design of a banker represented as a skeleton in a suit, or a picture of an elderly woman having tea, labelled 'banker'? To my mind, the latter is more effective at subtly defying the power of financial regimes.

There are clear limits to these small, symbolic efforts to reclaim a sense of broader ownership of the sector, but we should not underestimate the power of rehumanising and diversifying the images of finance. In computing, a Distributed Denial of Service Attack (DDoS) is an attempt to make a network unusable for its normal users by bombarding it with requests. A mass attempt to make a network available to a *much wider pool of users*, on the other hand, might be called a *Distributed Denial of Distance* (DDoD) attack, whereby a system is bombarded by those traditionally excluded from access. It would be fantastic to see a flourishing of artists like Hayley Newman, who cheekily labelled herself as the 'Self-appointed artist in residence for the City of London' and used the financial landscape as the basis for experimental art pieces and a book of short stories called *Common*.

Fun areas that can be developed under a DDoD programme include technological 'psycho-geography', designing playful conceptual ways for people to experience the physical space of finance, perhaps via audio-tours, maps and technological mediums such as augmented reality viewers. Tech-savvy people can get involved in hyperlinking financial institutions into the Internet of Things[1] via physical QR codes. Film-makers can explore guerrilla film-making, creating the financial equivalent of the *Blair Witch Project* or Banksy's spoof documentary *Exit Through the Gift Shop*. Composers can represent an algorithmic trading strategy through music, helping people to understand such things audibly. Poets can satirise CNBC financial analysis by creating Homeric epic slam poems of the spurious attempts to explain the markets. Designers can create infographics and visualisations that can break down complex systems. Coders can create computer games that enable people to explore the sector in virtual space. The *Art as Money* team produces psychedelic financial installation art, wearing outfits that blend from workers overalls into swish suits.[2] Can a fashion designer create a financial subversion suit, with Karl Marx cufflinks and a cyberpunk tie with Bloomberg prices streaming through it? Most importantly, could I use this to engage in the ultimate financial performance art: To walk into a financial institution, sit down at my desk, and turn on my computer?

GETTING EMOTIONAL: SUITING UP FOR DEEP LEVEL CULTURE-HACKING

There is no greater symbol of finance than the suit. Putting it on gives one a strange freedom, much like a mask does, to walk unnoticed amongst large crowds of other people in suits. When I first arrived in London in mid 2008, I used my suit to get into a number of hilarious interviews. In my first interview I had to write about the prospects for the Brazilian currency amid a noisy room of analysts, while having almost no knowledge of either Brazil or currencies. I was interviewed by austere investment managers who owned the rights to the James Bond book portfolio, and who asked me whether I took drugs. I nearly

---

1. A term used for physical objects or buildings that are connected to the internet via a physical beacon or barcode.
2. See http://blog.artasmoney.com/blog

failed maths at high-school, but I did a maths test for an options trading company while they played Gnarls Barkley music at high volume to distract me. I sat on the 36th floor of 25 Bank Street in Canary Wharf, in the offices of Lehman Brothers, having a comical interview with two managers who were insisting the firm was in fine health, just weeks before it collapsed.

For people with a passion for open exploration, this type of mischievous infiltration of alternative worlds is *fun*. The process of flying by night on the dark side becomes like a game, but a very emotional game. In the two years spent with my motley crew of young colleagues and old financial rogues, I could literally feel my thinking shift, pulled along by the emotional currents that come with building such relationships. As a broker, I spent time with intellectual derivatives traders, fund managers and practical corporate directors, but brokers as a collective are often renowned for being 'barrow boys' – rough, hard drinking, extroverted, not particularly prone to political correctness, and frequently identifying as working class. The lives of these individuals imprinted themselves on me, as I uncovered their different personal stories and how they'd come to be doing what they were doing.

Take, for example, Oscar (not his real name). He was from Eastern Europe. He had originally worked for a company called Enron – which infamously collapsed after a huge accounting fraud scandal and, upon its demise, drifted to Goldman Sachs. He used to say that Enron was an exciting, creative, company to work for, whereas Goldman was controlled and rigid, which is probably the reason why Goldman is still around. When I was working with him, Oscar became fascinated by the intricacies of a wind-farm securitisation called Breeze – consisting of a bundle of wind-farms that investors could lend to via the structure. He spent long hours trying to work out how the value of this structure would be affected if European wind-speeds changed. Others, such as 'Seamus', used to look on in bemused fashion at such eccentric activities. He'd spent a long time working for Brazilian institutions, most of whom had little interest in obscure products like Oscar's. His business was in broking high-yield emerging market corporate bonds – simple, laid back, and prone to occasional default. He had very little idea how the swaps that my team were working on actually worked – and neither, for that matter, did we. But as our big boss used to frequently shout: 'Sell the sizzle, not the sausage!', his subtle way of saying 'you don't need to understand how it works, you just need to broke them'.

Such small and frequently unremarkable day-to-day experiences slowly build up, and if you spend enough time in a suit it does strange things to you. You begin to realise that others are using it for the same purpose as you are – to gain and maintain access. Diversity becomes apparent as you take on the guise of uniformity, and previously single notional categories – such as 'hedge funds' – and the beliefs you attach to them, begin to fragment into sub-categories. As I spent time in the sector, it ceased to be scary or abstract. I built up the resources needed to move around, and acquired the intellectual frameworks to understand its operations from its own perspective. Within six months it was possible to feel the emotional currents inside myself, feeling the fears and excitement of money flows and meetings. In other words, I began to become part of the structure.

One word to describe the process of acculturation is 'Grok': It's used by the Martian protagonist in Robert Heinlein's 1961 novel *Stranger in a Strange Land*, referring to the fusion process whereby a person's body merges with the water they drink. In his words 'Grok means to understand so thoroughly that the observer becomes a part of the process being observed— to merge, to blend, to intermarry, to lose identity in group experience.' One meaning of the term 'Grokking' – now in the Oxford English Dictionary – refers to the idea of 'drinking cultures' in order to incorporate them within oneself. It's like deliberately electrocuting yourself to develop an emotional theory – or intuition – about electricity.

This is, of course, disconcerting. Identity, to some extent at least, is constructed via one's interactions with others who validate it. As I put myself in alien situations I was disrupting my pre-existing world of social relationships, which led to some strange situations. For example, in April 2009, after a day talking about derivatives to fund managers, I went to the Climate Camp G-20 protests in Bishopsgate, and was kettled for six hours by police. A high-spirited activist approached and shouted 'High five, awesome that you came disguised as a banker.' He was visibly shocked when I told him what I did, struggling to reconcile the act of protest with the idea of a broker.

Immersing yourself in cultures that hold alternative beliefs thus disrupts the status quo of your own mind, introducing conflicting reference points that create *cognitive dissonance*. This is well known in hardcore postmodern anthropology, but also in other areas: For example, in the 1970s, the undercover agent Joseph Pistone (aka Donnie Brasco) infiltrated the mafia so deeply that he incorporated the cognitive structure of their thoughts into his own. He developed a discontinuous personal identity, like a double-agent occupying alternative worlds in chameleon-like fashion. The point of doing this is to hack the concept of the barrier, keeping a foot in two worlds and adapting the structure of your thoughts to accommodate and explore the conflicting viewpoints. Your mind naturally seeks to create hybrid principles, and you begin to uncover the deep level fault-lines and trade-offs between arguments. This, perhaps, lies at the basis of becoming a heretic, as described by Thomas Aquinas: One who has access whilst simultaneously corrupting dogmas. You turn yourself, in other words, into a culture-hack.

The Chartered Finance Activist: Four Areas for Exploration

So, why not apply for the most notorious positions possible, just 'for the lulz', or the hell of it? Walk down the corridors of J.P. Morgan, and put interesting questions to the commodity traders, fossil fuel financiers and deal-makers you find inside.

It's a slightly tongue-in-cheek idea, but perhaps we could set up two programmes to encourage the process:

1. *The Chartered Financial Activist (CFA) programme*: In mainstream finance, the CFA normally refers to a 'Chartered Financial Analyst' – someone who has sat the gruelling CFA exams, which teach financial analysts all sorts of investment trivia. The Chartered Financial Activist, on the other hand, undertakes a three to six month culture-hacking mission in

a financial institution – perhaps via a summer internship programme – getting to know the environment.
2. *The MPhil in Financial Heresy*: A more in-depth programme, entailing immersion in financial culture for one to two years. Entails more commitment than the CFA, and more personal dislocation.

Any such CFA or MPhil programme though, needs to have as one of its aims the production of a dissertation on some aspects of the financial power structure. In the remainder of this chapter, we'll go through four possible dissertation topics, including the values of finance, the risk illusion, technological impacts on rationality, and the problem of institutional amorality.

Topic 1: The Values of Finance

In previous sections, I suggested that there are people with a diversity of backgrounds and personalities within the financial sector. That though, says little about what drives bankers, traders and fund managers. In many discussions about finance, there is the assumption (whether explicitly stated or not) that these diverse individuals are battling it out in a singular search for money. For example, the neoclassical economic vision presents bankers as agents who self-organise through self-interest maximisation. This informs the mainstream banking reform debates, which constantly refer to the need to 'shift incentives' (aka place money in different places) in order to steer the profit-maximisation impulse positively.

The very word 'incentives' though, is linguistically loaded to imply *extrinsic* rewards – such as large bonuses – that make people act. The casual discourse about greed driving the financial sector, however, has many shortcomings. We can illustrate this with an analogy. An aggressive person is more likely to join the army than the Royal Ballet. But it does not follow that everyone in the army is aggressive, or that aggression is the dominant motivating factor for joining the army. Some people join simply because it's perceived as the 'thing to do' in their family. Some join for the adventure, or because they're looking for work or a sense of belonging. Some go for ideological reasons, while others find the strategic analysis interesting. Once they arrive, the army has structures in place to bring out controlled aggression, but that remains only one part of any individual's story.

Adverts for military service thus tap into various motivations, from 'providing service to your country' to 'having an adventure and making friends'. Likewise, financial recruitment teams do not use the 'banker driven by greed' concept as the basis of their campaigns, realising that many graduates do not want to think of themselves in such a way. Try watching the graduate recruitment videos on investment banks' websites, or on Goldman Sachs' YouTube channel. They go to great pains to present a vision of their firms as a route to self-empowerment, explaining how appreciated graduates are, how they can use their skills, and how they will be given responsibility. They pose a series of challenges – 'Are you good at analysis?' 'Can you think clearly under pressure?' – generating a sense of elite belonging and 'can-you-make-it?' dynamism. These types of messages resonate with individuals in different personal situations, who are perhaps already being pushed towards finance for a variety of reasons. Consider the following, for example:

- *Social expectations*: Many people are pressured by family and peer-groups into entering professions such as finance, law or accounting. In the UK, for example, finance is one option for a son from a respectable 'posh' family to enter, couched in an elite sense of honour. A person from Eastern Europe might be inclined to view UK finance jobs as an opportunity their parents did not have, and which cannot be turned down lightly.

- *Dominant industry status*: In Detroit, people ended up in the car industry simply because jobs were available there. Likewise, the financial sector is full of people who had no especial desire to join it, but who drifted into it because the jobs were available. A sector with growing job opportunities can appear 'obvious' to those in university peer-group networks, especially if earlier waves of friends and contacts help provide access.

Finance also has psychologically addictive elements that help to perpetuate it. The front ranks of an investment bank – like that of an elite army unit – are preceded by stories of heroic mystique, appealing to those who feel they are 'skilled enough to make it'. Once in those structures, financial professionals frequently report that the 'meritocratic' structure readily rewards them for doing well, which feels empowering. The public debate may be focused on the issue of bonuses – which can indeed be large – but people are kept locked in by far more subtle rewards. For example, many graduates find it exhilarating to be on a team analysing whether or not to back, for example, a nuclear plant. In contrast to academia, where analysis filters slowly through journals, this analysis has immediate and direct consequences. This creates an adrenalin buzz, especially as the cost of mistakes becomes serious.

Most frequently overlooked in public debates though, is the *intellectual challenge*. Finance can be very intellectually stimulating for those who enjoy systems analysis. Many graduates would easily get bored of repetitive tasks after a while, but analysing changing economic conditions requires a constant process of juggling information. The multi-billionaire hedge fund manager Bruce Kovner, interviewed in the book *Market Wizards* (1993) by Jack Schwager, talked about trading as follows:

> For me, market analysis is like a tremendously multidimensional chess board. The pleasure is purely intellectual. For example, it is trying to figure out the problems the finance minister of New Zealand faces and how he may try to solve them. A lot of people will think that sounds ridiculously exotic. But to me, it isn't exotic at all. Here is a guy running this tiny country and he has a real set of problems … My job is to do the puzzle with him and figure out what he is going to decide, and what the consequences of his actions will be that he or the market doesn't anticipate. That to me, in itself, is tremendous fun.

The ability to get rewarded monetarily for having a direct impact on a variety of intellectually challenging deals can attract arrogant glory-boy types who believe they can beat the market with an innovative new technique. It can also, however, attract eccentric intellectual oddballs who enjoy being able to use their skills in an industry that 'appreciates' them. A good example of this can be found in *My Life as a Quant* (2004), a book in which Emmanuel Derman describes how he was drawn into building financial models in the banking fast lane, leaving a sideways-moving academic career in theoretical physics.

If you spend time with financial professionals, you'll quickly discover that many have this 'nerdy' side, and can be extremely passionate about analysis. There is a cottage industry of popular finance books which spin tales about traders as esoteric adventurers and oddball outsiders. While they may over-play the point for journalistic effect, they do provide anecdotal evidence of the almost playful roguishness of certain star traders. *The Quants* (2010), a book by Scott Patterson about the mathematical 'geniuses' of Wall Street, describes Peter Muller, the creator of Morgan Stanley's internal hedge fund PDT, who was also a regular keyboard busker on the New York subway. *Market Wizards* profiles Larry Hite, who drifted into trading after working as an actor, screenwriter and rock music promoter.

One particular point emphasised in this literature is the complexity of the motivations behind risk-taking in finance. Investment bank trading floors are routinely referred to in the press as being akin to a casino where money is gambled recklessly. We're used to associating the casino with the concept of greed, because in its purest form greed is that internal drive which draws one towards the possibility of *outsized returns for almost no effort*. Casinos are indeed havens for people with get-rich-quick mentalities. On the other hand, a lot of the best casino gamblers live on the intellectual thrill of beating the system, or bucking the odds. For such professionals, their adventures are often an elaborate game of skill measured in money, and fought against those who are too greedy to be clear-headed. If money is fetishised too much as an end-in-itself, the gambler will readily feel elation when they win, and distress when they lose, leading them to act stupidly. Professional gamblers bend the system to their advantage by teaching themselves to be emotionally detached from individual cases of winning and losing, focusing rather on the longer-term probability of winning more than they lose. This applies to financial gambling too: The best traders are often less overtly 'greedy' than the average ones, and think of trading in terms of a disciplined game.

It is thus surprisingly difficult to pinpoint quickly the values of individual people in finance, and if I'm hypersensitive towards negative interpretations of external behaviour, it's questionable whether I will be able to see the values at all. Depending on one's inclination, the individualism or aggression of the sector can be portrayed positively in terms of innovation, freedom and adventure, and indeed is frequently understood like this by financial professionals. Certainly, when set against the complacent figure of the conservative old-boys'-club banker, the diverse 'feral' bankers of financial crisis fame seem like a more interesting animal entirely.

Topic 2: The Risk Illusion

A day-in-the-life of most financial professionals is – in one sense – relatively straightforward. They will be phoning clients, interacting with software such as spreadsheets, and interacting with people in meetings and after work in pubs. There is the drudgery of admin, and the inevitable need to deal with office politics. Many people work late nights and are thus physically tired, and try to exercise to stay healthy. At the end of the day the older guys try to get out as soon as they can because they live out of London and want to get back to their families.

If, on their way home, a trader reads 'trading is socially useless' in a newspaper comment piece, they'll probably grimace. That may be because they have a vested interest they're trying to protect, but equally they may just fail to see a trading environment as anything other than entirely normal, having got used to it and incorporated it into their personal identity. It becomes hard for such individuals to understand public reactions to their lifestyle, and financial workplaces have a way of distancing workers from everyday conceptions of normality. An M&A banker might be working on five billion dollar deals. Many have international personas, having spent their lives working around the world. Operating in that environment, and being rewarded for being more efficient, more aggressive and more intelligent, may be exhilarating and empowering up to a point, but after a while it will come to seem ordinary, perhaps making financial professionals appear very arrogant to outsiders.

This is of course not inevitable, and financial professionals may deliberately attempt to keep themselves down-to-earth. Greg Coffey, a London-based Australian hedge fund trader who was paid an extraordinary £170 million in 2007, is known to ride the London Underground to work wearing casual clothes. There's no doubting though, the stark social distancing factor that large amounts of money can create. Don DeLillo's *Cosmopolis* paints a picture of the anomie (loss of norms) that comes with excessive wealth. In the book (and the film), a 28-year-old billionaire trader drives through town in an insulated limousine, dispassionately viewing riots, searching for something that might surprise him, or pose a risk to him.

Most people in major financial institutions are nowhere near that level of wealth, but the environment certainly encourages money to be seen as an abstract symbol of skill or status, rather than something used for day-to-day exchange. The tiered pay structures of the top investment banks set an initial hierarchy – base salaries may start at around £40,000 for a first-year analyst, moving towards £100,000 by the sixth year – but bonuses can vary from zero per cent of base pay to several hundred per cent, meaning juniors have the potential to make more than their managers.

This encourages a cult of meritocracy that is hard to escape. Those who have become wealthy have an interest in believing in the internally generated myth of their own unique significance. They tend to think of themselves as self-made successes, rather than attributing their success to luck, information asymmetries, or the brand name of their institution. When challenged, many will claim that the money they earn is 'deserved' due to their hard work, their willingness to take risks, or their personalities and intelligence. Many in the public intuitively reject that, but, within the financial environment, these claims hold much cultural weight.

While it's true that certain bankers are gifted individuals, many make their money off *economic rent* – being in an individual position of power within an intermediary institution with power, through which huge flows of money travel. The key question, within that environment, is whether the individual or the organisation is responsible for generating the wealth, and this is a major factor in deciding bonus payments to individuals. To put it in loose Marxist terms, there is a constant battle between financial institutions and financial workers over who owns the means of production.

Within the financial sector, contacts are one major source of revenue. If I develop a relationship with the financial director of a large housing company, I can legitimately claim responsibility for bringing a large-scale deal with that company to my financial firm, which in turn can earn the firm several million pounds in fees. If I've taken the time to build the relationship, I 'own' it. And if I leave the firm, then the emotional threads that constitute the relationship do not disappear – I merely take the relationship with me. The firm can try to claim intellectual property – such as details about the client – but not emotional property. I could 'give' the contact to the firm when I leave, but that would be meaningless, like me writing down the name of my friend on a piece of paper and handing it to my bosses.

Financial firms are paranoid about this power that individual workers have, and try to retain intellectual property through all sorts of confidentiality and non-compete agreements if workers leave. It seldom works. A person I worked with, for example, brought a USB stick with 3,000 contacts from his previous investment banking position and uploaded them onto our system. When he left our firm, he took the contacts with him again, and the firm tried to sue him. I still have those 3,000 contacts on my laptop – random structured credit traders who I've never met, but who theoretically constitute a source of potential revenue in the financial system, if only you knew them.

Contacts are one source of personal power in the financial system. Other sources might be specialist skills that are hard to come by, or deep experience in some niche area. It is however, very easy to overestimate these. Dealing desks, for example, generate their money in part from knowing clients, but also from taking risks in intermediation between those clients. A Morgan Stanley dealer is thus prone to claiming that he's paid for 'taking risk'. While they may insist that this is a stressful and skilful undertaking, being a trader for Morgan Stanley is a like being a soldier in the US Army – the institutional power greatly supplements personal power. You watch prices go up and down, and you take calculated risks with *the bank's* money. It's akin to being a sniper, hailed as a hero when your aim is good, but remaining some distance away from immediate personal danger.

This brings us to a point that is not often considered: The mere fact of an individual aspiring to a successful career in a brand-name company like Morgan Stanley or Goldman Sachs appears very conventional, perhaps even betraying a *risk aversion* in that person as they seek to conform to dominant conceptions of what success means. This is reflected in the huge 'how to get a job in an investment bank' advice industry aimed at individuals who put themselves under tremendous pressure to get in. Many such graduates obsess about the league table rankings of the banks they apply to, and make plans for how they will climb the career ladder from analyst, to associate, to associate director, to director and finally to managing director. They plump their CVs out to show how they excel at teamwork, leadership, initiative, facing challenges and making quick decisions. They waffle on about being go-getters, hungry to excel, quick to build technical knowledge, and how personable or charismatic they are. They flood in for 12-week summer internships, trying to secure a place for the following year's bank intake. In the back of their minds is the thought that you can't work in a hedge fund or private equity fund until you've put some time in at an investment bank.

Major investment banks, in other words, always run the risk of becoming clubs for bright but socially conservative people, buying into the hubris of their own giftedness but often without having the unconventional flair that genuine risk-takers have. Indeed, receiving a basic salary of over £50,000 a year does not qualify one as being in a truly risky position. People who enjoy true risk are more likely to start their own company, gamble their own money, or work for a firm where they are more likely to fail.

The cleaner at Morgan Stanley has probably been exposed to far greater personal risk in her life than the average derivatives dealer whose desk she vacuums under.

Topic 3: Technological Impacts on Rationality

Markets contain chaotic information that can easily affect people's emotions, especially if they are individuals who deep down seek certainty of belief and position ('risk aversion'). Whole industries of financial TV reporting, for example, are built on providing backward-looking narratives for 'why the Japanese markets are down', offering a comforting service by (arbitrarily) picking out reasons from among thousands of possible causal and interconnected factors.

Some of the world's best bankers and traders ignore such narratives and embrace the information chaos, displaying an openness towards uncertainty and accepting the inherently imprecise nature of investment decisions. Others though – perhaps because their jobs require it – often attempt to remove or quantify the uncertainty by looking to the past to predict the future. These attempts can indeed be interesting, and intellectually stimulating. There is, for example, a hedge fund that uses semantic analysis of Twitter posts to read the general mood in the air, from which they then make trading decisions. There is nothing necessarily damaging about this – we all try to create narratives about the past and future to some extent – but some traders come to obsessively believe that they can crack the secret of overall markets, searching for an abstract 'truth' amid the fluctuations of price information. This has been encouraged by the influx of mathematics and physics students into the trading environment, which has led to biases towards viewing price movements in the same way one views the movements of atoms. Statistics, and other forms of quantitative abstractions about past events, start to be seen as the ultimate source of insight into the future.

This process of increasing abstraction has also been encouraged by the advent of high-performance computing capable of crunching large amounts of market data to extract the imagined patterns. The average person tends to view Microsoft Excel as a useful spreadsheet program for everyday tasks. Financial modellers though, will tend to view it as a tool for creating their own programs, called models. Models are financial machines that are built to replicate the processes of human thought without a human having to be involved. They are used by corporate loan bankers to model loans, by M&A bankers to undertake valuations, by risk managers to calculate potential losses, and by traders to price financial instruments. Consider, for example, the Excel model (Figure 3.1) on page 125. It is used to work out what a longevity swap should theoretically be priced at. It does so by using a Monte Carlo simulation, testing thousands of permutations of possible future scenarios, a process that would take an individual human a very long time to do. It is a piece of financial technology, consisting of 6 MB of Excel file, that replaces the work of many people.

Such models can be useful, but they have serious shortcomings. Firstly, they are only as good as the assumptions they are based on. Secondly, they are only as good as the data you put into them. Thirdly, as Marshall McLuhan observed, technology contains embedded values that can feed back to its users. The combination of such intellectual machines and the physical machines that run them can distance their users – such as traders, M&A bankers and corporate bankers – from the ground-level reality of what they're modelling, encouraging a false consciousness of a statistical or hard scientific basis to social reality.

Textbooks on finance often read like vocational engineering manuals, and this is how financial professionals are encouraged to think about what they do. When enough people are schooled in such thinking, systems of internal groupthink develop that fail to encourage reflexive questioning of the methodology used. It's problematic if whole groups of people begin to view markets like physics, if in reality those markets are human ecosystems. Indeed, it could be argued that the financial crisis stemmed from disconnected groups of people 'rationally' creating an irrational overall outcome, by using a spurious pseudo-scientific paradigm that they collectively validated.

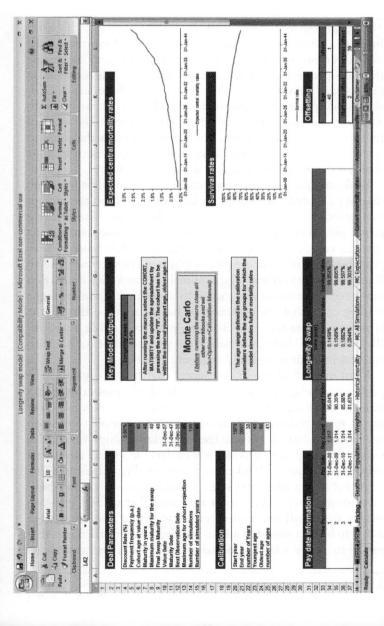

Figure 3.1

Topic 4: Institutional Amorality

In 2008 I wrote an academic paper for a legal journal on the topic of criminogenic (crime producing) structures,[3] suggesting that job-promotion systems based on achieving short-term targets tend to advantage – in an almost evolutionary sense – those middle managers who are most willing to tell partial truths to senior managers, while ignoring irregularities in the work of the junior staff beneath them. The worrying spectre this presents is that over time an entire institutional structure can become corrupted, thereby normalising deviant behaviour.

Banks certainly can encourage crude instrumental philosophies that serve as protective shields for individuals, such as the concept that 'greed is good'. It is a mistake though, to take these apparent moral philosophies at face value. In my experience, such belief systems can be quite shallowly held, and while bankers may pay lip-service to hardcore philosophers of self-interest like Ayn Rand, there are very few who genuinely act on a deep conviction in the righteousness of rampant individualism. Even in the rogue trading cases that are presented as having a moral thread, the rogues are often scared individuals who have made a mistake they then try to hide by betting their way out of it, rather than ruthless individuals wilfully engaging in fraud.

Most individual employees accept that fraud is wrong. The problem, I believe, is not one of individual immorality, but a much more insidious issue of *institutional amorality*. All the sector really requires and encourages is for people to develop specialist technical knowledge and relationships to achieve short-term targets. It provides few outlets for a wider emotional awareness. A junior banker may not see themselves as doing anything wrong when they engage in activities such as unethical investment. They work within a hierarchal structure, and each step is signed off and mandated by someone else. They were asked to build a model of a loan profile. Someone then uses that model to justify a lending decision, which is in turn vetted and

---

3. See B. Scott, 'Free market criminogenesis, corporate governance and international development', *The Company Lawyer*, Vol. 29, No. 8, 2008.

signed off by lawyers and accountants, allowing senior managers to demonstrate that they're fulfilling their legal duty to look after the short-term interests of their shareholders or creditors. The individuals are, all too often, distanced and disconnected from the collective consequences of their individual actions. Thus, while from the outside the activities of a bank may look like someone pulling off a robbery with intent, from the inside they appear like a vague slow-motion robbery, undertaken in steps by people with different ideas about what they're doing, where individually reasonable decisions lead to negative systemic effects.

Get Exploring

If we want to combat those effects, we have to dig into the rationality behind individual decisions in the financial system. A few hundred Chartered Financial Activists could go a long way in exploring how the human relationships that underpin the sector are distorted by psychological, institutional and technological factors that can alienate people from reality. They can also help to uncover how those dynamics might be used to engage in economic jamming, which is the subject we turn to in Chapter 4.

4
Economic Circuitbending

The term 'circuitbending' normally refers to the altering or customising of pre-existing electronic devices in order to create unusual musical instruments. Something similar can also be done with financial technologies. Financial activism, at its purest, is about using financial instruments in ways they're not supposed to be used, bending their initial purpose towards unorthodox ends. For example, *shareholder activism* may involve using a shareholding in an unorthodox way to divert a company away from its orthodox modes of operation, such as dumping toxic sludge into a river to maximise profits.

Shareholder activism and other forms of economic circuitbending are not intended to replace traditional forms of campaigning focused on mobilising public and political pressure. Rather, they are supplementary forms of activism that can enhance and augment existing campaigns. James Marriott of Platform London put it very well when he noted to me that 'We have long lobbied MPs on political issues, so why not simultaneously lobby investors on economic issues?'

Groups like Platform London, Greenpeace, FairPensions, BankTrack and various others have been proactive in developing new techniques of financial jamming to bend economic circuits. As more campaigners get involved, the concepts will be refined and pushed into the big time. Key areas that will be discussed in this chapter include the following:

1. Building up an understanding of capital flows, and developing DIY corporate finance advisory capabilities to help block them.
2. Expanding the boundaries of shareholder activism by unionising small-scale shareholders.

3. Developing activist hedge funds.
4. Using unorthodox methods to expose opaque areas.

WHERE THE MONEY FLOWS:
TRACING FOSSIL FUEL FINANCING

Sometimes we imagine that a corporation ends with its CEO; but corporations are investment vehicles for a combination of equity investors and debt investors. Management teams may co-ordinate the oil rigs, but any environmentally damaging project has financial backing that keeps it alive. Financial capital flows animate the economic landscape. We can imagine them in abstract form, pumping up whole industries, and letting them collapse when they flow out. Tar sands operations, and Arctic oil exploration, for example, are like sprawling dirty bouncy-castles, maintained by pumps pushing capital into them via corporate entities and joint ventures.

The deceptively simple thought that follows is this: if one wishes to shut down a tar sands operation, one needs to turn off the pumps that keep the capital flowing. It's a powerful vision, but it requires you to identify where the flows are coming from, and understand what activated them in the first place. It then requires you to turn them off. Importantly, it also requires that you offer alternative channels for the capital to flow into. This is very difficult to do in practice, but let's explore it anyway.

Who is Global Capital? Identifying the Channels

Where does tar sands and Arctic oil financing come from? And what about financing for destructive mining projects or land grabs? These are questions that can only be answered on a project-by-project basis. A major mining project could be funded by a consortium of commercial banks via a project finance arrangement. Money could be steered via bonds arranged by investment banks. It could be a sovereign wealth fund investing directly. It could be shady investors steering money via a faceless offshore vehicle called Acme Corp.

These individual investors might collectively be called 'global capital'. That makes it sound like a singular coherent force, but statements about 'where global capital is moving' can be misleading. The apparent movement is the result of thousands of independent decisions of disjointed investors. Each investor has different information and proprietary ways of analysing that information. You see them on Bloomberg TV, giving wildly divergent views on, for example, the Chinese property market.

On the other hand, investors do often *act in herds*. They attend the same conferences, and collectively perpetuate investment memes – pieces of intellectual code that install themselves into people's heads. For example, fund managers might previously have never considered investing in commodities. Then they begin hearing about it from colleagues. A pundit gets interviewed on CNBC, or writes an article, talking up the inflation-protecting benefits of commodities investments. Suddenly an investment meme takes shape. The investment banks catch on, and roll out investment vehicles to channel the herds while scraping fees off them.

One ongoing investment meme, for example, is 'China'. Type 'Invest in China' into a search engine and you'll find many articles making the case for investors to 'gain exposure' to the country. An American multinational might be bold enough to invest *directly* in Chinese factories (foreign direct investment), but a UK pension fund might invest indirectly (foreign portfolio investment), accessing investment opportunities via 'China funds', which buy shares in Chinese companies listed in Hong Kong. An investment bank might convince a Chinese company to issue a 'Dim Sum bond' via Hong Kong to sell to foreign debt investors. This is investment in China.

Investment involves taking liquid money, exchanging it to solidify it into real assets, extracting returns from those assets, and then later liquidating them into money again and redeploying it. As investors sell out of one investment (liquidate their position), they have to put the money somewhere else. Prior to the financial crisis many investors piled money into property, via investment vehicles such as mortgage-backed securities. As the crisis hit, they attempted to liquidate those positions in order to redeploy the money elsewhere, such as in US government bonds and gold investment vehicles. In the process the property market imploded, and the price of both US government bonds and gold skyrocketed.

These capital flows have major impacts on currency markets as investors reassign capital from one region to another. A US private equity fund that buys an Indian textile business needs to use American dollars to buy Indian rupees which they then exchange for a textile firm. If they wish to liquidate that position, they sell the firm for rupees, and use those rupees to buy US dollars, which now are looking for a new home. Both the 1997 Asian financial crisis and the 2002 Argentinean debt default saw 'capital flight', as panicking foreign investors liquidated their positions and dragged dollars out, draining the countries of foreign currency reserves and placing huge downward pressure on local currencies pegged at fixed exchange rates. The local currencies subsequently collapsed in value as their governments abandoned the pegs.

Thinking as an Investor: What Makes the Money Flow?

In 2006, I was commissioned to write a report on private capital flows into healthcare in Africa. I imagined this process as the 'privatisation of healthcare'. In my mind, I had visions of big US firms baying eagerly at the prospect of extracting profit from the ills of vulnerable people. Investors though, are not thinking of themselves as 'collectively privatising healthcare'. They are often isolated individuals sitting in offices in Johannesburg or Mumbai thinking, 'is it worth me investing in Ugandan private clinics?' What kind of investor would really put money into Ugandan healthcare? If you were a sober fund manager at Fidelity Investments, looking after pensions, would you do so? Many larger investors will only invest in proven industries, such as German car manufacturers. Moldovan car manufacturers, or private healthcare companies in developing countries, are bound to be risky investments, and the expected returns may not be high enough to justify the risk.

Big investment flows begin to happen when a generic business case in a specific industry appeals widely to a lot of individual investors. This occurs when an industry offers relatively high *expected returns* that can be gained for relatively low *risk*. Thus capital does not simply flow to where returns are potentially high – it flows to where expected returns are high relative to expected risk. South Sudanese oil fields offer potentially very high returns, but the risk is also high, which dampens an investor's enthusiasm. Little foreign private investment will flow to Somalia. The expected returns from many industries there are often low, and the risk entailed in extracting those returns is high. From an investment perspective, it only makes sense to embark on dangerous quests across the desert if you imagine fabulous chests of King Solomon's gold to be hidden in the dunes. Investing in Moldovan car manufacturers is like embarking on a dangerous quest in search of a chest of tinned foods. You could get the same return, for *much less risk*, by walking to your local Tesco. Alternatively, you can go to China and get *much higher returns* for the same level of risk. Eccentric thrill-seekers, governments and NGOs may go on quests to places like Somalia, but 'rational' investors, most likely, do not.

Investor Types: Risk Averse or Risk Prone

Most investors are not adventurers. They are more likely to be risk averse, especially if they are hired as stewards, like pension funds are. Funds often have mandates, legal charters that set out their internal rules for investment. They may be legally barred from speculating on highly risky ventures. Even prior to the financial crisis, when the animal spirits of excessive optimism were high, money from such investors was flowing into the less risky 'tranches' of securitised mortgage products. The conservative sheep got excitable and ran with the wolves for a while, but only at a distance in large protective huddles. When such products were revealed to be riskier than expected, such investors were forced to liquidate their holdings and flee to safer investments.

Risk aversion is one source of investor herding behaviour. Risk is normally experienced as a subjective perception. If I don't know what's lurking under the dark waters of the lake, I view it as risky. Money thus most readily flows along well-trodden paths to where the waters have been tested. It's akin to successive waves of gentrification in a 'rough' area – pioneering arty adventurers reduce the risk perception, suddenly leading to a flood of eager yuppies and coffee shops. At that point the artists sell their dilapidated squats at a huge premium to the yuppies and move on. Emerging markets are likewise viewed as comparatively risky by Western investors, who may not understand the country's language or how business is conducted there. The apparent 'risk' of investing in Vietnam, for example, is partly attributable to cultural bias and sometimes to plain ethnocentrism. As a country's boundaries are loosened, more adventurous foreigners make forays, and the perceived risk goes down. Suddenly investment magazines begin running articles on Vietnam, and *voilà*, a herding meme starts to spread.

Investor Types: Local or Foreign

At any one point there will be a series of 'frontier markets', such as – today – Kenya, Nigeria and Bangladesh, which are one rung down from emerging markets. Investors in these apparently riskier environments are either bold foreigners or local (or regional) investors who don't perceive the environments as risky. Indeed, when foreign investors go into a frontier market, they may be more comfortable doing so via joint-ventures with a local investment partner, or else as part of a consortium that can spread the risk. There are major political factors too. Foreigners may be *required* to co-invest with a local partner, and be limited to certain industries. Developing country Special Economic Zones and tax havens may suck in foreign investors with promises of low tax or low regulation.

Foreign equity investment in major emerging markets is comparatively well established, but debt investment is less so – in other words, it's comparatively hard for Western investors to lend to Vietnamese companies. In many poorer countries, both share and bond markets are underdeveloped, which means any type of foreign investment is constrained. If I can't buy ownership on a stock market, I will have to negotiate *privately* for it, which means I need relationships with local power-brokers on the ground. Politically unstable environments such as the Democratic Republic of Congo (DRC) have local gatekeepers who can facilitate access to investment. It might be a rough-necked ex-mercenary from South Africa who has invested time in making friends with local generals, offering a conduit for posh foreigners to gain access.

Investor Types: Diversified or Undiversified

A mutual fund run by Fidelity Investments is unlikely to invest directly in the DRC however. It's much more likely to invest in a London-listed mining company, which in turn invests in a joint-venture company in the DRC, which in turn co-invests in a huge copper mine with an opaque entity registered in the British Virgin Islands.

A Fidelity fund might thus have a tiny slice of DRC exploitation in it, and a tiny slice of tar sands, amid slices of weapons production, hair products, Barbie dolls, magazines and airlines. The mentality of such a highly *diversified* investor is clearly different to that of a locally based DRC investor with half his savings invested in a mine. Fidelity has a different perspective on risk: They don't put all their eggs in one basket, and have a more abstract connection to any individual egg. The undiversified investor, on the other hand, carries one or two ostrich eggs. Some of the dodgiest operators in the world – the cowboys who set out on gold-rush adventures – are often undiversified investors who live by their wits on the ground. For example, the Toronto Stock Exchange and London's AIM stock exchange are full of mining or oil 'juniors' – smaller risky companies that try to hit it big prospecting in uncertain environments.

Investigating Investment

A UK FTSE 100 corporation attracts investors from all over the world. A private Russian company, on the other hand, may be held by a group of closely-knit and secretive private shareholders, augmented with money from Russian banks. Uncovering which investors are behind any one venture can be a fascinating and difficult detective job. A very useful, but very expensive, tool for this is a Bloomberg Terminal, the source of raw financial data used by virtually all financial institutions. Using a terminal, I can trace the equity investors in Coal India, the huge Indian coal producer. It shows me that the Indian State owns 90% of the shares, that the Indian investment fund Reliance Capital owns 0.16%, and that the foreign investor Templeton Asset Management owns 0.02%, along with many others.

Campaign groups might consider pooling funds together to get access to a terminal, but it's much easier to make friends with people who work in financial institutions, who can email you Bloomberg screenshot 'grabs'. A terminal though, cannot provide access to deeply private information. Private companies often refuse to disclose who their investors are, and banks often refuse to disclose where they make debt investments. Bondholders in companies can be very hard to track too. Bond dealers and brokers may know who is holding Gazprom bonds, so private relationships need to be built to access that information. Take a look at economic detective agencies such as Kroll that specialise in 'corporate intelligence' and due diligence. They work on behalf of investors – who may be concerned about who else is investing in a Russian oil venture – and find innovative means to track down that information.

Build the Activist Bloomberg! A Wiki Project

Activist groups like BankTrack have done great work on building platforms for forensic investigation of capital flows. They and the UK Tar Sands Network, for example, have begun tracking investment in tar sands. The Rainforest Action Network works on tracing money going into coal in the USA, and the London Mining Network focuses on the financing of major London-listed mining companies. Nick Hildyard at The Corner House has great expertise in tracing investors in large infrastructure projects, and the Berne Declaration has worked on tracing investment in physical commodity trading. A major task for the future is to build up an effective overall clearinghouse for all this information, so that activists too can have their own version of Bloomberg.

DESTABILISING INVESTMENT CASES: EXPLORING INVESTMENT RATIONALITIES

Large investors like pension funds have a *fiduciary duty* to look after the money entrusted to them. They distribute it to fund managers constrained by legal mandates. If a fund manager advertises their fund as low risk, and subsequently blows money on ill-fated attempts to dredge up pirate treasure, they can be sued for breaching a mandate. Large investors though, can also hide behind concepts of fiduciary duty and mandates to justify unethical, but 'prudent' investments. It's a hired-gun rhetorical device similar to that used by advertisers: 'We're not responsible for tobacco deaths, we're just paid to make the adverts.' This mentality can be contrasted, in theory at least, to lawyers and accountants, who are supposed to uphold ethical principles that may go against their client's immediate interests. Groups like FairPensions are working to shift the legal definitions of 'fiduciary duty', such that fund managers cannot use it as a convenient excuse for ethical blindness.

Be a DIY Investment Advisor

In building cases against unethical investment, however, it can be helpful to tap into the intellectual frameworks of fund managers. If I approach a fund manager and say 'tar sands extraction contributes to global warming, therefore you shouldn't be investing in it', I would be assuming that he agrees with the argument, and that he sees himself as having individual responsibility within a broader swathe of investors, and that he has the ability to act on it. All three of these assumptions are uncertain. It's similar to pointing out to a truck driver that driving is wrong because it contributes to global warming. Does a truck driver *really* feel that they are personally responsible, especially if they have a vested interest in keeping their job? This is not to pose an amoral view of the world, but to point out that such constraints on positive action need to be taken seriously.

Risk is a different taste sensation to morality. It's like sweet, or sour, versus spicy: One can sense them simultaneously. A powerful campaign against an investment might combine a spicy sting of morality with an unnerving base of sour risk. Imagine then, that you're a corporate finance advisor with-a-difference working for Heretic Partners LLP, out to advise investors on their investments in corporations, and corporations on their investments in particular projects. If you wish to cast doubt on an investment case, you may either:

1. Increase its perceived risk (heighten the sour taste).
2. Lower perceptions of its expected returns (reduce the sweet taste).
3. Add moral indignation (load up the spice).
4. Serve all of the above together.

Blagging it on Risk and Return

Investment involves exchanging money (a cost) for a stake in a venture that you believe will yield positive cash flows in the future (a benefit). The amount you have to outlay, relative to those expected future cash flows, gives rise to an expected return: 'It will cost me £7,000 to cross the desert, but I expect to find £14,000 in the dunes. 100% return. It's a no-brainer!'

The rationality of investment though, is one of taking risk – outlaying money that you possibly will not get back – in exchange for a return that's expected to compensate you for that risk: 'There is a 10 to 20 per cent chance that I will die in the process ... hmm ... is £14,000 worth it? No, I would only go for the possibility of £21,000 ... or if I could reduce the investment cost to £4,600...' Such an outlook is used to assess whether investment opportunities are good value, or alternatively, what you'd be prepared to pay to invest. Here is another way of conceptualising valuation, incorporating time into the mix:

- Imagine a magic box that's guaranteed to open up and give you £100,000 as soon as you buy it. What would the fair value of that box be? Answer = £100,000.
- Now imagine that the box has a time lock and will open up in a year's time to give you £100,000. It has zero risk (it's guaranteed), but also requires you to wait. If you paid £100,000 for it *now*, you would actually be losing money, because an alternative option would be to make a zero risk investment in government bonds,[1] which pay an interest rate. If that rate was 2% for a year, you'd end up with £102,000 in a year's time. In the face of this alternative opportunity, why would I buy a box that only gives me £100,000 in a year? I might, however, buy the box if it was priced at around £98,000.
- Now imagine a less magic box that *wasn't guaranteed* to give you the £100,000 after a year. Perhaps there's only a small chance of it giving you the full amount. Would you be prepared to pay £98,000 for it now? No. Now there is true risk. The price would need to go down significantly to make it worth my while taking that risk...

Notice the interplay between how much you can potentially expect to get out of the box, the time involved, and the chance of getting it. The theoretical fair value of the investment is actually the expected cash flows, *discounted* by the time and risk. Discounting is a means to perceive the present value of an investment that will play out in the future. A 'discounted cash flow valuation' takes all the expected future cash flows, adjusts them for time and risk, adds them together, and *voilà*, this is how much it is worth.

Remember though, that risk is experienced as a subjective perception, and thus different people have different fair values for investments. A fund manager looking at a Chevron share is looking at a series of time-locked boxes extending into the future,

---

1. Lending money to the government has historically been thought of as *risk-free*, because the government has an army, can tax people, and controls the mint. The current interest rate on government bonds is thus called 'the risk-free rate'.

into which they can extend the personal hopes and fears that they've formulated in the present. They're imagining the potential cash flows embedded in that future (paid out to them in dividends), while considering the likelihood of those materialising, the cost of the share, and whether the expected returns will cover any obligations they have to others – for example: 'my pensioner clients are relying on me to earn them a decent but stable return', or 'the investors in my hedge fund require high absolute returns'. As thousands of these players make these decisions, it gets reflected in the price of Chevron shares. Share prices thus, generally speaking, reflect projected future scenarios – the higher the price, the more confident the view of the company's future. If Chevron's future outlook begins to look more risky, the value of its shares re-adjusts downwards to reflect that.

That's the theory at least, but it's important to take it with a pinch of salt because many investors don't actually attempt to guess the intrinsic fair value of Chevron based on its future outlook. They may simply look at similar companies and do a *relative valuation* – akin to working out the value of a house by looking at the values of similar houses around it. In fact, technical traders and other short-term speculators may make little effort to do valuations at all, simply riding with the fluctuations in prices. Also remember the psychological herd effects. A shift downward in price can spook more conservative investors, giving them a cold chill down the spine: 'Why is the price going down? Do other investors know something I don't?' That might cause the risk perception to increase, the investment flows to reduce, and the price to go down even further.

Chevron Managers Investing in Projects on Behalf of Investors

Increased risk perceptions depress the value of a company. That can displease conservative investors, causing them to back away, but might draw in investors who have higher risk appetites. If Chevron's management team, for example, were to start selling all their safe operations, and begin focusing solely on South Sudanese oil projects, they would be refocusing the company towards *a higher risk investor base*. As the risk increased, conservative investors would flee, the share-price would lurch downwards, and the higher risk investors would be induced in.

Theoretically though, the management team and CEO are supposed to serve their current shareholders. Those shareholders have invested because they perceive that what the company is doing suits their risk appetites and their return expectations, and they, in a theoretical sense, 'hire' the managers to maintain that. They have an expectation of the managers and the latter are supposed to treat meeting that expectation as an *obligation* they owe to shareholders. In a massive corporation, however, it's often not entirely apparent who the shareholders are, because there are thousands of them. The shareholders though, are given a face by the Board of Directors, a group of luminaries voted in by the shareholders, who are supposed to represent their interests to the company management team.

Every time Chevron decides whether to invest in a new project, such as a new tar sands operation, the managers are supposed to take into account their shareholders' expectations, referred to in the abstract as their *cost of equity*, or 'what return our shareholders expect from us' (e.g., 'our shareholders expect a 15% return'). Chevron's management will add that together with the interest rates they owe debt investors such as banks and bondholders, to come up with an overall *cost of capital*, representing all the demands from those nosy shareholders and parasitic lenders.

In the context of assessing a new project, this cost of capital is sometimes called the 'hurdle rate'. A new project may be worth taking on if it's imagined future returns can jump over that hurdle rate. In the technical jargon, they may invest in a project if it displays a positive *net present value* (NPV), or expressed another way, if the project's *internal rate of return* (IRR) exceeds the hurdle rate. If, on average, Chevron's individual projects don't do this, they'll be dying a slow death as investors demand more than Chevron produces.

Despite sounding very technical, this whole process is very subjective, and it's the kind of thing Goldman Sachs advisors charge extortionate fees to give advice on. The end game here is that there's a junior analyst sitting at a desk at Chevron trying to draw up spreadsheets of tar sands projects. The project is like a series of time-locked boxes of oily treasure, which the company may pump their investors' money into, trying to unlock a return. The analyst has no flawless crystal ball to tell her the exact future. She makes a series of predictions, helped by petroleum engineers, about how much oil can be extracted, how much it can be sold for, and what the costs of doing that are, thereby guessing the cash flows and the return to Chevron's investors. She needs your input.

OWN THE SYSTEM: SHAREHOLDER ACTIVISM

In every large public company there is a trade-off. The company raises money by selling shares of ownership, but in so doing they open themselves up to democratisation. Owning a share makes the shareholder a 'citizen' of the company, giving them a right to vote on company matters. A share is thus a financial technology of *access*, giving an inside voice to a shareholder to make demands within the company's city walls, as it were. Consider the following table of various corporate stakeholders:

Insiders
The employees, including lower and middle management
The senior management team
The board, representing a bridge between managers and shareholders

Equity investors (shareholders)
The large institutional equity investors who often own significant slices of the company
The smaller funds and hedge funds, who might have an interest in disrupting the status quo
The scattered and poorly organised retail investors, often including retired employees who own shares

Debt investors
Banks
Institutional bondholders

External influencers
The government, regulators and tax authorities
Financial journalists
Financial analysts who advise investors
Ratings agencies, accountants and lawyers
Civil society and pressure groups

The democratic power of shareholders is seldom used effectively. Large-scale fund managers hang out at the same cocktail parties as CEOs, often being vested in the same elite social groupings and modes of thought as the company managers. More flamboyant investors such as hedge funds can cause trouble, but only when it suits them. Small-scale retail shareholders often don't even realise they have any power, or are too poorly organised to activate it. It's akin to an Athenian democracy: The conservative city males vote, but the hills outside are dotted with peasant smallholdings in a state of proto-democratic submissiveness.

Democratic Reform: Awakening the Shareholder Democracy

One pressing agenda is to awaken this dormant democracy of small shareholders. And one method to do this is for campaigners themselves to join their ranks, becoming embedded rabble-rousers in the shareholder ghettos. This can entail four elements:

1. Become an agitator: Engage in personal shareholder activism.
2. Unionise the shareholders: Start building unions of small shareholders who agree with your concerns (see page 147).
3. Lobby the powers that be: Influence larger institutional investors to engage in socially responsible investment (see page 149).
4. Start Das Kapital LLP: If all else fails, start your own guerrilla group, a hedge fund of conscience (see page 160).

Individual Shareholder Activism

To infiltrate the ranks of ordinary investors, it's important to get deeply into character. You buy shares in a mining company. Now you're a shareholder. You become enraged by the way the patronising managers are running the company you partly own. They treat you, and your fellow small shareholders, like ignorant annoyances while cutting corners and creating environmental damage. You don a suit and attend their *annual general meeting* (AGM). You raise your concerns publically, requesting a response from the managers, and a meeting with them to discuss your concerns further.

Ideally, shareholder activism should in large part be aimed at other shareholders. It is counterproductive to arrive at an AGM like an unruly vagabond demanding to be heard, accusing the managers of gross ethical deviance, because this alienates you from other shareholders, who'll boo you down. In your heart of hearts, you may believe Shell's operations in Nigeria reveal a flagrant disregard for local ecosystems and communities. You may know of the persistent political abuses, and of the toxic artificial daylight created by the gas flaring. You are, however, a shareholder of the company, and your words should come authentically from the perspective of such a shareholder. The ideal though, is to position oneself as an enlightened and holistic shareholder. Potential approaches that fit that include:

1. Raising the risk bulwarks against damaging projects.
2. Factoring in their true long-term environmental and social costs.
3. Demanding legitimate returns.
4. Showcasing alternatives.

Raising the Risk Bulwarks

As a shareholder, corporate managers take risks on my behalf. Poor management of that risk damages the value of my investment. Consider the political backlash against Shell over the death of Ken Saro-Wiwa, or the huge damages and negative publicity that BP attracted in the wake of the Deepwater Horizon oil spill.

Shareholder activism should always play on the idea that company management teams are taking excessive, unnecessary, or hidden risks that are artificially enhancing the returns of the company in the short-term, but that will come back to bite them. The argument needn't be absolutely accurate in every case, but phrasing it emotively in terms of risk will make it more readily heard. There are many types of risk in the world. Market risk is the risk that a particular market is heading for a fall. Political risk and regulatory risk is the risk that an investment will be targeted by politicians and regulators. Reputational risk is the risk that people who buy a company's products will begin to view it negatively. Model risk is the risk that incorrect assumptions or methodologies have been used in investment decisions.

A large corporation owns a collection of individual assets, each with unique risks. A multinational commodity corporation may have mines, ships and grain terminals all around the globe. It is thus diversified, with each mine or individual project constituting one small slice of its overall operations. A major institutional investor that owns a chunk of that corporation is also likely to be highly diversified. Those two degrees of diversification lessen the risk of any individual project to that shareholder. Corporate managers though, still need to show 'good governance', managing the perceptions of major shareholders by showing that they are *generally* in control of the corporation's collective risks. A lone little shareholder activist berating them for irregularities in a single copper mine in Zambia will concern the CEO because it can cause *contagion*. If their major investors become aware that one mine is potentially badly run, what's to stop them imagining that the rest are too. The company could then become seen as a hornet's nest of potential future controversy.

The 2012 Libor scandal caused both a lurch downwards in Barclays' share price, and the toppling of CEO Bob Diamond. It wasn't that investors only cared about a single scandal among a handful of traders. The concern was equally about what the scandal revealed about the general governance of the organisation. Small scandals can focus unwelcome wider attention on CEOs. Bear in mind that they, and other senior managers, will always own shares in the companies they run, giving them a vested interest in keeping risk perceptions at a low level. A sole shareholder activist who threatens to raise risk concerns thus perhaps has more power than might be expected. Ideally that activist needs to generate an internal campaign, such that the message seeps into the general community of investors and into the financial press.

Questioning Long-term Social and Environmental Costs

An alternative to raising risk perceptions is to raise questions about projected returns. Chevron's internal analysts may have overestimated future returns from Arctic oil for instance. In their projections, such analysts would have incorporated monetary costs, but will they have incorporated the long-term *social and environmental costs*? The Carbon Tracker Initiative, for example, has been effective in arguing that investors have been misled by oil companies that report oil reserves that can only be burnt at the expense of long-term runaway climate change. The spurious reporting of unburnable reserves means such companies are overvalued based on false assumptions about their future.

CEOs are well-trained at fending off questions like 'why are you creating pollution?' They use utilitarian arguments like 'we're creating jobs, and we do our best to minimise any pollution created in the process'. They suggest that pollution is not within their control or within their remit. Another way of seeing pollution, though, is as an environmental cost that the company has simply 'externalised', i.e., *not accounted for*. Questioning why they haven't accounted for that cost elicits lame responses such as 'well, no one else does', or 'we don't understand how to account for it'. The shareholder activist will thus spin it as an issue of accounting incompetence on the part of management – something that should be in their control. Most importantly, as a shareholder, I need to know this information, because such externalised costs can be retroactively 'internalised' via fines, taxes and bad publicity – as in the above case of BP. I need this information in order to make a rational long-term investment decision.

Investment is a concept based on returns over time, so in asking whether an investment decision is a good one, one also has to ask about the time horizon. For example, is investment in infrastructure worthwhile? If it's judged over five years, the answer is clearly no – I outlay large amounts of money for little return. Governments tend to invest long-term in infrastructure because it opens up latent opportunities, and therefore tax revenues, that take shape over many decades. Major institutional investors, like pension funds, are supposed to have a long investment horizon too. Publically listed corporations though, are required to release quarterly results reports for transparency reasons. This is important for giving investors information, but also contributes to a short-term mentality in corporate managers. As they jockey to win investor money, they prioritise short-term returns that can be immediately showcased, at the expense of longer-term losses. Shareholder activists should thus position themselves as long-term shareholders, reminding managers of their long-term responsibility, and demanding that they account for the true long-term costs.

Demanding Legitimate Returns

A capitalist system theoretically creates situations of industrial 'necrosis' – stagnant industries should die as they show diminishing returns, and their life should be redistributed into dynamic industries via capital moving from the one to the other. Schumpeter referred to this as 'creative destruction'. In the current system though, health is measured in monetary returns relative to monetary costs, and many industries are given artificial life by failing to account for their environmental and social costs. They are animated, as it were, by our collective blindness to such costs. Other businesses remain unborn due to our blindness to their positive social and environmental returns.

A major source of profit in an environmentally or socially destructive company is thus its ability to not account for such external costs. What you have in that situation, is *animated death*, a zombie organisation living off illegitimate returns. In a situation of shareholder activism, you should be an enlightened investor who demands legitimate returns. I don't employ the company management to eke out illegitimate zombie returns for me.

Showcasing Alternatives

Many campaign groups think of shareholder activism as a novel means to advance a single issue. In the context of a single AGM, where one only gets to make a single request of management, that's often the most viable approach. It's easy to spot an outsider pretending to be a shareholder though. Deeper, and more long-term shareholder activism requires true immersion in the culture of a company, such that you truly feel like an owner, and act like one. From that perspective, the natural impulse is to complement critiques with suggestions for alternative paths. After all, as a shareholder, you want the company to succeed: 'I'd like you to shift our company's investment towards boosting our solar technology portfolio, which has much greater long-term viability.'

Shareholders of the World Unite!

All the above positions, however, are likely to be more effective if the individual shareholder activist has the backing of other investors. Shareholder activists thus need to be rallying other small-scale shareholders, who often include retired 'little old ladies' and ex-employees of the company. They need, in a sense, to be unionised. A group of 50 small shareholders coming together under a manifesto could be a surprising challenge for a CEO. Imagine a scenario where shareholder activists embed themselves within all major companies, gradually building collectives that grow powerful over time. The Vedanta CEO may refuse a single shareholder a meeting, but imagine a union of 850 shareholders, including many retired individuals with a passion for pursuing causes for their grandchildren's future. Over time, all companies should host these embedded unions, which can act as entry points for NGOs and campaign groups to get causes heard. Here are two other potential projects:

- *Share-price carrot mobs?* They concept of 'buycotts' was pioneered by Carrotmob in San Francisco. The idea is to use coordinated crowds to reward companies for good behaviour. A Carrotmob organisation might issue a pledge such as, 'If you implement this policy, we'll send 250 shoppers your way.' Could this idea be applied to company investment, rewarding companies for good behaviour by sending a vast mob of retail investors to buy their shares?

In reality, it would take a *lot* of people to have any impact, but crowdpower groups like Avaaz have shown that many thousands can be mobilised in clicktivism campaigns. Perhaps this is an idea for someone to develop further in partnership with such organisations.

- *Impact angels.* Rock stars and celebrities would make powerful shareholder activists. Picture Jack Black at Barclays' AGM, singing 'Hit the Road Jack' to the latest CEO. Would it be possible to build a network of 'impact angel investors', individuals with media clout who can join forces with shareholder unions of small investors?

Becoming a Broker of Dissent: Building an Activist Stockbrokerage

Stockbrokerages are intermediaries that facilitate access to shares. They seek to develop strong relationships with fund managers and retail investors, and produce research for those investors. A powerful shareholder activism movement requires an activist stockbrokerage. It's a slightly cheeky idea, but it could develop organically over time in several phases:

- *Phase 1: Building shareholder activism networks.* In the UK, FairPensions has done much to build awareness of shareholder activism among NGOs and civil society groups, helping to co-ordinate shareholder activist activities, and facilitate activist access to shares. More of this is needed.
- *Phase 2: Developing a specialist research firm.* In 2012 Platform London, FairPensions, and Greenpeace UK collaborated in producing *Out in the Cold*, an investor report detailing the hidden risks of Shell's Arctic oil exploration. It was a great piece of work, but again, much more of this is needed. How about setting up a permanent research firm that specialises in providing such reports for justice movements?
- *Phase 3: Developing corporate relationships.* All companies have in-house analysts providing input into strategy. Campaign groups need to be actively developing

relationships with such employees. For example, I've become friends with an analyst at a large oil and gas company who models the carbon impacts of their operations, maps out future scenarios for potential costs, and advises the company on how to respond to them. We have open conversations about it, and influence each others' thought. Being within corporate city walls, engaging with employees, is the quickest way to working out the strengths and weaknesses of your position.

- *Phase 4: Cold-calling the Brontosaurs*. A major fund management company like Fidelity can be a serious political force in a company, entitled to seats at high tables inaccessible to most shareholders. Gaining access to specific fund managers requires a concerted effort to build relationships with them.

As a broker, I spent large amounts of time trying to build a rapport with fund managers. Brokers are engaged in an endless opportunistic attempt to speak to people who don't want to speak to them. One has to debase and embarrass oneself in the process. You get the fund manager's number off the internet, or reverse engineer their email addresses with tools like Rapportive. You pay £6 to send them messages on LinkedIn. You phone the Fidelity reception and try to get past the gate-keeping secretaries. You engineer ways to bump into them at events, or find ways to get yourself introduced. You ask them out for coffee or beers, and tell them your agenda. Every time they put the phone down on you, you've learned one more thing not to say.

A rock band often has to play terrible gigs and get booed many times before they develop a unique sound that people stop and take notice of. If you've got something truly valid to offer, such as a fresh perspective on risk, a fund manager will eventually respond. If nothing else, they're probably sick of ordinary brokers trying to flog them products, and may welcome a fresh perspective from a well-informed activist. Engaging in these conversations quickly shows you where the faults in your arguments are too, and will enable you to strengthen them.

Relationship building should also be extended to those who influence fund managers, such as research analysts at major investment banks, and financial journalists. These individuals are paid to produce content and need fresh ideas, especially when they're tired and hung-over. If you can consistently provide them with ideas, those ideas can filter into their reports and indirectly influence large investors. A constituency that is comparatively sympathetic to justice movements is the socially responsible investment (SRI) fund industry. They constitute a small fraction of the overall fund management arena, but you can get in touch with them to discuss how to get your issues heard. Check out groups like EIRIS and PIRC who promote responsible shareholding, and who've developed ties with such investors.

Getting Into Character: Investor Webcasts

One effective way to build greater understanding of corporate politics is to listen to investor conference calls held by corporate management teams. Recordings of these are found on the investor relations sections of their websites. They normally last for an hour, beginning with the CEO and financial director explaining how the company has performed, before taking questions from bank analysts and investors. It's a quick way to get a feel for what a corporation is actually like behind its public facade. You'll also detect an elaborate cat-and-mouse game played between the company management and the analysts who try to assess how much their shares are worth.

ROLLING BACK FINANCIALISATION: ENGAGING INVESTORS ON FOOD SPECULATION

In 2008 there was a rapid hike in commodity prices. The financial press hauled in various experts who used a variety of well-recited reasons to explain the volatility: '*Meat consumption is rising in China, leading to greater demand for corn to feed to pigs.*' Then suddenly the price crashed, and other explanatory factors emerged: '*The global economic downturn will lead to reduced meat consumption in China.'* Global supply and demand clearly affect food prices, but are these arguments adequate? Do long-term incremental societal changes, such as a growing middle-class in China, really lead to short-term price rises and crashes across all commodities? In the wake of these spikes it is little wonder that dissenting outside voices began to suggest that the price volatility was related to investors, rather than consumers, piling money into commodity investment vehicles.

Commodity speculators – who bet on short-term commodity prices – have long existed, and continue to exist today in commodity futures markets. What are 'commodity investors' though? Traditionally, we might have thought of an investor in corn as someone who invested long-term in, say, a corn farming business. Since the 1990s though, and especially in recent years, *commodity structured products* created by investment banks have offered an opportunity for fund managers to synthetically invest long term in the *prices* of perishable commodities, almost like an investor-speculator hybrid.

The subjectivity of financial market prices, however, means that the debate as to whether these various players impact on prices is bogged down in extensive technicalities. In the US, groups like BetterMarkets have produced reports arguing that financial players distort commodity futures markets, and in turn distort physical commodity markets. They and others advocate 'position limits' to curb the amount of speculation in commodity futures, and indeed, provisions for such limits have been incorporated into the US Dodd-Frank Act. The issue resonates deeply with activists and NGOs, who see the major implications for food justice: Vulnerable people should not be subject to arbitrary food price changes caused by investment whims. In the UK, the World Development Movement (WDM) took the lead in campaigning on the issue, followed by others like Christian Aid and Oxfam.

This is an area which really needs to be taken up with the large institutional investors who are involved in the process. Politicians and CEOs are used to taking personal blame for decisions. Individual fund managers though, almost never take the heat for the politicised decisions they make with money.

Find out who they are and put the heat on them. During the 1980s, students on American and European campuses drove successful anti-Apartheid disinvestment campaigns. Is your university endowment fund, or company pension fund, investing in commodities without considering the potential impact? Below I discuss some ways to think about this issue, to help people design 'not-in-my-name' disinvestment campaigns.

Getting to Grips with Intuitive Concerns

In mid 2010 I helped out with WDM's campaign against Barclays Capital's involvement in commodity speculation, helped various other activist groups with the issue, and wrote an article for *The Ecologist* titled 'Food Speculation: How to argue with a banker'. Looking back, one observation stands out. Many campaigners across a whole range of groups are intuitively concerned about food speculation, but they often fight a 'proxy war'. Their technical arguments about why such speculation distorts markets frequently contain an implicit philosophical argument that it is simply not right to 'invest' in food commodities, regardless of whether it impacts on prices or not. The philosophical principle may be this: *An investor in food prices is explicitly relying on a situation that must entail the suffering of vulnerable people (especially those who are not farmers, such as urban slum dwellers). In positioning themselves to gain while others suffer, an investor lacks empathy for, or solidarity with, the sufferers.*

This sense of intuitive wrongness, however, may cloud the technical debate as justice campaigners seek to prove their intuition by appealing to statistical studies and other such data. The problem though, is that as with climate change this helps set up a 'prove vs. disprove' mentality which opens the issue up to being apparently 'disproven' by those with a counter-intuition. Indeed, among those who have an interest in countering the claims made by justice groups, this mentality is rife. Particularly telling was the response to a single 2010 report, written by Scott Irwin and Dwight Sanders, which used a statistical analysis that returned no evidence of financial players causing the 2008 commodity price spike. There is nothing wrong with a study coming to such a conclusion. The disturbing aspect of it though, is the way it's repeatedly trotted out by financial groups to 'disprove' the problem in a manner reminiscent of climate change denialists citing single studies to disprove climate change. There are many alternative studies that *do* find a connection. Food prices, like climatic changes, are subject to highly complex arrays of factors and feedback loops. The only way one can make scientific statements about such complex systems is by focusing on the weight of evidence, such that we come up with *probabilities* about the issue being a serious problem.

'It is Possible': Building an A Priori Base

A good approach to food speculation is thus initially to avoid the vagaries of the technical debate and to focus on setting up a framework for how it is possible that it is a problem, a framework that can then act as a base from which to view the evidence. The first step is to recognise the difference between *food* and *bets on food*. Food is physical stuff, bought and sold around the world in fragmented 'spot markets',[2] or via contracts between raw commodity producers and manufacturers of food products. Bets on food are synthetic, getting arranged in futures markets, or in futures markets via OTC swap markets and structured products. From this we can derive three separate debates:

1. Do short-term speculators distort agricultural futures prices?
2. Do long-term commodity investors distort agricultural futures prices via structured products?
3. Do distorted agricultural futures prices feed into distorted spot prices for actual food?

Debate 1: Short-term Speculation

Hedge funds are the stereotypical speculator, betting on markets and betting against them. Commodity hedge funds might buy futures directly via brokers, or indirectly by entering into contracts-for-difference (CFDs) and swap contracts with investment bank

---

2. As in a market where transactions are negotiated 'on the spot'.

dealers. In the end, all bets mostly wind up in the futures market. If you want to get a feel for it, open a spreadbetting account and bet on corn. Your bet, or at least some of it, will be expressed indirectly in the corn futures market via a dealer.

When you entered into the spreadbet did you feel yourself pushing the price of the futures upwards? It's a very tricky question. You were buying the contract, but in so doing, you were allowing another person to sell the contract. This is a reason why economists frequently suggest that speculators are *good for markets*. Perhaps there was a corn producer who wanted to hedge themselves by selling a futures contract, which you enabled by buying. You thus *increased liquidity* – finance-speak for the ability to transact easily in a market. Having worked in highly illiquid derivatives, I know the positive effects that speculators can have. Without them, a market works on 'back-to-back' matching of trades, a clunky process of trying to find an exact end-buyer for an exact end-seller, which is time consuming and expensive. By taking on trades, speculators ease that process, and improve the ability of a market to show prices (price discovery) which might be hidden in the minds of more shy players.

There is a self-reinforcing relationship between dealers and speculation. To kick-start a new market, dealers have to take risks to coax participants in. As they shout 'I will buy and sell', dealers increase the ease of trading, and the whole market structure might enter into a positive liquidity feedback loop as pure speculative players begin to enter and increase the liquidity further. This can eventually culminate in dealers being forced out entirely, as people trade directly with each other via computers. It is thus true that speculation increases liquidity.

Ever greater levels of liquidity, however, do not naturally equate to ever greater accuracy of price-discovery. The real food speculation debate actually concerns whether its *extent and nature* has gone past the point of being useful, to the point of being damaging. A market where perhaps 40% of the trade volume was undertaken by speculators might be efficient, allowing real end-users to trade easily. Let's assume that the speculators in that market based their decisions on *fundamental information*: Perhaps you, as a speculator, enter into your spreadbet based on an FAO report you read on the supply of corn, in conjunction with a USDA outlook report for corn demand in 2013. You use a unique methodology to decide that corn futures are currently underpriced, and you enter the bet, thereby helping to draw out prices that give a more accurate reflection of real world supply and demand.

Imagine, by contrast, a market where 90% of the trade volume was undertaken by speculators, and that of those 80% were the kind of *technical traders* that we discussed on page 77–8. Perhaps you enter into your spreadbet without paying any attention whatsoever to the fundamentals, rather basing your trade on the price patterns created by other players: 'It seems to be going up, I'll jump on.' If most other players are also technical traders, doing the same thing, would the market contain enough independent connections to the real world? Could an earthquake occur, but not be noticed, because everyone is speculating on each other's speculation rather than watching the real world? I call this a self-referential market, or a navel-gazing market that makes trades based on information internal to itself. It may be highly liquid, but this could be a parasitic liquidity that leads to arbitrary swings in prices.

This is admittedly an extreme thought experiment, because in reality large numbers of market participants do base their decisions on the situation in the real world. The problem though, is that technical trading is becoming more and more prominent, especially with the advent of high-frequency trading. In May 2011, Gary Gensler, head of the Commodity Futures Trading Commission (the US futures market regulator), reported that nine out of ten traders in the oil markets were speculative players.[3] It is not unreasonable for us to be concerned by this.

Debate 2: 'Investing' in Commodities

There might be thousands of short-term speculators in a market, but perhaps their trade sizes are small, like piranhas nipping

---

3. See Kevin Hall, 'Key Regulator: Speculators Swamping Oil, Grain Markets', *McClatchy News*, May 2011.

away while the large sharks or whales set the real prices. Perhaps the big players are actually corporates like Kellogg's, buying futures to 'long hedge' their future exposure to the corn they have to buy to make cornflakes.

On the other hand, picture yourself as a pension fund manager. A salesperson at an investment bank emails you a report from their commodities research analysts, suggesting that commodities are in a 'super-cycle', set for price increases over the next 30 years. The salesperson follows up with a call to tell you about their new commodity structured product, based on the Goldman Sachs Commodity Index (GSCI), which allows you to invest in the price changes of a broad 'basket' of commodities. She says you should invest for four reasons:

1. Outright returns: Commodity prices are set to go up!
2. Protection against inflation: Commodity prices are naturally correlated to inflation because they are a component of inflation (the definition of inflation is increase in prices).
3. Diversification: Buying this will lower the overall risk of your portfolio.
4. Volatility: Buying this will lower the overall volatility of your portfolio.

She knows that pension funds think differently to short-term speculators like hedge funds. For a start, big funds have no inclination to engage in day-to-day betting. Secondly, they are *long only*, which means they buy things to invest, rather than betting against things. She knows they're concerned about inflation, and that they want to diversify to spread their overall risk. A hedge fund is preoccupied with bets on single trades, but a pension fund manager doesn't care about the random fluctuations in short-term prices. They are, as it were, price insensitive. The salesperson and her colleague have a name for clients like you: *Dumb money*, because they can induce you to plough money into things with little regard for the short-term price outlook. Hedge fund traders call you that too.

This is a fictional story, but it illustrates one reason why lots of the money flowing into commodity markets is not from short-term 'speculators' per se. Futures have short-term expiry dates. In order to actually invest in them in any long-term sense, you have to constantly 'roll them over', meaning you buy one, sell it before it expires and then buy a new one. No pension fund has the time to do that. Commodity structured products – like commodity index funds, commodity notes and commodity exchange traded funds – are managed conduits which do it for you and pass the returns on to you via a legal swap contract. The CFTC produces reports on participants in commodity futures markets, and one huge category is 'swap dealers': These are the banks hedging out their exposure to the commodity products they've sold to big institutional investors. In other words, players like pension funds create a shadow in the futures market via swap dealers.

The growing acceptance of commodities as an investment 'asset class' among large institutional investors raises serious concerns. Efficient price discovery in markets only works if no individual participant can dominate, but what if a *herd* of pension funds act in concert, simultaneously deciding to allocate 'dumb money' to commodities? It could lead to swings in price across all commodities at once, inducing further herd effects among short-term players who want to ride the momentum. Markets are like see-saws – moves upward in price can induce more sellers in to bring them down again, so there is no inevitability to momentum effects. If, however, big funds become entrenched as a *structural buyer* of short-term futures in order to express a long-term investment mentality, then they'll constantly place weight on the buying side of the equation. They may, in other words, increase 'buoyancy', or the resistance to downward price pressures.

Debate 3: Can this Change the Real Price of Food?

Can the price of futures on the Chicago Mercantile Exchange affect the price of local food in Mozambique? There's no way to answer that question generically. In local food markets around the world both local and international factors are always in play. If you looked for an answer in a financial textbook, though, it would generically tell you: 'No, the physical spot prices of commodities determine futures prices, in the same way that the results of horse races determine the value of horse bets.' They'll argue that if a futures price goes up too much relative to on-the-ground prices for commodities, then *arbitrage* will kick in: If it's possible for me to buy oil in Abu Dhabi for $80 and simultaneously sell it on a futures market for delivery in three months in America at $120, and it only costs me $20 per barrel to store and transport, I make a risk free $20 profit per barrel. Arbitrageurs, in financial theory, provide a reality check on futures markets, keeping them in line with real world prices.

It's a nice theory, but buying commodities on a spot market in order to arbitrage a futures market is actually very difficult. What is the spot market in wheat? There are many varieties and they are being sold via bilateral contracts all over the world. There is no central location for 'wheat prices' ... other than the *futures market*. Indeed, for many commodities, the futures market is the only centralised, visible market that can be used as a *benchmark*: A physical wheat trader like Cargill offering to sell wheat to the Egyptian government in three months' time is likely to look at the futures price before they quote and negotiate a contract, and so is the Egyptian government. In other words, futures prices can feed directly into real world prices. In the case above, the Egyptian government may take the hit on behalf of its citizens by selling the wheat on at subsidised prices to local bread manufacturers; but in other countries, the price could hit consumers directly.

The Future and the Precautionary Principle

We've now set up the conceptual edifice for explaining how this could be a problem:

> Markets with high degrees of short-term speculation, especially by technical traders, in conjunction with herd effects and buoyancy from large long-term institutional funds, could be a volatile combination, which in turn can be reflected in real world prices via benchmarking processes.

Commodity markets are complex global systems, and teasing out price causalities is very difficult. The need is thus firstly to build up evidence, and secondly to shift the terms of the debate away from the prove vs. disprove mentality, towards a *risk management* mentality. A risk management outlook entails planning for several different future scenarios, rather than having blind faith in one outcome. For example, many people were intuitively concerned about securitised mortgage products prior to the financial crisis of 2008, but were unable to prove that they were distorting real estate prices. Lack of confirmation, in a risk management outlook, does not equate to 'no need to worry'. It doesn't matter whether a single econometric study finds no *current* causality, and belief among economists that any particular issue is resolved ignores the fact that financial markets are dynamic and evolving. We have deep current concerns, based on market evidence and historical experience, about the disruptive potential of future food speculation and commodity investment, especially as it gets bigger. It's thus crucial to apply the *precautionary principle* to the situation: The onus should be on financial market participants to prove that it is safe, not for others to prove that it is unsafe.

The precautionary principle is, to some extent, a conservative impulse which says 'don't tamper with an existing set-up'. It potentially stands in opposition to innovation in general. To justify using it in the context of commodity investment, you've got to suggest that a financial innovation is either an unnecessary or gratuitous add-on to markets that were otherwise fine, or alternatively that the markets are too vulnerable to be subject to unchecked innovation. In both of these cases, agricultural futures markets count. They worked perfectly well prior to excessive speculation, and, most importantly, they deal in food, which has massive welfare impacts around the world. The precautionary principle should apply especially strongly here.

Finding Allies: Get Out and Talk to Traders

The average mainstream economist works in an air-conditioned office running regressions on data-sets. Their abstract papers lack any of the real colour of markets. Getting to grips with the growing issue of food speculation must involve a serious effort to build relationships with people within these markets.

I've had many anecdotal experiences with traders who openly talk about the changes taking place, and how they are finding ways of taking advantage of them. They talk about how they fleece dumb-money index funds that are trying to roll over futures contracts. They talk about how hedge funds use options strategies to try to corner markets. Traders in metals futures markets are very concerned about investment funds that literally buy up physical metal, and large companies like Nestlé have attacked speculators too. These are the rational markets, and you can go out and speak to them.

Food price speculation is not the only issue on the cutting edge of commodity financialisation. Efforts to build contacts and models of potential impact need to be extended to the area of land commoditisation too. People have invested in land for a long time, often developing an emotional connection to the actual soil and earthworms, but when large institutional investors buy land via managed 'farmland funds' in order to gain generic exposure to land as an asset class, there is a serious disconnection process occurring. Another understudied power group that inevitably has fingers in the commodity pie are the physical traders like Cargill, Bunge, Glencore, ADM, Vitol and Trafigura. Unlike most financial traders, they are uniquely placed to engage in geographical arbitrage, drawing on their global networks of physical commodities to offset them against each other, and against fluctuations in futures prices. Employees in these companies are well placed to explain the many factors that go into determining food prices, including the raw commodities, the fertilisers, the labour, the intermediary fees, the cost of shipping, the cost of processing it and the final distribution. Once you've got access, you can explore many more areas of skulduggery beyond derivatives distortions.

DAS KAPITAL LLP: GOING LONG THE REVOLUTION WITH MARX'S HEDGE FUND

In 2011 the *Guardian* blogger Joris Luyendijk quoted me as saying 'Karl Marx would have made a fantastic hedge fund manager.' It predictably caused howls of outrage in the comments section, but I never meant it in a literal sense. I was suggesting that the best hedge fund managers are characterised by a certain disruptive tendency, an ability to cut through herds of conventional investors. This is not to romanticise hedge funds, but deploying money into a situation is similar to making a statement of belief – if your money goes against the herd, it's a bit like saying 'up yours' to them. There are even hedge funds that set themselves up as 'corporate raiders' or 'activist funds' that deliberately challenge company management. Well-known examples include:

- The Children's Investment Fund: A fund started by Chris Hohn. In 2012 it launched a campaign against Coal India's directors, suing them for breaching fiduciary duty (aka ignoring shareholders). They have an attached charity which receives a portion of the firm's profits.
- Greenlight Capital: A fund run by a poker-playing manager called David Einhorn which publicly bets against firms, much to their annoyance.
- Carl Icahn: A corporate raider famed for terrorising corporate management teams. He views himself as a predator on a mission to destroy complacent CEOs: On his website, icahnreport.com, he quotes himself as saying 'A lot of people die fighting tyranny. The least I can do is vote against it.'
- Dan Loeb: A hedge fund manager infamous for buying stakes in companies and then writing incendiary letters of withering scorn to the company management teams.

Others, such as Pirate Capital, have been less successful, but are based on similar principles. Could it be that the mindset of a hedge fund manager can be strikingly similar to that of a campaigner? Certainly, the belief systems of hedge fund managers are expressed in *financial direct action*, albeit mostly for their own gain. Could campaigners battle it out in this realm too, by setting up truly activist hedge funds?

Activating the Financial Drag Queens

Any large fund planning to invest on behalf of retail investors or pensioners has to be vetted and regulated by the authorities. The bar for starting up a small hedge fund, on the other hand, is much lower. Any NGO will have the intellectual resources to run one: Why isn't there an *Amnesty International LLP*, gradually buying up stakes in companies with poor human rights records, demanding accountability while using the dividends to fund the dissent?

For many NGOs, part of the answer is lack of funds, and the rest is ideological opposition to the idea. The financial system though, like the internet, is a networked technology of power which can be used in unusual ways. If you feel authorities and large corporates are dominating the internet with patents, firewalls and intellectual property lawsuits, you don't turn off the wireless, you get creative. Who's to say that we can't wear the garb of a notorious financial institution in a heretical fashion.

A friend of mine who worked for 12 years in an investment bank had an idea of starting a hedge fund that would attempt to extract money from the oil sector and redirect it to the renewable energy sector. It's interesting in principle, but incredibly hard to execute in reality. It's important to take these ideas with a pinch of salt. Perhaps the point of an activist hedge fund is not actually to work in a conventional sense, but rather to create publicity, to learn, and to act as a subversive 'drag queen' joker bending the rules. On the other hand, so few people have experimented with the idea of creating subversive hedge funds that it's hard to know what the potential might be. The only way of finding out if the dynamics of trading can be harnessed in a positive way is to experiment boldly. There is nothing to lose ... except money.

I propose three phases in the process:

1. Altering hedge fund DNA.
2. Developing the strategies.
3. Harnessing normal hedge funds.

Phase 1: Altering the Structural DNA

Current hedge funds are *exclusive* – relying on institutional investors and wealthy individuals to fund them – and *for profit*. The financial drag version would thus be *inclusive* and *non-profit*.

- *Crowd-powered*: Many people who do not have the personal time to engage directly in shareholder activism may be willing to contribute small sums to a hedge fund via a crowd-funding platform like Kickstarter. The resultant fund could represent a large network of individuals, all of whom would have access to the fund's decision-making processes.
- *Non-profit activist enterprise*: The fund would need to maintain non-profit status, both to keep the spirit intact, and to avoid the legal issues that come with soliciting for-profit investment. A social enterprise is a company with a social or environmental mission that generates revenue to expand or to be self-sustaining. A variant of this could be the *Activist Enterprise* – a company structure that funds its own campaigns via the success of previous disruptions. Robin Hood's activities, for example, are an example of an activist enterprise.

Phase 2: Designing the Strategies

Normal hedge funds are categorised according to a number of established trading philosophies. Activist hedge funds could build up alternative philosophies, either for real economic effect or for symbolic effect. Here are some ideas:

- *Bloodhound funds*: In 2012, following the Barclays' Libor scandal, I published a piece in the *Guardian* arguing for a hedge fund that would specialise in sniffing out financial crime in companies. The idea would be to bet against them, and then release the information to cause a drop in the share price. To some extent the idea was inspired by Muddy Waters Research, who specialise in uncovering fraud in Chinese companies, and Anonymous Analytics, who uncover fraud by 'unconventional means' (aka spying). It was clearly a controversial idea, treading close to the illegal realm of market manipulation and insider trading. The idea though, remains interesting: Is it possible to create hedge fund structures that act like antibodies attacking fraudulent cells?

- *Robin Hood funds*: The fund makes money off projects that have negative consequences, and then uses the proceeds to fund more positive projects. It could for example invest in weapons companies, engage in shareholder activism in the process, and steer all dividends into refugee relief. The fund taps into the negative value produced by a company in order to release it in the form of positivity. This clearly has limitations, but would complement a shareholder activism strategy.
- *Exposure funds*: Symbolic funds to demonstrate system vulnerabilities, and uncover information. See page 166 below.
- *Carbon retirement funds*: Funds that attempt to corner carbon markets to raise the price of carbon credits and encourage companies to invest in renewable energy. See page 196.
- *#FutureOfMoney funds*: Funds that explicitly support alternatives to mainstream finance. See page 241.

Phase 3: Running With the Wild Wolves: Harnessing Networks of Hedge Funds

Imagine if it became commonplace for all global NGOs to create networks of hybrid hedge funds that represented their interests within financial markets. For one thing, many normal traders looking for a more challenging trading paradigm might find this fascinating, offering them an opportunity to jump ship and try something different.

Alternatively, such hybrid funds could form partnerships with normal hedge funds to activate greater resources. Back in 2003 Max Keiser and Stacy Herbert started an organisation called Karmabanque, characterised as a 'broker of dissent': An intermediary between hedge funds looking to bet against companies, and activists looking to bring down company share prices by making them targets of boycotts. The idea petered out, possibly because again it comes close to market-manipulation, but the concept of collectively altering a company's behaviour via a *network* of small funds is worth experimenting with further.

One tool in the armoury of investors is *proxy fights* – getting other shareholders to back them in a resolution or takeover bid. Want to cause a real stir and get onto the front page of the FT? Why not launch a *hostile takeover bid* for a company to stop it from doing something. It sounds outrageous, but there is a precedent for this in the 2007 TXU buyout. TXU was a huge US electricity utility that was bought out by KKR, TPG and Goldman Sachs' Capital Partners (Goldman's internal private equity fund) in a gargantuan private equity deal. They were backed by two environmentalist groups, the Natural Resources Defense Council and the Environmental Defense Fund, who gave the buyout team environmental credentials in exchange for concessions to scrap 11 planned coal power plants. It was controversial – the internal deliberations of the Environmental Defense Fund reveal their concern about being accused of selling out their green ideals in a Faustian bargain[4] – but the deal went through, and the plans for the coal plants were all scrapped. It's a deeply interesting case study of the dynamics of swimming with the sharks.

DEMONSTRATE VULNERABILITIES: SHINING A LIGHT ON SHADOW-BANKING

In much traditional activism, the boundaries between the activist and the target remain intact: We might investigate something, and explicitly campaign against it. Nick Shaxson's excellent

---

4. See EDF, 'TXU Leveraged Buyout: Challenges and Opportunities for EDF', February 2007, available at www.docstoc.com/docs/38411180/TXU-Leveraged-Buyout

book, *Treasure Islands* (2011), is an example of an external investigation into the issue of tax havens, explicitly pointing out something that is going on. The regulatory campaigner picks it up and uses it to say 'banking is too opaque'. Frederick Kaufman's *Bet the Farm: How Food Stopped Being Food* (2012) is another excellent external investigation, used by a campaigner to issue statements of concern about food speculation.

A more *implicit* form of activism though, involves asking open-ended questions in the form of 'what dubious things might we personally do within this system?' It bends the boundary between activist and target by personally demonstrating the vulnerabilities of the financial system. It's a subtle concept, and a problematic one, best highlighted by the example of IT systems: A major task of 'security researchers' (aka hackers) is to demonstrate how to 'crack' something in order to showcase its vulnerability. If finance was conceptualised as a human software system, much of it would be written in obfuscated code, involving unnecessarily complex structures that increase opacity and risk. Could a rogue trader like Kweku Adoboli[5] be retrospectively imagined as a subversive agent who demonstrated the vulnerabilities of UBS's lax risk management systems?

Exposure Funds

We spend too much time brooding over the opaque inner workings of complex hedge funds from the outside. It's like suspiciously watching a magician who dazzles the crowds with his black magic. But how about setting up a structure that exposes its inner workings, so that you, the magician, can reveal to everyone how your tricks work? *Exposure* is a pejorative term in magician-lore, referring to the act of revealing the secrets of tricks: '*You spoil it for all of us!*' shout the other magicians.

In the November 2011 issue of *New Internationalist* Hazel Healy describes how she invested in commodity structured product to understand how it worked, in order to write an article on food speculation. Pushing that one step further, if I set up my

5. A trader at UBS who allegedly lost the bank approximately $2 billion in 2011.

own small commodity trading fund, I could write about myself, exposing the dynamics of commodity trading from within. The fund needn't actually be funded with lots of money – it could be a purely symbolic use of the structure of the hedge fund to demonstrate a negative phenomenon. A normal fund takes speculative positions and then shows financial gains or losses. A symbolic fund could do the same, except it would present the financial gains or losses along with the social and environmental losses or gains. Movements in prices thus become proxies for food justice, gender rights and conflict, displayed via an interface that interprets prices as such. Such a commodity fund would twist 'positive financial returns' into 'negative social returns' in the eyes of the public.

Killing Two Vultures With One Stone: Learning via Demonstration

I've sometimes been asked to explain the financial crisis, or to explain a vulture fund. I'll be relaxing with a friend who has a hazy idea about the crisis involving 'toxic securitised products'. They're focused on a known negative consequence, and slowly and painfully attempting to grope backwards to an unknown cause. In the process there is a tendency for them to over-complicate the issue, viewing the micro-level through the lens of the sprawling mess of the macro-level outcome. A more intuitive means to understanding is to start from the micro-level and recreate the macro-level forwards, simply seeing what would occur if you were in that position.

In 2012 the *Planet Money* team ran a series of excellent shows, exposing how opaque shell companies registered in tax havens work. They cut straight through the conceptual fluff simply by setting up two shell companies – Unbelizeable in Belize, and Delawho? in Delaware (a tax haven state in the USA). They invited listeners to make suggestions on what dubious things the companies should do. Jason Sharman of Griffiths University used a similar approach of 'soliciting offers for prohibited untraceable shell companies' for his book *Global Shell Games: Experiments in Transnational Relations* (2013).

Deliberately participating in dodgy activities allows you to learn about them in an intuitive way, creating Frankensteins that you can demonstrate to the world.

Get in on the Shell Game

Tax havens like the British Virgin Islands (BVI) don't only facilitate tax avoidance, they facilitate secrecy. Richard Murphy of the Tax Justice Network coined the term *secrecy jurisdiction* to refer to places that offer this 'service'. A person can use such jurisdictions to set up webs of companies that hide their identity. How about creating an elaborate structure that documents the process of setting itself up and then 'leaks' the information about itself via an ongoing blog? *Confessions of a Window Cleaner* was a 1974 sex comedy film about the ongoing exploits of a promiscuous cleaner. Could our blog be called *Confessions of a Window-Dressing Money Launderer?*

First of all, you have to set up a special purpose vehicle (SPV), a shell company to conduct your business. Contact a tax haven company registration service (easily found on Google), and ask for advice on where to incorporate a shell company. Even if you have no intention of starting one, this process is strangely fun. A man in Bermuda tries to sell his services by explaining the high level of secrecy they offer. It costs some money to set the company up, but if you can raise that, open a shell company and give it a name. Perhaps *Jackass Ltd*? Now you can find uses for it.

Use 1: Catch a Vulture

Vulture funds – sometimes called distressed debt funds – are investment funds that buy up the debt of collapsing companies, or the defaulted debts of poorer countries at a major discount, hoping that they can sue them for default. The Jubilee Debt Campaign, alongside investigative journalists like Greg Palast, have previously uncovered vulture funds like FG Hemisphere. The fund paid $3 million for a debt the old Zaire owed to Yugoslavia, and then used it to sue the Democratic Republic of Congo for $100 million.

It's no easy task to locate 30-year-old loan certificates from the old Zaire, and a Barclays Capital bond dealer is unlikely to have 1980s Argentinean bonds stored in their inventory. It's also unlikely that investigative reporting alone will uncover the secrets of how vultures find these pickings, so perhaps the best way to expose their practices is to look like a vulture fund yourself. You use your shell company to go undercover into the dodgy world of second-hand third-world debt. Who is dealing in it? Can you convince FG Hemisphere to believe you're in possession of old Haitian debt? Who's the vulture now...

Use 2: Create a Spoof Securitised Product

In the lead-up to the financial crisis, the purpose of setting up an SPV was to use it to hold assets that investors could then make claims on. A securitised product is just a claim on an SPV that holds a collection of, say, residential mortgages (RMBS), or commercial mortgages (CMBS), or high-risk corporate 'junk bonds' (CLOs), or car loans (Auto ABS), or rights to credit default swap payments (synthetic CLO), or airplane leases, movie rights, legal cases pending settlement, or any other source of potential future cash flows. What do you want your SPV to hold? Lottery tickets?

In normal banking, the operations of the bank are centralised. It acts as a conduit scraping the difference between the long-term loans it holds, and the short-term loans it funds itself with. The shadow-banking system of financial crisis fame though, exploded the centralised functions of a bank outwards into multiple stages, each one separately funded. A bank might originate mortgages, and then sell them to an investment bank, which sells them to an SPV they've set up in a tax haven, which in turn offers investors access to them via 'tranching structures' that fragment the cash flows from the mortgages into a rainbow with different shades of risk and return. Low-risk investors such as pension funds might debt-invest by lending money via the least risky tranche, which offers a stable but low return of light blue. High-risk cowboys might equity-invest via the highest risk tranche, offering wildly volatile deep red danger and high returns. The end result is that boring mortgages suddenly satisfy everyone's utopian dreams.

In your own SPV, you could offer three tranches: *Jackass Class 1*, *Jackass Class 2*, and *Jackass Class 3*. Jackass Class 1 is low risk, so it gets paid first if the lottery tickets have a few small wins, but it has a low maximum cap on what returns it can claim. Jackass Class 3 is high risk, so it gets nothing unless there are big jackpot wins, which it has unlimited claims to. Try selling access to this structure to your friends. Which tranche do they buy into?

Rewind Fast-forward: Spinning a Narrative of the Future Results

Imagine you'd undertaken these types of exercises *prior* to the financial crisis, starting from one point, and imagining the various future scenarios:

Act 1: In 2005, you decide to put yourself into the mind of a credit structurer in an investment bank. 'Hey guys', you say, 'Do you think we can sell institutional investors portfolios of shitty loans?' Then it's all go. Your team purchases the loans from various Florida and Arizona lenders. You hold onto them ('warehousing' them) while setting up a Cayman Islands SPV. Your structurers are designing a tranching structure with catchy names like Jackass 1, 2 & 3, and your sales team is on the phone lining up investors. The pieces all come together. The loans detach themselves from you as you transfer them to the SPV that's getting funded by the investors. Arrangement fees are taken, as are bonuses and champagne for all. You've had some trouble selling the higher risk equity tranches though: *Don't worry, we'll hang on to those for a while, and sell them later.*

Act 2: Now Florida houses are being financed by a whole collection of disparate investors. Can you feel how this might alter the incentive structure for your new persona – the bank manager originating mortgages: *I can sell them to those clowns in the investment bank who sell them to Norwegian investors...*

Act 3: Why are the property prices going up? It's probably because a much wider pool of disassociated investors is now lending to people to buy houses. *Who cares, I'm willing to lend because if the house owner defaults I just claim their house, which is worth more than the loan I give them...*

Act 4: Investment banks operate in a situation of unstable disequilibrium, borrowing short-term from 'money-market' funds and other banks to fund their operations. That short-term borrowing is cheaper, but it means we constantly have to *refinance* ourselves: As each short-term loan comes due, we borrow more to pay it back, thereby 'rolling over' our funding. *What happens if you can't?* Not sure, I guess we'd suffocate to death.

Act 5: A slowly collapsing property market feeds on itself, as the imploding prices create a violent tide that sucks the value out of mortgages that were secured against the property, and by extension, all the structured credit products that were secured against the mortgages. Back in the investment bank you suddenly realise something: *Oh shit, we've still got those high-risk tranches on our balance sheet. We forgot to sell them!*

Act 6: A crisis of confidence chokes your investment bank's ability to refinance itself in the money markets, and forces it to sell assets to pay off the short-term debts that are coming due. That's like trying to sell hot potatoes that nobody wants. We are forced to sell them at fire-sale prices, and write off their value through write-downs. Our share price is now crumbling, and our commercial banking operations must retreat from lending. We must 'consolidate' and build up our reserves and 'capital ratios'. *Will you lend to normal companies?* Hell no, tough times call for tough love. *Might the overall economy start deteriorating from lack of access to finance?* I guess so, but times are tight and friends are few. *Might this in turn jeopardise your entire commercial loan portfolio?* Um, yes. *Houston, we have systemic breakdown.*

This is, of course, but one of many potential scenarios from my initial viewpoint in 2005. In another scenario, a near utopian world ensues as perfectly rational actors create perfect markets that create global prosperity and equality. Which scenario plays out?

INFORMATION ADVENTURES:
RELEASING TRAPPED INFORMATION

In late 2011, I undertook an investigation into a mining deal that a multinational company was involved with in the Democratic Republic of Congo. It appeared that the company's business partners in two mines that it co-owned and operated were two shell companies, registered in the British Virgin Islands, which had obtained their stake in the mines from a state-run mining firm in a very non-transparent manner. The situation was of concern, not because there was any proof that anything corrupt had occurred, but simply because there was *no information* to explain it.

My attempt to clarify it with the multinational was met with a refusal to acknowledge that I had any good reason to be asking for this information. Many corporate managers around the world – no matter what industry they are in – will not help you find out about their operations by providing such information. They place the onus on underfunded NGOs to trace the opaque offshore structures they do business with, or the loan agreements they enter into, or the transfer pricing arrangements they use to avoid tax. Campaigners are forced to buy into an asymmetric power dynamic, searching for inside information they're legally barred from getting.

There is, however, another way of responding to an information blackout. Think of bats, or underwater creatures like dolphins, who mostly use *sonar* to navigate. They send out sound signals, and build up a picture of what lies further ahead based on whether the signals return or not, a process called echo-location. They construct a sense of reality without explicitly seeing it. An analogy can be made with positive and negative shapes: Positive shapes are explicitly 'seen', or, in a sense, visually proven, but negative shapes are *implied* by the absence of resistance. A creature that seeks out positive shapes is disadvantaged in a system that provides none. Sonar, in a sense, enables bats to 'see' the absence of obstacles, or negative spaces.

People in the financial sector, likewise, build pictures of reality from fragments of both positive shape and negative shape information. The expert on Bloomberg TV confidently explaining why the gold price is increasing might seem as if they can see a positive shape, but they're often actually sending out sonar: If nobody disagrees with them, their opinion solidifies into received wisdom. Likewise, if a company refuses to release private information about their operations, they also implicitly cede their right to control the public narrative about their operations. This allows us to flip the onus back on them in sonar form, and say 'here is our reality'.

Playing Joker's Poker

If you type 'how much money does Barclays Capital make off food speculation?' into Google, you will find an answer. But it doesn't come from Barclays. I estimated the amount based on various fragments of information I collated when working on food speculation with the justice group WDM. I compiled a report based on various assumptions to suggest a spectrum of possible amounts that Barclays made. We then sent it to Barclays' for comment. They did not respond. In refusing to falsify anything we said, they thereby implied that we were roughly accurate, and those numbers now stand as current truth until proven otherwise. If Barclays' wants their version out there, they must give it: They are stuck in a pincer trap of either letting a public truth form, or releasing a private truth.

I call this playing *Joker's Poker*: A company stonewalls you. You use re-enactments, Exposure funds, and your back-of-the-envelope corporate finance skills to say: 'Here is a poker hand of five possible scenarios for what might have happened.' Show it to them and ask them to pick a card. In offering a spectrum of options, one does not accuse them of anything directly. If they refuse your offer, they implicitly suggest that the worst-case option could be true, which now enters the public domain. The invention of truth by playing Joker's Poker is necessitated by the asymmetric nature of information in the corporate world. Perhaps this is a form of 'information arbitrage': When a market is out of kilter with reality, arbitrageurs are supposed to bring it back down to earth. If the truth we project is out of kilter with reality, a company must do likewise.

Project: Creating a Financial Wikileakipedia

Corporations are huge unstable political networks, holding their 'collective intelligence' in small slices within many individuals. Some of those individuals want the information out, others don't. In general though, the legal structures in place prevent any of them from doing so, even if they know it would be in the public interest. Excessive corporate confidentiality facilitates the centralisation of power rather than the dispersion of power. It allows fraud to occur, but more importantly it masks the more mundane processes in which individually legal actions collectively add up to toxic systemic effects.

One project could thus be to build an online educational initiative aimed at increasing transparency about areas of general concern, such as the offshore system, shadow-banking, speculation and unethical lending. Whistleblowers are encouraged to contribute mini-leaks to the site, uncontroversial fragments of information that collectively begin to illuminate a bigger, darker picture. WikiLeaks releases its information in dramatic bursts, while Wikipedia slowly builds it up. The hybrid form – Wikileakipedia – creates a slowly unfolding mega-leak. Of course, we'll need the help of a few embedded anthropologists to help it along. Anybody interested in going gonzo in the Cayman Islands?

Part 3
Building

5
Building Trojan Horses

CREATING BYPASS CIRCUITS

In January 2012, a small band of campaigners launched MoveYourMoney UK, an initiative to encourage people to shift their money out of megabanks and into smaller, more socially responsible co-operatives, building societies and credit unions. The campaign, inspired by a similar effort in the US, sought to empower people who would otherwise have little time to engage in straightforward activism, encouraging them to contest an existing financial regime while simultaneously supporting more positive models of finance.

It's little use creating dams to block money flows without simultaneously considering how to build canals to steer it more positively. Triodos, Charity Bank and Ecology Building Society are examples of small financial institutions that attempt to do this, lending exclusively to projects that create positive social or environmental value. Imagine a hypothetical scenario in which campaigns such as MoveYourMoney were successful in convincing UK savers to switch, and that over 25 years they become the UK's biggest lender. What might the economy look like? Here's one vision I drew up based on the lending criteria of the three banks:

The UK would support an extensive network of co-operatively run organic farming and food processing businesses. They would be connected globally to other networks of localist food producers, sharing resources and information. There would be an intricate distributed renewable energy network, supplemented by offshore wind turbines, wave turbines, and a large-scale energy efficiency infrastructure, partly funded via the capital markets with 'green bonds'. There would be a major 'green silicon valley', with top graduates applying their skills to developing hyper-efficient products, smart grid technologies and internet 'sharing economy' technologies that reduce waste. A major source of employment would be in social business and social enterprise, judged on their ability to generate social value and meaningful employment. Poorer people would have access to financial services, including microfinance for small businesses that promote community resilience. The banking sector would support vibrant arts and culture projects, charity and third sector organisations, as well as philosophy of life initiatives. Mortgages would encourage green retrofits and energy efficient housing. There would be ups and downs, but the banking sector would make serious attempts to combine local community resilience, global equality and creative enterprise.

The vision, for those with an explicitly socially minded world-view, may be tantalising. Normalising the idea of socially responsible investment in the broader public imagination clearly has some way to go however. I was on the original MoveYourMoney UK team, and it quickly became apparent that while many people agreed with the message, actually getting individuals to act on it was a difficult process. Many people are simply unaware that there are other ways to manage their money, and have lingering doubts about shifting away from what they're used to.

To shift the financial sector requires groups raising awareness about alternatives, and think-tanks (such as the New Economics Foundation) that nudge the policy framework towards those alternatives. And there need to be people who actually build alternatives, spanning a range from more conventional ideas (such as SRI funds), through to more radical innovations such as alternative currencies, disintermediation technologies, co-operatives and sharing platforms.

A major issue though, is that much energy is locked within 'silos': Those building alternatives are often disconnected from those in the policy world, and those involved in reform initiatives are disconnected from those with a more explicitly activist mindset. To create a vibrant and critical Do-it-Yourself financial system going forward, those silos need to be broken down.

ORTHODOX UNORTHODOXY:
GETTING TO GRIPS WITH MAINSTREAM REFORM

Recent financial reforms such as the UK Vickers reforms and the US Dodd-Frank Act gained their political traction in reaction to the financial crisis. Many of their provisions – such as Vickers' call to ring-fence retail banking away from investment banks – relate to the crisis. Other initiatives, such as calls for a financial transactions tax to reduce speculation, and calls to regulate compensation, have had mixed success. Much of this post-crisis regulatory debate though, has been undertaken in a reactive fashion, in response to short-term instability. The nature of democratic politics is to demand less risk when things are bad, and more risk when things are good. That's a lot better than stagnant dictatorships, but it also means that campaign groups, following the political fluctuations, get used to reacting to the 'here and now' of finance rather than planning campaigns ahead of time.

It's easy to get distracted by the periodic financial scandals that cause public outrage and widespread condemnation of the culture of finance. These include the 2012 Libor scandal, the mis-selling of financial products, rogue trading and money laundering. These overtly criminal or fraudulent actions flare up and then get subsumed into the broader debates on 'socially useful' finance. Socially useful finance is often narrowly defined in terms of how to create a down-to-earth style of finance that helps ordinary people in the present live ordinary fulfilled lives, from the standpoint of their current expectations. Ordinary retail banking is thus socially useful in so far as it helps people in everyday transactions. The financing of small and medium-sized enterprises (SMEs) is often considered socially useful because of the jobs it creates. Pension fund management helps people survive in old age, and insurance protects them from risk.

The battles over socially useful finance usually revolve around the extent to which the financial sector actually prioritises these things. They might focus on the reluctance of banks to lend to SMEs, and their proclivity to lend in ways that create economic instabilities, like property development bubbles, or to lend to 'useless' hedge funds. Laments over the ethical deviance of individual banking CEOs blend with macroeconomic debates on the booms and busts created by credit expansion and contraction. Politicians point out perverse short-term incentives created by huge bonuses, ironically backlit by tax-payer subsidisation of banks. Public sector workers get viscerally enraged by the ability of the sector to privatise gains and socialise losses, while they face job cuts to take the hit for RBS's cowboy antics. Pundits warn on the excessive political power that a banking oligopoly with an unhealthy domination of the economy possesses, holding governments hostage with threats to relocate elsewhere.

The debates can easily end up going around in circles. Much of the complexity concerns the *trade-offs* involved in reforms, particular sides of which are emphasised by different parties with different interests. Financial lobbyists point out the large numbers of jobs created in the sector, while avoiding the topic of what else those graduate students could be doing instead. The fund manager points out his role in helping people in retirement, while glossing over the collective effect of funds disrupting markets as they pile into them with a herd mentality. The derivatives community emphasises the narrow usefulness derivatives have in shifting risk around, but underplays how 'useful' they are for risk escalation via speculation. Structurers explain how an exotic structured product may be useful for a single fund, but are at a loss to describe the systemic risk engendered by their widespread use. A single hedge fund may boost the returns of a pension fund invested in it, but on average hedge funds may simply extract value from them, reallocating it via management fees to a small number of traders. High-frequency trading may improve the liquidity of markets, but only by drowning them in a sea of orders that dilute useful information, create instability, and to top it all, use up excessive amounts of electricity.

In the mean time, various kinds of regulatory reforms or innovations are incrementally driven forward. They're often politically pragmatic compromises, weighted towards existing power groups. In the following sections, we'll engage with them in outline, and to explore their strengths and weaknesses.

BANKING REFORM:
LOCAL BANKS AND FINANCIAL INCLUSION

In the wake of the financial crisis, many politicians stressed the need to reform the market structure of banking, including splitting commercial banks from investment banks, and reducing the size of megabanks. Some forms of reform though, are more acceptable than others. Tony Greenham of the New Economics Foundation, for example, suggested breaking up the UK state-owned bank RBS into chunks, in order to revitalise local banking networks, a proposal that makes some people in suits twitch and grimace. Other think-tanks, such as Civitas, have joined the discussion of how to shift the structure of banking in the UK away from centralised oligopolies, both to improve resilience, and to serve financially excluded populations and small businesses.

Continental capitalism in Europe has historically had a stronger focus on traditional bank lending to businesses, and countries like Switzerland and Germany have strong established traditions of *local banking*. Germany's financial system, for example, includes a network of local savings banks called Sparkassen that have mandates to develop long-term lending relationships with SMEs in particular regions. Those Sparkassen are linked to a tier of larger Landesbanks, via which they can gain access to larger capital markets. The result is a more decentralised system that can connect capital markets to SMEs. There are many interesting examples of alternative banking structures around the world: Kiwibank, for example, is a post office bank which has risen to become a major lender in New Zealand, operating via local post offices. A point to ponder is whether local banking offers a means for small communities to reconnect to a sense of ownership of finance. Can local municipalities be enabled to create their own banks that fund local businesses and community projects?

A deeper challenge to banking structures are *monetary reform* initiatives that seek to limit the power of private banks in credit creation. Scholars such as Prof. Richard Werner, and pressure groups like Positive Money, question the received wisdom of allowing banks free reign to extend credit into housing, speculation and inflation-fuelling consumption, and advocate greater public control of credit. Can a national community collectively decide, via a government, where money is steered, and do so more productively than a banking oligopoly? In a 2011 talk on banking reform, Lord Maurice Glasman characterised the Anglo-American model of private finance as one of *promiscuous capital* – where investors attempt to avoid long-term engagement in search of 'quick bangs'. He suggested that the role of politics has always been to entangle investors, containing their restlessness towards a model of faithful capital.

Governments though, are fearful of the connotations of 'telling banks where to lend'. Such language is easily portrayed as a form of creeping centralisation. It's more politically acceptable to enter into gentle agreements like Project Merlin, a UK government initiative encouraging large banks to lend to small institutions. The problem though, is that major banks themselves are now highly centralised, diminishing their ability, and their desire, to lend small sums to individual SMEs. They're adept at lending large amounts to hedge funds, or to generic portfolios of home loans that can be statistically modelled. The ancient art of on-the-ground relationship banking is not really their forte.

House Rent Blues: Community Banking and Microfinance

All major global banks pay lip-service to boosting financial inclusion to show that they're paying attention to the 'little people' in developing countries, and to financially excluded individuals within wealthier countries. The administrative costs of offering banking services to individuals, however, tend to be fixed, and if an individual is only depositing a small amount, it's doubtful whether it's worth having them as a customer. This is especially the case if the bank is beholden to shareholders that demand higher returns for lower risk. It's more profitable, and less risky, to win the business of wealthier individuals.

Freelance life has its ups and downs, and in 2011, I ran out of money. I had an informal contract with my landlord and he allowed me two extra months to gather rent. I approached a payday loan company in Brixton to borrow £400. The interest on the loan would be 25% for a single month. In other words, I would have to repay £500 within 30 days. There were two ironies to the situation. Firstly, people who are struggling to pay £400 are also the people who are least likely to be able to pay £100 in interest within the course of a month. Secondly, due to me being unable to give proof of future income, the company wouldn't even lend to me. In the end, I was able to borrow from friends, but imagine the situation of a person with no social safety nets, no regular income and no tolerant landlord. They would have to rely on loan sharks, back-alley lenders specialising in short-term loans attached to long-term shackles.

In wealthier countries, community banking and mutuals attempt to target these problems. Faisel Rahman in the UK, for example, set up a financial inclusion initiative called Fair Finance. In developing countries, *microfinance* was pioneered by institutions like Bangladesh's Grameen Bank and BRAC. Their idea was to lend to small co-operatives of rural women in marginalised communities, empowering them to start their own microenterprises. The principle could perhaps be summed up as follows: Give a person $1, and they'll eat for a day. Give them $3, and they'll eat for 3 days. Give them $10, and they'll eat for ten months. The idea is to enable people to buy their own means of production – such as a sewing kit to manufacture clothes – from which they can sustain themselves.

Ordinarily, the financial 'kudos' of a bank increases in line with the perceived status of its customers. Microfinance, though, deals with customers that are *so* marginal, and loan sizes that are *so* small, that the sector generated a real buzz around itself merely for having the audacity to pull it off. It has endured many scandals though, including a micro-financial crisis in certain parts of India where providers went on lending binges. But despite the ups and downs, financial inclusion is now an established goal of the international development community. There are also emergent forms of *micro-insurance*. MiCRO, for example, offers insurance to small-scale entrepreneurs in Haitian slums who face tropical storms. A hot technological area is mobile phone banking, which can lower the cost of banking for marginal communities. A major success story in this regard is M-Pesa, the huge mobile payment system in Kenya.

ENVIRONMENTAL FINANCE

Luke previously designed algorithms for financial trading systems, but is now one of a growing number of green entrepreneurs, building businesses that seek to move society away from fossil fuel reliance. I met him randomly in a London coffee shop where he was drawing sketches for a system that used mirrors to concentrate the sun's energy onto a special photo-voltaic solar cell. He was searching for venture capital to back his efforts to build these arrays in Portugal.

The term 'green economy' though, is ambiguous on many fronts, and is subject to many forms of political misuse and sophistry. For example, it often gets used to refer simply to a 'less bad' version of business-as-usual. Rio Tinto, for example, might 'go green' by hiring a sustainability consultant to calculate how much water they use in their mining processes, and to offer options for how they can minimise that within a certain budget. Such supply chain initiatives are clearly needed, but Rio Tinto is not likely ever to be a company that actively improves our surrounding environment.

The terms *green finance* or *environmental finance* can, likewise, refer to numerous practices. They may refer to attempts to fund explicitly green businesses, but equally can refer to an outlook towards financing that attempts to minimise ecological impact within a framework of maximising profit. Green finance, as it currently stands, does not refer to investment in an economy that de-emphasises material accumulation and material growth. That kind of thing is more likely to be seen as 'new age finance' or perhaps 'hippy finance' by many traditional financiers. A question like 'how do we finance a geothermal plant in Indonesia?' is more tangible to the average deal-maker, and indeed, provides more of an intellectual challenge than the well-established field of financing oil companies.

Cleantech venture capital firms are on the lookout for interesting opportunities in smart grid technologies, energy storage technologies, water desalination processes, electric vehicles, hydrogen fuels and desert solar, but it nevertheless remains comparatively more expensive to produce energy via renewable technologies. This is largely because fossil fuel companies still externalise most of their environmental costs. Alternative energy, and green businesses more generally, thus remain comparatively less profitable than 'normal' businesses, and have a comparatively more difficult time securing financing. They often rely on government subsidy systems (such as feed-in-tariffs) which boost their returns relative to fossil fuel power, thereby opening up finance for them. Such subsidy schemes are subject to political vagaries, perhaps dependent on whether key members of government are connected to a Texas oil family or not. On the surface, governments are aware of the need for greener infrastructure, but often lack the will, or the ability, to finance it through national budgets. In the UK, the government has set about launching initiatives like the Green Investment Bank, which in theory aims to pave the way for private investment in large green projects by, for example, providing guarantees to them (in the manner of a young person's parents standing as their 'guarantor' so that a private bank will loan them money).

Green Bonding

How does one get a pension fund, or other large institutional investor, to lend to environmental projects? This is a question that preoccupies various engineers of environmental finance instruments. Instruments they've designed include:

- *Green bonds*: Debt investment vehicles through which investors can lend to environmental projects. They have been issued by various institutions such as the World Bank's private finance arm IFC.
- *Green infrastructure bonds*: A special type of green bond proposed by Climate Change Capital, aimed at steering private capital into energy efficient infrastructure.

- *Rainforest bonds*: Proposed by groups like Enviromarket as a way to steer money into forest preservation. They refer to this, perhaps controversially, as 'ecosecuritisation'.

The relative merits of these various securities aside, the key question in the mind of any bond deal-maker is 'can we sell them to investors?' To make them attractive to potential debt investors, embellishments such as tax incentives or government guarantees are required. To help convince investors, the Climate Bonds Initiative has established itself as a green ratings agency to certify green bonds.

Environmental Markets for 'Ecosystem Services'

The environmental finance scene has an authentic energy, but it does remain constrained by many mainstream assumptions. In my experience, many of the people who work in the sector are ex-bank employees seeking to apply their skills to a new challenge, and they bring with them many of the modes of understanding found in mainstream finance. For example, many of them are keenly interested in the attempt to quantify (and monetise) the value of 'ecosystem services', such that they can be recognised within investment models. In 2011, the UK government released the National Ecosystem Assessment, an attempt at valuing, in monetary terms, the 'natural capital' of the British Isles. I've been subjected to surreal conversations with consultants telling me what the intrinsic value of the life of an African elephant is, or how to use options-pricing to value biodiversity and climate risk.

There is a trade-off at play here. In one sense, these efforts are trying to catalyse financing for positive environmental change. On the other hand, trying to value abstract categories like 'nature' or 'elephant life' is at best incredibly crude, and carries the risk of further alienating us from reality. Herman Daly, a heretical former World Bank senior economist, rightly stated that 'the economy is a wholly owned subsidiary of the environment, not the reverse'. There is a distinct pseudo-scientific feel to some of the less nuanced debates on natural capital, akin to a teenager trying to calculate the monetary value of their parents.

Then again, I have a distinct bias against such language. I grew up doing things like sleeping in mountain caves and was an obsessive birdwatcher for many years. I hold strong deep ecology views, and do not even use the term 'nature', believing it to reinforce a false distinction between humans and other animals. I instinctively align with more hardcore environmentalists, who often literally *loathe* the human-centric concepts of 'ecosystem services', 'natural capital' or 'environmental markets'. For many such environmentalists, one market that stands out as embodying everything that is wrong with mainstream approaches to sustainability is the *carbon market*.

Carbon Trade-offs

The carbon markets were originally given life via the Kyoto Protocol, an agreement flogged out in 1997 in a violent stable of political horse-trading, and first coming into force in 2005. The protocol set a controversial vision for the future of international climate relations, allocating carbon reduction targets to countries based on their historical emissions. One method the EU countries devised to hit their targets was the European Union Emissions Trading Scheme (EU ETS). The scheme covers around 12,000 European companies with the highest emissions. It calculates an upper limit on how much carbon equivalent[1] they can emit, and then allocates allowances (EUA's) to them,[2] equal to this cap. At the end of each year, the companies are required to surrender these allowances from their allocated quota to cover that year's emissions, a bit like showing your fishing licence to the marine coastguard to prove you're allowed to catch six tonnes of fish. If they emit more than their quota, they're forced to buy allowances from other businesses. If all are emitting too much, the price of the constrained credits should skyrocket,

---

1. 'Carbon markets' are actually 'Greenhouse gas markets': They also cover gases like methane and NO_2, which are converted into a 'carbon equivalent' for the purposes of calculation.
2. Most allowances are given for free, but a proportion are auctioned off too.

inducing some to stop emitting and to sell credits instead. This is a Cap and Trade system: You set a cap. And then you trade.

The Intellectual Backing Behind Cap and Trade Systems

'Externalities' is one term economists give to the ancient problem of the individual good relative to the collective good. A *negative externality* occurs when private benefits are accrued by an individual at the expense of society or the environment, like someone on a public bus rocking out to heavy-metal music while everyone else glares at them. A *positive externality* occurs when benefits accrued by society or the environment come at the expense of an individual, like someone building a lighthouse that they never get paid for, but that ships use all the time. In this case, a private individual takes the hit to make society better off, which they may be very happy to do, though it may be unviable for them to continue doing so in the longer term.

In the case of positive externalities, governments may attempt to step in with subsidies or public provision. In the case of negative externalities, society subsidises the individual by bearing an unequal cost, and thus society should exact a tax in return. A Pigovian tax is thus one that attempts to force private individuals to internalise the social or environmental cost of their actions. In the case of Pigovian carbon taxes, a government fixes a price on carbon pollution, and quantities emitted by private parties are allowed to fluctuate in response.

The alternative though, is to fix the *quantity of pollution* through allocated credits and let the prices fluctuate in response to that. That's what cap and trade systems seek to do. It comes from Ronald Coase's theory that externalities arise in situations of poorly defined property rights. It interlocks with the 'tragedy of the commons' theory – the belief that people are more likely to trash things that nobody explicitly owns. Anthropologists have long documented agricultural societies that do not conform to this theory, but it is true that the intangibility of the atmosphere certainly does make it easy to pollute it without perceiving personal responsibility. Coase's theory aligns well within the dominant economic paradigm: The concept of handing out limited rights to pollution, and then letting people distribute them via markets and prices, appeals to those who believe in market efficiency.

The EU ETS has, however, been through turbulent times. At first, far too many permits were given out, and then it fell into general malaise amid the economic downturn and uncertainty about the Kyoto Protocol's future. The cat is out of the bag though, and a patchwork of nascent environmental markets has emerged. They're all based on a similar principle of creating a legal commodity out of an environmental cost, or an environmental outcome, and then allowing participants to trade it amongst themselves.

Offset Schemes

The EU ETS is but one element of the global carbon markets. It exists alongside 'offset' markets, also called 'baseline and credit schemes', which offer a way to *manufacture* carbon allowances. The biggest of these is the UN Framework Convention on Climate Change's *Clean Development Mechanism* (CDM), which enables offset projects to be set up in developing countries. Outside my hometown of Durban, for example, is a landfill site that hosts one of South Africa's first CDM projects. Left as is, the rubbish in the landfill would rot away and release methane. This is called the baseline scenario. The local municipality decided they would harvest the gas, and burn it within a turbine to generate electricity to sell to the electrical grid. Two sets of carbon reductions are thereby achieved relative to the baseline scenario: Firstly, methane is prevented from escaping into the atmosphere. Secondly, the electricity created displaces the more carbon-intensive electricity produced by Eskom, South Africa's coal-guzzling electricity giant. The project thus displays 'additionality', being able to prove that these carbon reductions wouldn't naturally occur in its absence.

The UNFCCC formally recognises additionality by promising that if a project goes ahead, it can be credited with creating a stream of certified emission reductions, or CERs. Those CERs in turn are given value by the fact that they can be sold to companies in the EU, as *substitutes* for their allocated allowances under the EU ETS cap and trade scheme. Through this, companies in the EU ETS can theoretically subsidise green projects in the developing world that otherwise wouldn't be economically viable. This concept is highly appealing to multilateral agencies like the World Bank that need an ideologically friendly mechanism to resolve the dilemma of increasing growth while reducing fossil fuel emissions: If you want economic growth in Laos, link it to a growth of renewable energy resources, subsidised by coal-fired power stations in the UK, smoothly co-ordinated and powered by market forces.

The devil, of course, is in the detail. Calculating carbon offsets is an imprecise science at best. To get a sense for it, browse through the carbon offset methodologies in the UNFCCC's CDM manual. Examples include:

- AMS-II.J: Replace incandescent lamps with compact fluorescent lamps.
- AMS-III.M: Recovery of caustic soda from waste black liquor generated in paper manufacturing.
- AMS-III.D: Methane recovery in animal manure management systems.

These sound like positive actions to undertake in principle, but the methodology that's generated the vast majority of CDM credits is AM0001: 'Incineration of HFC 23 gas streams that would otherwise be vented into the atmosphere.' HFC 23 is a greenhouse gas that is around 11,000 times more potent than CO_2, so destroying one tonne of it will earn a project a whopping number of credits. This created a perverse incentive for factories in China and elsewhere to produce more of it, just so they could destroy it. That methodology is under review, but a more general concern is how to establish baseline scenarios. Projects are measured in isolation, but what if you pay a Brazilian farming operation to reduce emissions via land management on one field, only to discover they simply increase their normal activities on another field? 'Leakage' like this can easily occur, and the difficulty in actually proving that you've offset CO_2

leads to different standards of offsets. The CDM requires a fairly high standard of proof, making it comparatively expensive for a project to produce them. There are other 'voluntary' offsets schemes though, that produce lower quality, and much cheaper, credits that individual people like us might buy in an attempt to offset our airplane emissions.

The Carbon Traders

Financial institutions view carbon markets as something new to intermediate in. Despite sometimes being referred to as financial instruments, however, carbon credits are actually just legally created commodities, and carbon credit traders thus sit on commodities desks in banks. They're also found in large energy companies, in physical commodity companies like Vitol, and in specialist carbon trading firms.

Compared to other commodity markets like oil, carbon markets are tiny, and in my experience, the participants all tend to know each other well. The straightforward business in banks like Deutsche Bank is in *secondary markets*, intermediating in credits already in existence. The specialist firms often get involved in *primary carbon markets*, helping to source and originate new CDM credits. This latter activity is the dirty ground-level stuff, with buccaneering deal-makers dodging red tape and local politics, flying in small aircraft over Peruvian mine dumps, looking to sign contracts for offset projects. That's a comparatively expensive process: The employees sent in search of new credits might have fun in Lagos nightclubs, but the origination companies back in London are prone to collapse as many of these deals fail to deliver.

Despite being characterised as a market solution, carbon markets are highly dependent on political forces. The participants in the EU obsess about whether the USA will get involved, but the political feasibility of that is dampened by the lobbying efforts of large polluting corporates in America who don't have an interest in paying for carbon pollution, whether it be in the form of carbon credits or carbon taxes. With uncertainty over a successor agreement to the Kyoto Protocol, the future of CDM markets is subject to much uncertainty, and carbon credit origination companies have become somewhat subdued in this area. On the other hand, new cap and trade systems are emerging in China and in the state of California. Banks are thus waiting for more clarity on where the next carbon action might come from.

Kurtz in the Land of Forest Carbon: REDD

One newer controversial area is 'forestry finance'. The destruction of forests accounts for a significant percentage of global emissions, not to mention devastating biodiversity loss. The huge swathes of remaining tropical primary forest is thus the focus of REDD, *Reducing Emissions from Deforestation and Forest Degradation*. The first major REDD deal occurred in 2010 when Norway agreed to pay the Indonesian government $1 billion to limit licences for forest logging. The Indonesian government obtains an alternative source of cash to selling logging concessions by instead selling REDD credits to Norway to offset Norway's emissions.

The basic idea behind REDD is to pay people for the ecosystem services offered by the trees, thereby preventing them from cutting them down for lumber, or clearing the forest for agriculture, mining and palm oil plantations. A cynical take on this type of 'payment for ecosystem services' (PES) is that it's like paying a ransom to individuals who are threatening to harm a friend of yours. A more positive take sees PES as paying people to act as stewards for ecosystems that they're otherwise under economic pressure to damage. REDD is based on the same baseline and credit concept as CDM projects. Measuring and then monetising the carbon sink ecosystem service by selling REDD credits is an alternative for people who might destroy a forest for short-term gain, but it depends firstly on the ability to measure, and secondly on whether the payment is high enough. While World Bank agencies undertake scientific surveys to establish measurement methodologies, the deeper political question is *who gets paid and who loses?* If the Indonesian government limits logging concessions in order to secure REDD payments, does the new limit affect palm oil companies and coal miners, or do small-scale farmers and indigenous forest people bear the brunt?

Joseph Conrad's *Heart of Darkness* features the ivory trader Kurtz, practising unsavoury methods deep in the forests of Central Africa. Are the bars in Kalimantan hosting a new school of Kurtzes, replaying scenes from the Scramble for Africa, signing treaties with local chiefs by buying them off with whisky? I've investigated projects based in the Philippines that use pyramid marketing and 'pump-and-dump' techniques to con retail investors into buying low-quality REDD credits that don't even exist yet. The World Bank couches the chaotic process of setting up REDD in euphemistic language, calling for 'capacity building' to prevent abuse. In the absence of strong oversight, REDD could become a snakepit of controversy.

REDD Ain't Black and White

A few years ago I was having dinner with a group of friends involved in climate justice campaigns. Someone was describing a great renewable energy project they'd heard of. I knew the project, and explained that it stayed afloat by selling carbon credits it created while generating solar energy. The table instantaneously went silent and people were noticeably uncomfortable. Somebody hissed 'false solution'. It was as if I had broken a taboo raising a subject that shouldn't have been brought up.

Carbon markets activate an uncomfortable mental circuit for many environmentalists. I intuitively understand the near primordial resistance to the concept of allowing people to monetise environmental issues. Putting a price on the air we breathe seems to have a jarring callousness to it. It seems to leave future sustainability in the hands of the subjective and short-term price views of individual disconnected people. Such approaches appear to reduce the process of protecting life to shallow considerations of the immediate *individual* costs and benefits. In describing this as the natural way things get solved, mainstream economics seems to endorse narrowly selfish behaviour as normal. It leads the individual to ask, 'Is it worth me stopping polluting?' rather than encouraging them to think 'It would be good for the world if I stopped polluting.' Many in the climate justice movements insist people shouldn't need external incentives to act morally. They may suggest that change should come from internal ideals, expressed via a grassroots upwelling of environmental enlightenment, or via government action from the top. The disturbing question for the activists at the table, however, was whether it is better to have no solar project, or a solar project sustained via carbon markets.

The Rosy View: Individual Inclusivity

Like many areas of the financial markets, individually positive activities within carbon finance can be separated from the overall implications of the system. On an individual basis, a carbon market is clearly very useful. As I produce solar energy, I can simultaneously produce a legal commodity called a credit. I can now approach a bank and say, 'I have *two* sources of future income from my solar project, please help me finance it.' It unlocks financing for me by increasing my return.

In 2010 I helped a South African pineapple farmer who wanted to meet carbon traders in London. He ran a farmers' co-operative that collectively owned a pineapple juice factory. After juicing the pineapples, they'd discard the husks, which rotted to create methane. He wanted to fund the installation of an anaerobic digester to harvest the methane, which he could then convert to electricity to power the factory. An industrial-sized anaerobic digester is expensive. Even if his ideals told him it was good to prevent emissions, it would be unviable to install such machinery without some assurance he could pay back any money he borrowed to finance it. The CDM, which offered him carbon credits for installing the digester, was one route to securing this.

In the absence of credits, it would be more viable for him to create externalities by leaving the pineapples to rot on a landfill. Such are the kind of individually 'rational' actions that lead to a failure of collective rationality over time. One can fight that failure through regulation (you must all harvest the methane from your pineapples), or one can tap into the individual's rationality via external incentives (we will reward you for doing so). Sometimes these questions get framed in economic justice circles as integrity vs. compromise. The complexity though, is that 'compromise' can equally mean 'inclusivity'. Initiatives that monetise carbon reductions do actually open up climate action to people previously excluded from it. Our thinking about climate change is often abstract, and clouded by shorter-term constraints that block actions yielding benefits far in the future: 'I'd like to install an anaerobic digester, but I'm tight on cash right now.' Carbon market advocates believe a well-designed trading system can mobilise coherent collective action, based not on imprecise ideals, but on tangible cash flows. Are such systems thus *inclusive*, accommodating people's short-term limitations and imperfections? Are green ideals an *exclusive* view held by intellectuals with little grasp of everyday practicalities?

The Less Rosy View: Collective Disconnection

The real issue at play though, is not really whether CDM markets are empathetic towards small-scale pineapple farmers. The real issue is the power relations embedded in those, and other, environmental markets. It's often pointed out that various charlatans inevitably abuse environmental language to sell dubious credits to make a quick buck, but this is to be expected in any new market. The much more serious concern is that carbon markets appear to allow the largest *buyers* of credits to 'absolve' themselves of carbon sin by presenting those credits as offerings at the global confessional. If the carbon price was very high, this could incentivise them to invest in new green technology, to avoid visiting the demanding priest, but this has not been the case. Pressure groups like Sandbag, and many others, have shown that the carbon price has often been kept artificially low due to political pressure to hand out too many allowances, and to hand them out for free. The supposedly market-based price for carbon, in other words, is subject to political lobbying, and this threatens to turn the market into a sham.

It is theoretically possible to overcome the shortcomings outlined above, but at the deepest psychological level the carbon markets impart certain messages to society. They are, after all, a form of social technology, and in using them we have the potential to inadvertently alter the way we think. The use of market systems to distribute private ownership rights to areas previously perceived as commons raises the spectre of communal disconnection from a sense of environmental responsibility.

Building a Hybrid View: Getting Out and Meeting People Involved

In 2010 I did some gonzo exploration of carbon markets, intrigued to meet the people involved and to get to the bottom of it. I discovered a much more holistic mix of people compared to some more straightforward areas of finance. It involves scientists, technologists and policy wonks interpreting the political manoeuvring among huge global power blocs. There are roughnecked rogues a world away from UN agencies, and young Indian entrepreneurs out to be next generation businessmen. There are good-hearted ex-development professionals working on small-scale solar projects in Tanzania. There are people who genuinely believe they can radically improve the earth by harnessing the power of enterprise, and there are cynical CEOs who shallowly use the markets for self-serving purposes.

To get a sense for the energy, start by reading the coded language within the original Kyoto Protocol. Explore the bureaucratic channels of the UNFCCC. Look at the websites of the banks and brokers, and then the individual projects in Nicaragua and Papua New Guinea. It all forms a morally ambiguous mass that challenges straightforward ethical notions about those that care and those that don't. Exploring such areas also allows us to consider whether the markets can be hacked in any way.

Carbon Retirement Funds: Squeezing the Dark Spread

In 2010 the financial heretic Max Keiser believed that J.P. Morgan had taken a huge bet against silver. He set up the *Buy silver, crash J.P. Morgan* campaign, encouraging people to buy physical silver to drive the price up. Theoretically the campaign could have induced a runaway 'short-squeeze' in which J.P. Morgan, seeing the price going up, would attempt to back out of its bet and thereby cause the price to rise even more, potentially bringing about its own demise. The idea was always more symbolic than practical, but, on the other hand, it's something hedge funds try do all the time. Armajaro, for example, infamously hoarded cocoa futures to squeeze other participants in the cocoa markets. If Armajaro can corner the cocoa market, there's nothing to say a hedge fund of dissent couldn't corner the carbon market to force up the price.

Carbon traders talk a lot about 'dark spreads' and 'spark spreads'. A 'dirty dark spread', roughly speaking, is the price of wholesale electricity minus the price of coal. It leaves you with an indication of the profitability of a coal-fired power station. The 'dirty spark spread' is the same, except it measures the profitability of a gas-fired power station. Ordinarily, European dirty dark spreads are higher than dirty spark spreads, meaning it's more profitable to produce electricity with coal than gas.

The 'clean dark spread' and 'clean spark spread' adds the price of carbon to the equation. It indicates the profitability of a coal-fired power station and a gas-fired power station in the context of a carbon market. Coal power is more carbon intensive than gas power, so in the context of a carbon market, gas power can become relatively more profitable. Theoretically speaking, as the carbon price moves higher, power companies are incentivised to 'mothball' or decommission their coal power stations, and rev up their standby gas power stations instead. Carbon prices thus have feedbacks into coal and gas prices.

So how does the hedge fund of dissent fit into this? Groups like CarbonRetirement buy credits from the EU system, and 'retire' them, preventing anyone else from getting them. If this can be scaled up, using a fund to gobble up available credits, the carbon market could theoretically be squeezed, inducing a shift to relatively cleaner gas power. It's not a solution to climate change, but in opting for the market system, power companies simultaneously open themselves up to a potential hack.

GENTLE BRONTOSAURS:
SRI, ESG AND ETHICAL INVESTMENT

In mid 2012 J.P. Morgan Asset Management closed down its Catholic Ethical Fund, due to lack of investor demand for it. It had been set up to invest only in companies that fitted a Catholic world-view, screening out alcohol companies and pharmaceutical companies that produced contraceptives. Investors put a mere $5 million into it, which was hardly enough to express a Catholic view on the future economy. This raises tricky questions: Is an ethical fund the same as a socially responsible investment (SRI) fund? Comparatively few people would believe it's 'socially responsible' to avoid investing in contraceptives.

SRI funds are supposed to invest money in firms that display good environmental, social and governance records (sometimes shortened into the acronym ESG). They've been extensively critiqued over the years for using negative screening – not investing in negative companies – rather than investing in stand-out positive companies. They're often run by major fund management companies that offer far more 'non-SRI' funds than SRI funds. They've also been found to frequently invest in companies that have terrible environmental records, such as BP. This may be due to mandates that require them to invest across a diversified range of industries, forcing them to pick 'the least bad' companies in each industry.

For all the critiques though, the SRI community is an important outlet for individuals who want a mainstream alternative to normal funds, and they do push forward the cause of transparency. SRI funds have developed useful mechanisms and metrics to pry beyond the frequently shallow world of corporate social responsibility (CSR), and to look deeper into companies' labour and governance standards. They have supported side-projects such as the Carbon Disclosure Project, which has made some progress quantifying the carbon footprint of companies. They are signatories in the UN Principles for Responsible Investment, and the UNEP Finance Initiative, which attempt to provide companies with palatable guidelines for sustainable behaviour.

Index Activism

They also offer one interface for campaigners to engage with the fund management world, as well as the potential for activist strategies. Sam Gill, for example, is a young activist entrepreneur who runs the Environmental Investment Organisation, which has set about building a series of indices to rank companies by carbon emissions and carbon disclosure. These are intended as the basis for an investment fund: As people put money into such a fund, the money would be steered to those companies with the highest index ranking, incentivising low emissions and high disclosure. The concept remains on the margins of the investment community, but it is a bold design hack with interesting future potential.

SOCIAL FINANCE AND IMPACT INVESTMENT

If SRI was the first wave of socially aware investment, *social finance* and *impact investment* is the next wave. They are distinguished by their deliberate attempt to finance activities that have overtly positive social outcomes. Here are some interesting social finance projects that I have come across in recent years:

- *Social shares on social stock markets*: Pradjeep Jethi and Mark Campanale have been working on the Social Stock Exchange, aiming to channel money into financing social enterprises via shares. Similar examples include the Nexii exchange (based in Mauritius), and Ethex.
- *Charity Bonds*: UK-based Alia has developed a Charity Bond, in which investors lend to a housing charity, and divert the interest into another charity of the investors' choice. InvestingForGood also helped the charity Scope issue a bond in order to expand their network of charity shops and their fundraising programmes. London-based Numbers4Good is working on developing a Youth Employment Bond to fund occupational training for unemployed young people.

Social finance is a diverse field. At the larger end of the scale, it may concern how to finance public necessities like health and education. A reason why governments have traditionally 'invested' in public education is that the financial returns from education take the form of tax revenues from a more productive population, which only manifests over the long term. No private investor would normally do that, because it takes too long, and they can't capture tax revenues like a government can. They'd only invest in *for-profit* private schools, which exclude most pupils. The question of whether it is possible to design equitable privately financed schools is the type of knotty and politicised issue taken on by social finance professionals.

At a smaller scale, social finance might concern how to finance social enterprise. Imagine you were running a restaurant that explicitly hired recovering drug addicts as waiters and chefs. Such staff are comparatively costly to train, and are subject to uncertain behaviour. Who could you get to invest in such a comparatively high-risk venture that produces low financial returns? It goes completely against the grain of the mainstream finance mantra of risk commensurate to return. Social finance professionals though, aim to help you unlock financing by recognising the 'social return' you offer society.

In every social investment, the return comes in two parts. There are the financial returns in the form of actual cash flows, and social returns in the form of non-tangible well-being to society, such as increased education, beautiful surroundings or freedom from oppressive structures. Traditionally, subsidising social returns (a type of 'positive externality') is the realm of government and philanthropy. When a wealthy foundation gives money to an underprivileged urban dance troupe, they in a sense exchange the money for a purely social return.

Social gains though, do not come in clearly denominated units. They are subjectively experienced in the ebb and flow of societies, and it is very doubtful that one can quantify them. A philanthropist might require feedback from charities they've supported, but they don't require a spreadsheet with a percentage return of health and social benefits from youth dance. To unlock money beyond grant-financing from governments and philanthropists though, methods are needed to internalise the positive externality of social returns. Two ways in which this can be done are as follows:

1. Creating hybrid 'impact investors' or 'blended value' investors who can accept a combination of social and financial returns.
2. Finding a way to monetise social returns, such that 'normal' investors can invest.

Blended Value Investing: Accommodating Yin and Yang

Impact investors can invest via specialist social investment funds – offered by managers such as Bridges Ventures, Venturesome and Root Capital – that offer access to ventures with low financial returns but high social returns. The Acumen Fund, for example, specialises in deploying 'patient capital' – long-term investment that is happy to wait – into areas like rural agriculture and health services in developing countries. These social funds are often styled with an explicitly NGO-like image that is much less macho than traditional financial institutions, and, in fact, the major NGO Oxfam has recently launched a small impact investment fund for international development. In my anecdotal experience, they also hire a comparatively high number of women compared to normal financial institutions. Much of the language in the scene is a hybrid between financial and charity sector terminology, such as *social return on investment* (SROI).

An impact investor is happy to receive a comparatively low financial return from the projects they invest in. One might be inclined to imagine this investor as a single individual, but consider the following example: Imagine a group of 50 individuals, half of whom are philanthropists, and half of whom are normal investors. When mixed together and viewed collectively, the group becomes like a synthetic impact investor that needs higher returns than a pure philanthropist, but lower returns than a normal investor. If we think back to the securitised products discussed on page 169–70, there were higher risk tranches and lower risk tranches. In normal securitisations, high-risk tranches are taken on by hedge funds. They shield more conservative investors in exchange for claiming the potential for huge gains. Using this as an analogy for social investment, we could imagine philanthropists as being almost like hedge funds protecting the financial returns of normal investors, in exchange for a much higher social return.

For example, a philanthropist funding a small clinic might ordinarily exchange a £5 million financial loss in return for £5 million worth of social return. What if though, financing for a medium-sized hospital could be catalysed due to a philanthropist being prepared to take a £5 million hit to act as a buffer for normal investors – who are worried about the risk and return – to fund the hospital. The philanthropist takes some of the risk out of the deal, heightens those investors' financial returns, and thereby creates a 'leveraged' social return worth much more than £5 million. Another example could be a social housing development, where tenants will pay low rent. The returns are too low for normal investors, but a philanthropist might induce them to invest by being prepared to take the financial loss. In 2009 a colleague and I referred to this concept irreverently as the *Jesus tranche*: The philanthropist *unlocks* a greater social return than the financial loss they take, a bit like Jesus breaking the five loaves to feed the multitude.

'Leveraging' social return via a synthetic social investor admittedly sounds a little dubious, but most aspects of social finance are indeed controversial, often because they're closely tied to political questions of state provision versus private provision. A particular example of this, which has received significant press attention, are *social impact bonds*.

Monetising Social Returns: Social Impact Bonds

Initial waves of privatisation in a country might involve, for example, a government paying private social service providers to provide a pre-defined set of prisoner rehabilitation services. Over the years, more emphasis has been placed on 'payments by results' (or outcomes-based commissioning), where providers are paid to deliver a social outcome – such as reducing prison reoffending rates – using whatever means they feel necessary.

Small social service providers, however, don't have large cash piles to pre-fund themselves while they tinker about trying to achieve an outcome they can be paid for.

Social impact bonds (SIBs) have been presented as one potential solution in such situations. Strictly speaking, an SIB is not really a bond. It's more like a fund backed by investors, which enters into a contract with the government to be paid for a social outcome or for a saving it creates for the government. The fund then pays social service providers to tackle a social problem, and if those providers succeed, the investors get paid by the government. The investors attempt to monetise social returns by taking on the risk of social services failing to achieve outcomes.

The first small SIB was set up by London-based Social Finance Ltd., to reduce prison reoffending rates. To assess whether it succeeds, the SIB offers rehabilitation services to some cohorts of prison-leavers, but not others, thereby attempting to measure the difference in reoffending rates. Besides the inherently problematic and imprecise nature of such a measurement, it also takes several years to complete. This means such SIBs remain a difficult sell for many normal investors, locking them in to a comparatively high-risk investment with low-ish expected returns.

The field of social finance is largely driven by individuals working outside major financial institutions, many of whom are highly passionate about what they do. Nevertheless, while some social investors get involved in such ventures for the love of it, others may have more opaque motivations. Goldman Sachs, for example, received an outsized amount of press in 2012 for putting a small amount into the first American social impact bond. J.P. Morgan and Deutsche Bank have small social finance departments too, connected to their Corporate Social Responsibility departments. It's questionable whether such banks can truly claim to be 'social financiers'.

THE MAKING OF A REFORMED BANKER

Imagine a person entering a Morgan Stanley graduate programme straight after leaving a top university. She spends five years in debt capital markets, arranging for investors to buy the corporate bonds of European telecoms companies. At Christmas she always has to explain what she does to confused relatives, so she shortcuts it by saying 'I help the economy.' Her dad brags at the country club about his high-flying child, but deep down, she feels burnt out, and feels herself getting locked into the sector. *Is this really what I want to be doing?*

In a spontaneous moment she announces that she's taking a year out to go travelling. Perhaps it's a response to a lost sense of idealism that's been replaced with hard 'realism' since she left university. She always loved that film *The Motorcycle Diaries*, where the young doctor, Che Guevara, roams the highways of South America on a journey of self-discovery. It helps that she now has money to live without working for a year, so off she goes, surfing in Indonesia, volunteering in Kenya, and chewing coca leaves on the Inca trail. Upon her return she's rejuvenated, but has the same skill set, and meets the same friends. A headhunter offers her an attractive and exciting post at a large private equity firm. It's too good to turn down. She signs on for another five year voyage on the mainstream financial seas.

Three years later the money is flowing into her bank account, but the personal rewards are diminishing. She feels a growing sense of a disjuncture, and gives away significant amounts of money to philanthropic causes. She reads a cynical newspaper pundit dismissing this as a way for finance professionals to 'relieve their guilty conscience'. She doesn't feel that she's doing something 'bad' by working at a private equity firm though. It's more that her job only serves one aspect of her personality. Perhaps the impulse to give back is an attempt to achieve some sense of holism. She joins the board of a charity foundation to offer them her 'hard-nosed' business skills, and joins a programme to mentor underprivileged children.

A few years later the firm wants to make her a partner. That will definitely lock her in. She stumbles across an internet site called EscapeTheCity.org, targeting financial professionals who want to 'do something different'. It showcases niche areas like social finance and socially responsible investment. Suddenly it all makes sense. *This* is exactly the thing for her. Her skills are needed to rescue ailing young entrepreneurs with positive visions. She jumps on it with an almost religious fervour, embracing slogans like 'doing good by doing well', a catchphrase to describe the process of creating a positive social benefit whilst being profitable. She's asked to speak at conferences on impact investing, where people laugh as she refers to herself as a 'reformed banker'.

The Limitations of 'Doing Good by Doing Well'

I know many fantastic 'reformed bankers'. They bring great skill-sets and contacts, and combine mainstream credibility with an ability to cut straight through the kind of spurious arguments one might hear coming from an aggressive CEO. They're individually excellent at 'here and now' questions such as 'how do we make this social project work right now?' The concern though, is that the collective energy they bring lacks a radical vision.

What do I mean by this? Implicit in many debates on socially useful finance is the belief that the sector can be reformed without fundamentally altering basic economic precepts. More radical interpretations, however, may see in the financial sector manifestations of much deeper flaws built into economic models. For example, Marxist thinkers may deeply question the social relations between equity investors and employees, and whether this concentrates power and creates inequality as shareholders gradually extract value from wage earners. Religious traditions might deeply question the nature of debt investment. Is debt a tool of the powerful to extract unproductive rents and mask growing inequality? There are deep questions about the psychological dynamics of money itself, and whether it disconnects people from their social and natural environment. Ecological perspectives question the very concept of economic growth.

Most arguments against the financial sector contain combinations of shallower and deeper levels of critique, but the deeper we go, the more fundamental the disagreement, and the more we move into the realm of 'revolutionary' thinking. A surprisingly wide range of people may agree that the financial sector creates unsustainable levels of debt, privatises the gains that stem from misallocating it, and socialises the losses from the inevitable breakdown of that misallocation. Fewer are prepared to get deeply drawn into debates on whether the sector is hardcoded to breach the ecological limits of the planet, or whether money itself is a psychological disconnector. Those appear as obscure long-term battles, whereas designing methodologies for the accounting of climate risk in pension funds may be more immediate and pragmatic, naturally appealing more to those with practical experience.

Perhaps 15 years working for a bank puts someone in a great position to make cutting comments about the weaknesses of the financial sector. On the other hand, all those years of apparently hard-nosed business dealing might make someone susceptible to being constrained by ideas of what's 'realistic', having got used to a pre-existing set of assumptions exemplified in phrases like 'that will never work'. Reformed bankers, for instance, often have a deep affinity for concepts that resolve the dissonance between their definition of 'realism' and 'idealism': For example, they often are drawn to the concept of aligning the profit motive with positive social and environmental outcomes. They may also get animated about adapting concepts they already know, excitedly referring to social finance as an 'asset class'.

In many ways it is positive to break down the idea that there need be a trade-off between acting responsibly and 'business'. It's an inclusive vision that allows a businessperson to feel they have a positive use for their skills. The darker side though, is the risk that deeper psychological motivations make someone *want to believe* that positive social and environmental outcomes can be aligned with the profit motive. For example, perhaps they are locked into groups of friends who they don't want to alienate by challenging their deeper level assumptions about profit. Perhaps they're comparatively wealthy, constraining their ability to imagine the reality of true deprivation, leading to an excessively positive outlook.

Some social and environmental finance events can have a very mainstream feel, with 'happy-clappy' positive types mixing with harder-edged bankers and middle-of-the-road reformists. You arrive at Bank of America Merrill Lynch to hear a talk about Big Society Capital, which aims to build a social investment market in the UK. A certain politeness hangs in the air, a social etiquette, and an awareness of elite status. There's a muted ability to acknowledge the obvious conservative political undertones that underlie a concept like 'Big Society Capital'. Somebody stands up to proclaim an apparent change in culture. Static panel discussions are held, where older fund managers talk about what it is 'realistic' to expect from social investment. They trot out a J.P. Morgan report on the exciting, but nevertheless humble, future of social finance as a niche asset class. They explain that fund managers have fiduciary duties to deliver 'risk-adjusted returns' and that a social finance investment might be a slightly off-piste add-on to their normal strategies. A consultant suggests that the way to sell investors on the idea of investing in the Triodos Microfinance Fund, or the Ethical Property Fund, is to highlight the 'uncorrelated diversification benefits' of doing so.

All of this is perfectly reasonable. The legal structure of the fund management industry does indeed prioritise 'normal' investments like tar sands, and views socially responsible investment as a niche feel-good addition to their client offering, for those who wish to use it. However, when someone points out that a great deal of the philanthropy required to fuel social finance comes from bonus payments extracted from 'normal finance', people shuffle uncomfortably. The host moves the conversation quickly on, eager to not alienate their sponsors, Bank of America Merrill Lynch, who kindly provided the venue, the canapés and the wine.

ADDING THE RADICAL TO FINANCIAL INNOVATION

It's no secret that areas of innovation such as social finance tinker away on the edges of mainstream finance and are not viewed as 'threats' to entrenched financial regimes. Perhaps though, that is a source of strength. I have implied that 'mainstream-friendly' people are somehow non-radical, but that may be narrow-minded. The hybrid forms of social and environmental finance discussed above could be conceptualised as *design hacks*, using the language of mainstream finance to open small breaches in an existing structure. Individuals with a hacker outlook can see the subtly subversive potential that these innovations have, holding mainstream status while potentially bending it. Is there an entire class of 'positive deviants' within mainstream organisations, completely invisible to those used to viewing the black and white world of surface appearance?

A successful green energy entrepreneur once told me 'I wear a suit, and I go to the big energy conferences. I talk to all the Big Oil players, but I'm out to destroy their companies. You want to know how to bring down Big Oil? Firstly raise their cost of capital to choke them. Secondly, build a better business.' His language of entrepreneurial war is not to everyone's taste. It seems to buy into the ideology of relentless competition, with strains of a libertarian myth of the trailblazing individual who forges the shape of society through their sheer willpower. But let's cut to the heart of the issue. Critics of capitalism are often portrayed by the Right as stuck in a static intellectualism, having some access to academic and policy fields, but irrelevant beyond that. Why are there so many papers on the fundamental contradictions of capitalism, but so few project plans for an alternative bank?

I'm always struck by the lack of hardcore economic justice activists at social and environmental finance conferences. They occupy a parallel scene that is often deeply suspicious of such innovation. It ranges from outright disdain of environmental markets, to more muted suspicion of instruments like Charity bonds. There may be a relatively positive view of microfinance as an agent of international development, and of community finance initiatives that help less wealthy people, and the traditional activist might turn up at the credit union open day. For the most part though, the idea of being in the same room as Merrill Lynch's environmental team is a highly unappealing prospect for many in justice circles.

We theoretically want a financial sector that voluntarily steers money towards useful projects rather than destructive speculative activities, so why are we suspicious when something like a social impact bond tries to do the same thing? One possible reason is that justice movements are concerned that reform approaches implicitly reinforce the values of the things they are against. Social finance might get conceptualised as an attempt by finance to capture the social via a financialisation of social value. The perception is of an unequal partnership between two conflicting forces. It always implies an 'attack' coming from the side with the most perceived power, and allows little room to imagine it the other way around: Could social finance rather be the 'socialisation' of financial value?

Another question is whether those distinctions should even exist. By definition, if alternative forms of finance won out, it would entail them becoming mainstream. Purist thinking, positing strict boundaries between 'the financial' and 'the social', unnecessarily complicates this. For example, the socially responsible bank Triodos uses the mainstream bank RBS – known for its funding of fossil fuel projects – as a clearing agent. Does this taint Triodos? The real issue, as Triodos knows, is that building an alternative bank in a networked system is very challenging. The building process forces them to engage with questions like 'what happens if we're forced to deal with companies that extensively utilise tax havens?' Individuals with a revolutionary mindset struggle to accommodate these inevitable contradictions, and so will tend not to start an alternative bank. This is one reason why a hacker outlook is useful when thinking about building alternatives. It allows one to think of Triodos as hacking a network and co-opting RBS towards more useful ends. Triodos, from this perspective, is like a Trojan Horse with a radical vision, interlocking with a powerful financial regime.

Trojan Horses set up a breach in an existing structure, but they need constant radical input, otherwise they end up as tame rocking-horses for use in photo-shoots with Goldman Sachs' PR team. A Trojan Horse can be as simple as animating a fund manager by talking in terms of asset classes, but the linguistic hack needs constant critical input lest the manager box it in a mental comfort zone within their company CSR department. The social and environmental finance sector has set up many potential Trojan Horses, but to maintain their openness and to bring out their disruptive potential requires the sector to be inundated with people with radical visions that extend beyond whether or not a portfolio remains balanced, individuals who will aggressively cut canals for positive funds to flow. The point at which a room moves from 'we respond to demand' to 'we create demand' is the point where a Microsoft IT security conference becomes a true hacker conference.

6
DIY Finance

GETTING REAL WITH REALITY

Back in the eighteenth century, if you stood up in a room full of aristocratic music aficionados and said 'We need to make music more expressive, less rigid, less dominated by elite notions of composition, and more politically engaged', people might have looked at you askance, balked, and told you to get real. Likewise, when the experienced fund manager scoffs and says 'show me how your alternative finance vision will work in practice', their attitude is rooted in a particular time and place, and is hypersensitive to the constraints present in that time and place.

Businesspeople and politicians are very prone to throwing out statements about what is realistic in society. The very term 'businessperson' (and the related term 'businesslike') is a highly loaded word, referring to someone who apparently displays a no-nonsense pragmatism that is necessary to survive in the 'real world'. I appreciate the value of pragmatism: It's obviously true that if a venture has no revenue, it will die. On the other hand, pragmatism can be a code-word for a lack of willingness to test the bounds of rationality. For example, it was pragmatic to be a member of caste-like guilds in the Middle Ages. The prudent, pragmatic people of the time were merely parroting a static view of rationality validated by others in the society. Pragmatism should be taken seriously, but not so seriously as to forget that its underlying conceptual infrastructure, consisting of 'realistic' assumptions, has shifted many times.

Perhaps those who able to recognise the flaws in assumptions most readily are those with fewer stakes in the existing economic or social status quo – such as students, or marginalised communities, or particular individuals with an oddball outsider ethic that makes them less susceptible to being caught up in group dynamics. Going against the grain of a dominant paradigm is very difficult though, and when a particular economic system completely surrounds one, there is often an impulse to imagine how to get out of it completely. Sometimes this takes explicit forms, such as grand visions for an alternative society. Other times, it's more implicit. For example, embedded in the idea that you can 'bring down mainstream finance' is the implication that it can be replaced with something else. That's a heavy and abstract thought, because it seems to demand that a particular alternative be imagined and defined from the outset. In many justice movements, this culminates in a sense of despondency at just how far off this abstract alternative is from being created. It can also contribute to high levels of sectarianism as particular versions of the imagined alternative are pitted against each other in a virtual testing ground.

But making the financial system less dominated by elite notions of composition, does not have to have a pre-defined path. To return to our opening analogy, Jimi Hendrix's music was brought to life through a combination of incremental social awakening and political, economic and technological changes over many decades: In 1873 a prison chain gang in the Deep South develops ballads to the rhythm of their picks; in 1913 a young musician sees a stuffy rigid orchestra and thinks 'I wonder how I could jazz up that trumpet thing'; in 1947 a hotel lounge guitarist accidentally overdrives their amplifier by turning it too high, causing the refined patrons to howl in protest while the young disenchanted bartender looks up and says 'what is that amazing sound?'

Looking forward, something may appear crazy because we cannot envisage how it might be supported given the existing social structures – like trying to imagine Spotify when you've only experienced a cassette player. Thus, the answer to the question 'Where is your alternative?' should be 'Who knows? We're experimenting'. The imaginative bounds only get tested when someone takes the trumpet from the orchestra and uses it to play jazz, or takes the paint and throws it, Jackson Pollock style, to see whether it will stick.

BRING ON THE ROCK & ROLL FINANCE

Mainstream finance often reinforces an imagined distinction between the economic (rational, efficient, scientific) and the social (spiritual, experiential, artistic). It echoes the pop science distinction between left and right brain, the former working within rational assumptions, and the latter adept at playing with the boundaries of rationality. Everyone has the potential for hard-nosed, efficient behaviour aimed at maximising their resources, but we all similarly have the potential for activist behaviour aimed at redistributing those resources to the vulnerable. Everyone has the creative potential to re-imagine and tinker with structures, and everyone has a sense of a connection to other people and with our broader ecosystem. Current finance mostly serves the first potential, thereby alienating many from their activist, creative, communal and ecological possibilities.

Embedded in mainstream financial institutions are design principles that impart lessons to those that use them. As I interact with a Barclays' retail branch I am encouraged to believe that I am a passive drone who can be patronised with gimmicks. Their online platform never attempts to teach me anything about their workings, revealing design principles that ensure the *opacity*, and thereby an *inequality*, of information. People who work in such institutions are encouraged to believe that money naturally and efficiently moves towards the greatest return, or greatest stability, or least risk, and that it's prudent to behave according to this efficient rationality. The so-called reality is in people's minds, entrenched via the deep structures of neoclassical economic thought, displaying an elegant, even beautiful, internal consistency, and held in place by group psychology and economic power.

There are many alternative design principles that challenge this crisp neoclassical symmetry. Money can be charged with activist energy, the ability to respond to genuine issues of justice. It can be charged with artistic energy, the ability to embrace uncertainty and recognise beauty in things often ignored. It can be charged with ecological energy, the ability to move in accordance with ecological cycles. Creating heretical financial vessels, with alternative design principles, can shift deep thought structures: As I use a timebanking platform (see page 237), for example, I'm suddenly awakened to the fact that exchange can be deeply communal, and that market systems are underpinned by huge unrecognised gift economies.

The Financial Artist

Activists are fantastic at coming up with deeply disruptive visions, but to challenge existing rational dogmas in a technical area like finance demands that those visions be combined with pragmatic implementation. Indeed, creativity refers to both *deconstruction* – being able to see beyond existing structures – and *construction*, being able to translate that vision into new structures. Traditional artistic mediums like paint or clay give scope to creativity by allowing an artist to give *real form* to a creative vision that challenges or deconstructs a normal view of the world. Company structures too can be an artistic medium. Having a truly creative vision, and then constructing it with a legal entity and contracts, is, however, much more complex than moulding clay.

Take, for example, the process of setting up an alternative bank. This is a piece of financial installation art that needs to be implemented in several stages, and is a sure-fire way to fast-track one's experience of the difficulties of building alternatives. Anthony Thomson launched Metrobank in 2010, focusing on reintroducing the concept of personalised customer service into banking. In free market theory, the market is supposed to include *ease of entry* and *ease of exit*. Banking regulators though, are terrified by the idea of a bank failing, so the situation in the banking market is more like one of 'very difficult entry with no option of exit'. Metrobank took over two years to create, and required a lot of capital. Thomson not only had to convince the regulators that the bank was viable, but also had to deal with tricky laws around marketing financial services, the costly job of creating a robust, secure, IT system, and then the small issue of convincing people to switch to his bank.

Once embedded into systems though, such installation pieces can serve as templates for others. Ecology Building Society – which lends to sustainable housing projects – was started by a group of Green Party activists in 1981. They are very small, but that's what gives them an ability to focus on specific green construction projects in local areas. It's no good for there to be only *one* Ecology Building Society, though. There need to be many more, but we're faced with regulators who don't want lots of little banks and building societies that are hard to administer, and who thereby advantage major incumbents. What a regulator may respond to, however, is a system whereby small banks operate under a common *platform* that can be regulated like a franchise.

Fiona and Robin Brownsell have been working on developing 'plug-and-play' IT systems that new banks can lease. Thus, rather than each new bank having to build everything from scratch, they can tap into a collective economy of scale. There's a chicken-and-egg situation here though: In order for platform builders to cover their costs, they have to believe that enough small banks will eventually buy into their system. One bold piece of collective financial installation art would thus be to develop an *activist banking platform* consisting of a plug-and-play network of pop-up banks. Imagine a hypothetical situation in which you walk down the street and see an Oxfam Bank and a Greenpeace Bank. Imagine they are part of a tiered group of activist banks all using the same primary IT and clearing systems. An umbrella group of local religious charities could plug into the system too, using it to set up small community banks. The constituent nodes collectively own the backbone infrastructure, creating a decentralised yet centrally regulated system. Edinburgh, Brighton and London become major centres of global activist finance, connecting to other such networks around the world. Sound crazy? Many modern mega-banks built themselves up in a related fashion by incorporating numerous smaller banks under a common administrative platform.

The imaginative constraints on banking can be pushed at in many ways. Transform Capital Management has championed the idea of an 'impact investment bank' to fund environmental start-ups and social enterprises. Imagine creating an investment bank that hires vulnerable and homeless people, creating a class of financiers who actually have experience of deprivation. Absurd? No more absurd than current investment banks.

The Activist Entrepreneur

Among many on the Right, the use of pre-existing power to secure advantages within systems rigged to favouring power is often conceptualised as 'innovation' and 'entrepreneurship'. It's the type of economics-101-style of rational entrepreneurship of those who want to get to a conventional place by conventional means, starting from a position of power ('I've expanded my family's pin factory'). The conservative entrepreneur's 'creativity' may often involve perfecting a technical skill ('how do I do this better than anyone else?'), or applying an existing skill to a new area. It's the type of entrepreneurship that may appeal to those who've previously worked in large institutions, who are often trained to be good at short-term efficiency and robustness, prizing themselves on mastering a structure, on being an expert, or on outcompeting others in the same area, often while hiding behind faux-libertarian ideologies. Such entrepreneurship is often seen in the financial world when a group of traders break off to start their own hedge fund, or when an ex-banker decides to start their own flagship company – like Drexel Burnham's Michael Spencer starting ICAP. The financial start-up I worked for was set up by ex-traders and ex-brokers who came from large institutions.

Silicon Valley type entrepreneurs – exemplified by Steve Jobs – tend to be different to the standard economics-101-style entrepreneur. They still want to get to a conventional place, but want to do so by unconventional means ('Check out my uber-cool new way to sell advertising!'). While many of them claim to be 'normal' entrepreneurs motivated by profit, they often display an unconventional ethos, eschewing economic security and contrasting themselves to the corporate careerist looking for a stable job and a high salary. They're often obsessive about creating something of *beauty* they can be proud of. They very often have a desire to be different, and to be free. A major entrepreneurship buzzword is that of the *Lean Start-up*, referring to an on-the-fly bootstrapping style that many activists intuitively understand, focusing on nimbly bypassing incumbents rather than trying to battle them on their own terms.

In the financial sector, this type of 'cool' entrepreneurship is found in financial technology (fintech) start-ups. These are Silicon Valley style, internet-based start-ups that may not necessarily have an explicit social mission, but that do have the potential to shake up old banking models. Simple, for example, is an online financial service that touts itself as a 'worry free alternative to traditional banking'. Nutmeg is an online platform for personal investment management. Jack Dorsey of Twitter started Square, a payments processing technology. Some people in the fintech scene are ex-bank IT consultants who realised the shoddy job major banks do at mundane things like payments. Some are designers who focus on sweetening the 'UX' (user experience) of finance, for example, by creating apps that can present information about a bank account to people in more intuitive ways.

A good place to get a sense for the fintech scene is on the online community BankInnovation.Net. The energy is authentic, and is gaining momentum, and I really enjoy bouncing ideas with such entrepreneurs. On the other hand, entrepreneurs often romanticise themselves as *The Force* that drives change. People in start-up communities sometimes even label themselves as 'change-makers' or 'disruptors'. This in-built self-assertiveness can be a natural coping mechanism in face of the constant possibility of failure, but it can also lead to hype about entrepreneurship in general, regardless of whether or not it's truly disruptive. For example, many entrepreneurs aspire to be bought out by a large financial institution, in the same way that many Silicon Valley start-ups aim to be bought out by Google. Perhaps Barclays will buy out a 'gamification' platform, or an 'augmented reality' platform, to enhance the Barclays' experience.

There are though, frequently overlooked forms of entrepreneurship driven by a radical impulse. For example, hacker-style 'intrapreneurs' want to get to an *unconventional place by conventional* means ('I wear a suit, but I will destroy big oil'). Indy entrepreneurs and DIY artistic entrepreneurs want to get to an *unconventional place by unconventional means* ('Welcome to my steampunk record store. We're an anarchic collective that doesn't use money'). The radical with practical skills is a threat to the status quo of any economic system. They combine pragmatism with idealism, working towards robust but lean models incorporating principles that inspire and challenge people to think and act differently. These types of activist entrepreneur are driven by a rebellious impulse and social conscience, but, like Bob Dylan, rail against group thinking, displaying a lean, bootstrapping, 'shit-stirrer' outlook, critiquing both authorities and anti-authorities. They seldom attempt to show how to 'fix' things too literally, but rather seek constant experimentation. Here are some examples of fantastic financial shit-stirrers I know:

- Eli Gothill: A computer coder who has been experimenting with Twitter gift currencies called #Punkmoney and GiftPunk. He documents the challenges on his blog webisteme.com, exploring which aspects of his projects fail, and designing solutions to improve them.
- Agamemnon Otero: A Uruguayan artist who developed the Brixton Energy community shares project (see page 223) as a pilot that could be learnt from, with the aim of rolling it out on a much bigger scale to create a decentralised solar power plant across South London.
- Alistair Alexander and Jamie Perera: An activist/musician combo who worked on weekends to design a timebanking platform called Shmoney, getting it to a point where they could obtain funding to develop it even further.
- Josh Ryan Collins and the Brixton Pound team: Starting from a dinner conversation, they created a physical currency, and then an electronic payments system, which is now being used as a model for other alternative currencies.

There are many more of these unconventional entrepreneurs around the world. I like to refer to them as 'seedbombers'. Seedbombs were pioneered by the Guerrilla Gardening movement. They are little bags of wild seeds thrown into a rigidly controlled public garden. The seedbomb attempts to make public parks truly public. Using this as an analogy for the financial sector, we can see the current regime as running a 'public' garden with a dangerous level of monoculture, leaching the soil, and full of toxic runoff from synthetic fertilisers. A vibrant alternative-building community will seedbomb it, designing projects quickly, throwing them into the mix, aiming to create clusters of crazy, yet compelling, financial flora.

BREAKING FINANCE MONOCULTURES WITH EVOLUTIONARY ALGORITHMS

The field of evolutionary algorithms is a fascinating area of artificial intelligence, where a computer randomly tests thousands of possibilities for optimising specified principles within a set of constraints. For example: *'How can we optimise speed with robustness, within constraints X, Y, and Z.'* The real world version of this would be to seedbomb projects and rapidly feed the results back to see if they're achieving specified design principles. Such an approach makes no attempt to design grand solutions from the outset, focusing rather on building three elements:

1. Establishing design principles.
2. Undertaking experiments in financial fusion.
3. Feeding results back into a feedback structure.

Design Principles for Seedbombing

Alternative finance platforms should impart alternative messages through their use. So what design principles would you want to see embedded in the financial system? Design principles might include:

- *Simplicity of design*: Much innovation in mainstream finance is simply an increase in complexity, such as a derivative which more precisely matches some parameter, or an operation that gets done at increasing speed. It's often unnecessarily complex and more akin to obfuscation, further alienating people from the sector. To increase financial democratisation, simplicity of user-experience – which the fintech community is highly adept at – is empowering.

- *Holistic optimisation, not rational maximisation*: Much mainstream economics is built on the ideal of maximisation rather than optimisation. A corporation might maximise profit, but not the well-being of the people who work for it. Too high a degree of specialisation might maximise output, but leave you a miserable drone for ten hours a day. A financial instrument that optimises might provide an investor with a financial return, but also connect them to other things that are meaningful.

- *Diversity*: Many financial regulators have an implicit preference for a concentrated financial sector, believing it to be easier to monitor and less likely to cause panics. The irony is that while concentration brings a superficial sense of control, it leads to much deeper systemic risk. Monocultures are easier to spray with pesticide, but much more susceptible to single collapse. We need a distributed financial sector with diverse institutions.

- *Reconnection*: Returning to the hacker analogy, a financial activist should aim to reconnect parts of a system that are otherwise disconnected, thereby unblocking power concentrations. For example, both the user and the operator of a financial platform should be empowered in the process of interaction with it, and be led to connect to the underlying economic reality of what they're doing. Within Marxist frameworks, this might be phrased as reducing *alienation*.

- *Permacultural design principles*: The principles described above are fundamental to many ecological thought systems. Those who are familiar with the 12 Principles of Permaculture, for example, have an intuitive sense for them. There is no scope to discuss permacultural design in any detail in this book, but for those who are interested, it is definitely worth further exploration as useful basis for financial design.[1]

EXPERIMENTS IN FINANCIAL FUSION: THREE AREAS TO SEEDBOMB

There are many disruptive experiments for financial seedbombers to try out, including projects in crowd-powered finance, complementary currencies, social finance, risk management systems, activist funds, grassroots finance systems, social enterprise, ecological finance, anthropological exploration, psychological studies of money, and alternative conceptions of value. The following sections though, will focus on three broad and interlocking areas where activity might be fruitful.

- Experimentation zone 1: Disintermediating, democratising, decentralising
- Experimentation zone 2: Activating five-dimensional money
- Experimentation zone 3: The risk-sharing revolution

Experimentation Zone 1: Disintermediating, Democratising, Decentralising

It is theoretically possible that everyone in the world could be their own bank, investing their money directly into ventures. In fact, in a situation of perfect information where everyone knew all there was to know, banks would have little reason to exist: They exist because we lack both information about investment opportunities, and the skills to evaluate those opportunities. Furthermore, while we might individually invest in a single opportunity (e.g., my uncle's farm shop), we often don't have money to invest in a safer diversified portfolio of

---

1. Thanks must go to Ilana Taub of the sustainability consultancy *6heads* for alerting me to this idea.

opportunities. A lot of these constraints still exist. Technology though, has made it much easier to obtain information about investment opportunities, and has lowered the transaction costs for direct investment.

Gaining Connection: P2P

One major area of development is in internet-based peer-to-peer (P2P) lending platforms. Well-known examples include Zopa and Funding Circle, which allow individuals and companies to tender for loans directly from other individuals. MarketInvoice allows small businesses to borrow against invoices they've got coming due. Kiva's online platform shows me micro-scale projects in Ecuador that I can invest in. These are a world away from the centralised oligopoly of high street banks that refuse to disclose what they are using my money for.

Peer-to-peer technology is being extended into other areas traditionally dominated by large financial institutions. For example, CurrencyFair is a P2P currency exchange that allows me to buy euros directly from someone who wants pounds, and Friendsurance is a P2P insurance company, allowing groups of friends to insure each other. While most of these platforms remain small, the concept is catching on and gaining more widespread public attention, raising the spectre of *dis-intermediation* – otherwise known as 'cutting out the middle man' – for major banks.

Gaining Scale: Crowd-funding

Crowd-funding is another technology brought to life by internet communications, enabling projects to fund themselves by pooling money from lots of small contributors. Platforms like Kickstarter and Indiegogo, for example, have revolutionised the landscape of funding for creative projects. Thanks to them, I can post my plan to build a solar-power Noah's Ark and actually find oddball people around the world who are willing to finance it in exchange for a chance to ride on it. Social Enterprise crowd-funding platforms like Buzzbnk help UK social enterprises and charity projects raise money. Abundance Generation is a new crowd-funding platform for debt investment in renewable energy, allowing me to lend £5 to a wind farm. Crowdcube and Seedrs allow me to invest directly in ownership of small start-ups. A local food organisation called Big Barn, for example, raised £12,000 from 58 investors on Crowdcube.

Crowd-funding platforms received a lot of press due to their inclusion in the US JOBS Act (Jumpstart Our Business Startups), which sees them as a useful new source of funding for small start-ups. Much of the press debate focused on the potential for small dodgy projects to get funded by hapless retail investors. Leaving aside the fact that major banks frequently fund huge dodgy projects, it's certainly true that with decentralised power comes the possibility for decentralised abuse. If all finance was run as a peer-to-peer network, we would have to adapt to deal with the consequences. We're used to seeing the financial sector as something that serves us in a one-way fashion, like arriving at a DJ set and expecting to be entertained, and booing the DJ if they don't play the songs we want. Imagine, on the other hand, a system whereby the quality of the music was determined by the quality of the dancing, a self-supporting feedback loop in which everyone collectively created their experience. The idea of taking collective responsibility for financing ourselves is actually scary, and there are trade-offs to greater democratisation. In the short-term it probably means more failures, but in the long-term it can lead to empowerment and resilience.

Gaining Emotional Returns: Community Shares

Collective responsibility often works best in communities of trust: If I borrow from my community, I will be shunned if I use the money recklessly. One instrument being pioneered to tap into community dynamics are Community Shares, which allow people to invest in local projects. Brixton Energy funded a local solar power plant with community shares in 2012, and now all sorts of people around Brixton own a stake in a project they feel connected to. Brixton Energy aims to replicate this to create a network of locally owned solar plants all over South London. These types of instruments may have lower financial returns, but because the investors are local, their reward is often emotional. You literally *feel* the return embedded in a community that you experience on a daily basis. For many, this trumps a higher financial return from something you have no personal connection with.

Experimentation Zone 2: Activating Five-Dimensional Money

The term 'money', like the term 'love', is a word we use extensively, but find very hard to explain. Mainstream economists tend to portray money as a neutral technology of exchange, seldom capturing its deep cultural foundations, its creative energy and tension, and its potential to psychologically distort transactions. We often think about how people use money (e.g., wastefully, extravagantly, frugally), but we seldom think about how using it *affects us*. It's like obsessing about how a pen can write positive or negative things, but neglecting to consider how the act of writing affects the way we think. Money is an intermediary that facilitates exchange, but in the process it can disconnect us from the social nature of exchange. Many self-proclaimed capitalists, for example, argue that the object of business is to 'make money', which is clearly absurd given that money means nothing unless it can be exchanged with others for goods and services. If I'm shipwrecked on an island with a pile of golden treasure, it's worthless unless I can find *other people* who will accept it in payment for food and shelter.

Money is often objectified as a thing-in-itself, just like love is objectified in Hollywood films. Love is an emergent property created in the process of two people interacting, not a thing-in-itself that can be 'found'. If the people stop interacting, the love disappears. Likewise, when people stop interacting, money has no meaning. Its perceived value is mostly activated by its use in exchange. The belief that money is a thing-in-itself pervades society though. In the words of Max Weber, Money 'is thought of so purely as an end in itself, that from the point of view of the happiness of, or utility to, the single individual, it appears entirely transcendental and absolutely irrational.'

A connected view of exchange might involve perceiving oneself producing things, temporarily exchanging them for money, and then exchanging that for other things. The more common disconnected view is the inverse: I have money at the beginning of the month. I use it while engaging in production, either for myself or others, for which I receive more money, thereby 'filling up' my account with money again, as an end-in-itself, by the end of the month.

Searching for the Soul of Money

Activism, in challenging damaging concentrations of power, is a form of meta-level risk management. It seeks to hold the intellectual commons open in the face of authoritarian structures – such as cults of market fundamentalism, patriarchal dominance, state repression and religious dogma – that constrain thought. When it comes to the financial system though, we are often distracted by the spectacle of the huge looming towers of Canary Wharf and Wall Street. It is like the magician who diverts the eye with overt symbols of power, while the real tricks go on around you. The financial system is embedded in our use of money, but we seldom recognise that. Maybe one step to altering its structure is to first deeply reflect on our own relationship to money.

For example, have you ever considered why money seems to have exchange value, but not actual use value? I can exchange a £5 note for useful goods and services, but I seem to have no intrinsic use for the note outside of the exchange process. What exactly gives it exchange value without use value? One possible starting point is to realise that if money had intrinsic use value, it might be a poor medium of exchange. For example, coffee would be a poor commodity to use as money, because as soon as someone felt like drinking some, they'd just consume it and remove it from circulation. It seems, counter-intuitively, that money almost needs to have limited intrinsic value in order to work. It's interesting to note the fetishisation of gold as a currency throughout much of history. Gold is not a particularly useful commodity. It's mostly an aspirational good, something that you might find valuable only once you've satisfied basic needs. It has status elements, and in a pre-money society it would most likely be religious or military figures in positions of power who would waste energy on obtaining an over-the-top luxury item like a shiny rock. Monetary history is a lot more varied and complex than this, but the basic point stands that money needs to appear symbolically valuable enough for us to trick ourselves into believing it has value, but not valuable enough that we'd actually consume it directly. People can convince themselves that someone out there finds gold useful for mystical or vanity reasons, but in the interim, they themselves have no immediate practical use for it, allowing it to become a great medium of exchange.

Once that process locks itself in, cultures develop around it, and people begin to collectively validate the value by trusting that others will accept it. The soul of money thus becomes underwritten by human relationships of reciprocity – even if we know that the note has no intrinsic value, we *trust* that others will accept it, and they trust it by trusting that others will accept it back in the future. The note thereby gets imbued with a type of intrinsic value drawn from the collective reciprocity of the society, with the added backing that the government will accept it for taxes. Through such processes, currencies come to appear in the abstract as representations of all other goods.

Word-hacking Money

These underlying dynamics are easily obscured and forgotten though, and may only become apparent when you delve into, and disrupt, the linguistics of money. In my own life, for example, I don't use the word 'money'. A 'British pound' *sounds* like a thing-in-itself, so I rename it to explicitly break that illusion. I personally use the term *COGAS-UK* to describe a pound, an acronym for 'Claim On Goods And Services (within the geographic boundaries of the) United Kingdom'. That's what a British Pound actually is. A connected way to perceive money is to think of it like a lasso that you harness resources with. I go to the café, and harness a coffee via a societal relationship of trust, embodied in a coin or note. People often look at me askance when I say this. Try it though. Go back in this book and replace the word 'money' with COGAS. You may find yourself staring at the coin in your hand, feeling it lose its thing-in-itself qualities.

Perhaps the most simple, yet spectacular, money hack of all time is that undertaken by J.S.G. Boggs. His infamous 'Boggs Notes' are beautiful hand-drawn replicas of US dollar bills, almost indistinguishable from 'real' dollar bills. He uses them to 'pay' for goods. The authorities claim he's a counterfeiter. He claims he's an artist, exchanging his works for food. He's clearly both. He cuts right to the heart of issues like consumerism, which is a fetishisation of the act of *claiming a good*, not an obsession with the good itself. If we actually appreciated the goods themselves, we wouldn't throw them away so readily. Nobody throws away a Boggs Note.

As I begin to connect with the intricate human connections that underlie money, 'buying' my coffee begins to feel like a direct exchange with the hundreds of people who were involved in the process of producing it, including the investors that funded the plantations and processing facilities. Indeed, all monetary investment is simultaneously a play on money itself: It is simply the process of using claims on goods and services with the intent to produce more claims on goods and services. It's the process of expending current energy to produce more energy over time. Debt investment is not that different to deliberately giving someone some food, and asking that they give you an extra apple when they reciprocate.

You can even experience an internal 'financial system' when claims that you and others make against your personal energy leave you feeling burnt out, as exemplified in the phrase 'I'm overextending myself'. I've had a hard day at work, so I buy a coffee with money, thereby exchanging one set of claims I have, setting them off through the till on an energy circuit to who knows where. As I drink, I start another energy circuit within me. After all, where does all value come from, other than from our labour and the ecosystems around us? Finance, at its deepest levels, has got little to do with numbers, and much to do with people's energy, the claims on that energy, and inevitably, human relationships and power. Money is just an abstraction of all these things.

The Occult of Complementary Currency

These social and psychological phenomena are well-known to the small group of monetary mystics who design their own alternative currencies. Just like the characters in *The Matrix* who've seen that reality may not be as it appears, monetary mystics operate in the world in full knowledge that money is a powerful societal convention, and undertake hacking exercises into the fabric of such collective illusions.

The first monetary mystic I met was Tav, running a 'metanational collective' known as the Espians in London. I'd just left the financial sector, and cockily believed I understood currency. Tav casually chatted about The Terra, an attempt by a man named Bernard Lietaer to create a global currency backed by usable commodities. Tav talked of using electricity as money, and of currencies with inbuilt deflation that deliberately reduced in value over time. It quickly became apparent that working in the financial sector had never required me to actually engage with the deep cultural life of money. Money always seemed to have a hermetic, 'airtight' quality, that didn't require one to understand it in order for it to work, perhaps much like the entire financial regime.

Over time there have been thousands of alternative currencies and exchange systems. Some have sought to compete with mainstream currencies, others to diversify away from them. Many alternative currency builders think of themselves as helping to create an ecosystem of currencies, some of which are used to *localise* exchange, or *decentralise* the control of the medium of exchange, or *humanise* the act of exchange, or *energise* the velocity of exchange. Families of alternative currencies include:

- *Commodity-backed currencies*: These types of currency are issued against a store of commodities, or against a future claim on a commodity, and are frequently measured in a physical quantity such as KwH or litres of oil … or, once upon a time, pounds of sterling silver. As discussed earlier though, these currencies only work if people don't actually try to consume the commodity that is imagined to back the currency. An example is the Ven Currency, which is backed by a combination of other currencies, commodities and carbon prices. The Green Money Working Group works on renewable-energy-backed currencies.

- *Mutual credit systems*: The basic idea of mutual credit is to create an interest-free credit system based on reciprocity. You allow someone to claim goods from you, this is noted down in a central ledger, and they return goods and services in exchange over time. That is the gist of it, although the actual systems can be more elaborate. The most famous of these is the co-operative economic circle WIR in Switzerland, where businesses extend each other credit. Others, like LETS (Local Exchange Trading Systems), involve individual people in a certain area exchanging with each other.

- *Dominant-currency-backed local currencies*: A popular way to create alternative currencies is to back them with a dominant national currency. For example, the Brixton pound is actually a store of British pounds in a credit union bank account, against which Brixton pounds are issued. It thereby acts to ring-fence the British pound into a local area. Other examples of this include the Bristol pound, the Totnes pound and the Toronto dollar.

- *Digital currencies*: The most well-known of these is the digital-usage-backed currency Bitcoin, which is discussed below.

The Importance of Plug-and-Play: Local Currencies

Local currencies are a great way to complement local economic regeneration efforts and to build pride in communities. That said, there have been many alternative currencies designed by well-meaning individuals who have lacked the flair for user-experience or for scaling their ideas up. The currency languishes on a home-made website, or is presented in an overly complex way that doesn't grab ordinary people.

A good example of a group with flair is the Brixton Pound team. They mostly work on a volunteer basis, but they've managed to scale the idea up and gain much press attention. The Brixton pound notes themselves are beautiful, adorned with local celebrities like David Bowie and Luol Deng, and with urban street art designs. They host regular events and stalls at community gatherings. They've also created an online platform enabling mobile phone text-based exchange – when I'm in Brixton, I often pay for coffees by sending a text message.

Importantly, the same technology platform was rolled out for the subsequent Bristol pound. Developing this type of plug-and-play technology saves others from having to reinvent the wheel. That way, someone in Brazil might use the same local currency platform as someone in Spain. Arthur Brock's MetaCurrency project is one such effort to build common platforms.

The Importance of Underground Hype: Bitcoin

Bitcoin is very different to a local currency like the Brixton pound. It's a *global*, decentralised, online 'crypto-currency'. One way to obtain it is by 'mining' it – running an algorithm on a high-powered computer, exchanging extensive processing capacity for a chance at obtaining new Bitcoins. If like me you only have a laptop, you can buy Bitcoins on online exchanges from people who've mined them. They can be used to buy intriguing things from oddball vendors who'll accept it, including pizzas, online games, marijuana, consulting services and whatever else can be found in the electronic black markets. Digital currency gurus like Jon Matonis will accept Bitcoin donations via their blog sites. The Bitcoin community, who can be found hanging out in online forums like the Bitcoin Forum, has no leader, taking the form of a decentralised collective connected via internet relay chat, on a mission to subvert the global monetary system. It's popular among various anarchist and hacker communities, libertarians who fear government influence over national currencies, and, of course, American survivalists. It's captured people's imagination, not only because it is the most robust digital currency yet, but also because it has a mythical foundation story, involving the mysterious character of Satoshi Nakamoto. Satoshi has no traceable identity, but released tracts onto the web, describing how the currency could work. He then disappeared, leaving disciples to carry on the work. The mystery made people want to take part, giving the currency *soul*.

Alternatives – currencies or otherwise – need not only good design principles but also a sense of underground hype to charge them with psychological power and soul. Facebook and Gmail understood this, initially promoting themselves via closed peer groups, creating a sense that one was missing out by not using them. That can be the first step to going viral.

Experimentation Zone 3: The Risk-sharing Revolution

Countries like Malaysia, Saudi Arabia, and increasingly the UK, are leading centres for *Islamic finance*. Like various other religious traditions in history, Islam is very uncomfortable with the excesses of interest or usury. This means that Islamic financial institutions, unlike Western banks, do not engage in debt investment, viewing debt investors as rentiers free-riding on equity investors, or else as bad influences that encourage equity investors to engage in excessive risk-taking with borrowed money.

The natural corollary of this is that Islamic financiers basically advocate equity investment, often phrased as 'risk sharing', because a shareholder shares in the risk of a venture directly rather than indirectly. An Islamic fund thus might directly equity invest in a venture, receiving dividends in return rather than interest. An Islamic mortgage might entail an Islamic bank entering into a partnership with an individual who wants to buy a house, buying it for them on their behalf and then letting them slowly purchase it from them in instalments. In practice, it's questionable how different that is from a normal mortgage, and the boundaries of Islamic finance are up for contestation. More purist Shariah scholars, for example, may be deeply sceptical about the likes of HSBC Amanah, an Islamic finance provider attached to the major interest-earning commercial bank HSBC. These grey areas aside, a holy system of production and exchange, from many Islamic perspectives, is only achieved in the context of true risk-sharing between equals, but with the added proviso that the risks shared should not be the result of ill-informed speculation.

Superficially, this sounds fairly similar to socialist concepts of equality in economic ventures, but one difference is that Islamic finance focuses on the relationship between debt investors and equity investors, whereas socialist thinkers tend to focus on the relationship between equity investors and the employees in a venture (bosses vs. workers). When combining the two traditions, we find they explore a matrix of fractious economic relationships. On the one hand, debt investors extract value from equity investors, who in turn extract value from employees. On the other hand, both debt investors and employees are entitled to fixed returns (interest and wages) from a venture, whereas equity investors' returns *float*. In other words, owners of enterprises leverage their returns via both debt investors and employees.

The concept of 'risk sharing' is slippery, and it's not always apparent who exactly takes the most risk in a venture. Consider this example: I might spend two years designing a new series of interesting electric guitar pedals on the weekends in my garage. I decide to quit my soul-destroying job and start up my own guitar pedal business. I spend six more months designing a business plan and then enlist others to help me make it a reality. I might get some venture capital, and borrow money to help scale the business up. Over time this ends up taking the form of a company structure with employees. Initially I'll be low on cash, so I pay my employees partially in equity by giving them stakes in the company. If the company subsequently goes bust, the debt investors may be able to recover some of their money, the equity investors (including myself) are wiped out, and the employees are laid off with whatever they've managed to extract in the form of wages in the mean time. Thus equity investors, especially prior to limited liability companies and bankruptcy laws, perceive themselves to be on the hook for significant amounts of risk.

This is one source of the economic libertarian ideology that says equity investors accumulate wealth – over the long term at least – through the taking of risk and the creation of opportunities.

The interesting thing to note about this though, is the crossover with *workers' co-operatives*. Co-operative type economic relationships expose those taking part in them to the personal risk that comes with directing a venture, putting individuals on the hook for its potential failure. At the same time, they differ to an individualist entrepreneurial vision by spreading risk across all the participants in an enterprise. Workers' co-operatives in effect attempt to fuse the role of equity investors and employees into one. To start a co-operative, participants have to contribute either money or labour, and in exchange receive shares in the company. A co-operative – in some conceptions at least – is thus an equity-financed venture that pays people in dividends rather than wages, replacing labour contracts with share certificates. If the entity fails, all the workers fail too. If it succeeds, all the workers succeed too. I part-own everything I produce, and with it, I part-own the possibility of complete failure. Exposure to risk of failure is part of the definition of lack of alienation.

Bringing Sexy Back to Co-operatives

Within left-wing circles, there is a long-standing and frequently obscure debate on the desirability of workers co-operatives within a broader capitalist economy. The debate is sometimes traced back to the early nineteenth century, when the Scottish industrialist Robert Owen first tried to turn his cotton mills into planned worker-owned communities, and subsequently failed in his attempts to create utopian communities in America. His followers initially included figures like Josiah Warren, who later rebelled against Owen's attempt to collectivise property. Warren, who is frequently cited in individualist anarchist traditions, plays an important part in the history of alternative currency movements. For example, he created the Cincinnati Time Store in 1827, where people exchanged goods for labour time rather than normal money.

Many left-wing debates on the various strands of co-operative economies, and the financial systems that might accompany them, are, however, bogged down in heavy language that doesn't grab the public imagination. The Co-operative Bank in the UK has a fairly fresh image, but beyond that the co-operative movement still languishes in obscurity. Part of that comes from the fact that co-operatives are inevitably perceived as farmers' or village craft co-operatives – small, provincial, barely making ends meet, and not particularly sexy. We never think of technology or internet start-ups as co-operatives, even though they're normally entirely equity financed and consist of small groups of closely collaborating workers who are paid, at least in part, with equity rather than in wages.

Such start-ups, in mainstream circles, are very sexy. Thus, if there was ever an epic hack to be pulled off, it would be to create a modernised vision of a quasi-anarchist-meets-socialist economy as a collection of interconnected start-up companies, operating solely on dividends, financing themselves upfront via co-operative banking systems, and interlocking seamlessly into a global economy.

The Techno-hippies of the Sharing Economy

In many normal economic situations we produce separately and consume separately, mediated by arm's-length exchanges. Collaborative approaches seek to move us towards producing together and consuming together, mediated at least in part by reciprocated gifts. Various incarnations of collaborative economies can already be seen. Take for example:

- The Hub community, of which I am part, which is a series of shared working spaces for freelance individuals and social entrepreneurship start-ups. These Hubs have developed an internal culture similar to co-operative villages, with networks of individuals and groups that work for themselves, and for each other, and for the outside world. They also interconnect to other Hubs around the world via an online platform.

- 'Commons-thinking', which entails viewing resources being held collectively in trust over which people hold usufruct, the right of enjoyment. You see this principle underlying initiatives like the Creative Commons license, which relies on people sharing content that others can then build on, and the Open Source movement, where people collaborate to produce software and then share it. This also connects to Clay Shirky's concept of 'cognitive surplus', describing the situation, frequently seen in internet communities, where individuals loosely share with each other and contribute incrementally to each other's projects, collectively producing something in their spare time rather than individually and passively consuming things.
- Many new 'collaborative consumption' start-ups seek to get people actively collaborating in their consumption patterns, both to save resources and to build relationships. Localised versions of this are manifested in the Transition Town Movement, where people may seek to transform unused private space into common space, and minimise the use of resources via sharing.

Many of these principles of co-operative culture come intuitively to people. The market economy is in a constant dialectic with a largely unrecognised gift economy, and many of our day-to-day exchanges are in fact non-monetary. When I casually talk to my friend at the pub, I am exchanging information with him. I don't demand payment for it, but there is a subtle system of reciprocity at play. If, for example, he silently stared at me and said nothing, he would be in breach of this reciprocity, and I would feel wronged.

Sharing economy start-ups attempt to re-introduce this intuitive concept into areas that have been explicitly marketised and governed by monetary exchange. One theory of marketisation and monetisation is that it enables us to resolve co-ordination problems and trust problems: I don't personally know anyone who has a jacket that I need for winter, so I'm forced to go to a market to find it; the clothing store owner there doesn't know me, so they don't trust me to reciprocate in the future, so they demand payment 'on the spot' in money, which they do trust because society more generally trusts in it. Money solves the lack of immediate trust between two given individuals, but is almost too easy, perhaps reinforcing the arm's-length relationship. A sharing economy platform such as Freecycle, on the other hand, attempts to replace this monetary exchange with reciprocated gifts. You find someone who has a spare jacket they no longer need and you arrange to pick it up from their house. There is no expectation of payment, but there is an implicit expectation that they will be able to claim something from a pool of goods that you are also contributing to over time. Freecycle relies on reciprocity, and only works if everyone on aggregate gives as well as takes.

Sharing economy approaches have been greatly enabled by online network technology. StreetBank, for example, enables neighbours to connect up within an online community: If someone has a lawnmower in the neighbourhood, they can list it, and others can borrow it. Naturally, these platforms have limitations imposed by the capacity of individuals to connect personally with others: I may be happy to share my amplification system with someone on my street who is having a party, but what about a stranger who lives many miles away? One area of Sharing economy development is thus the creation of trust metrics – such as Trust Cloud – so that people who don't know each other directly can engage in sharing type exchanges by seeing someone's trustworthiness 'score'. Social media helps in this process – for example, via a platform like LinkedIn we can begin to see degrees of connection between individuals. Perhaps the stranger knows a friend of a friend of mine, and the relationship of trust can flow via our friends as intermediaries.

Platforms like Freecycle and Couchsurfing.org (which enables global travellers to sleep for free on peoples' spare couches around the world) can lead to vibrant communities forming in which monetary exchange is avoided altogether and where people get to meet each other. Some even begin to take on a cult-like significance to those who participate: Couchsurfers gather together for couchsurfing parties, while elaborate carpooling networks have developed into an alternative version of hitchhiker culture. Some sharing economy events, such as the Burning Man festival in the USA, take the form of self-governing celebrations of alternative exchange.

(Reciprocated) Time is Money

A comparatively well-known sharing economy innovation is *timebanking*. I spend two hours teaching you how to play guitar, and I earn two hour credits in return from you. A centralised exchange keeps a record of this, and allows me to use my credits with anyone in the system. Over time, people dip in and out of debit and credit – if I've spent too much time claiming services from people, I'll eventually have to start giving back. Some people have (incorrectly) seen timebanking as an attempt to live out the 'labour theory of value', loosely seeing an hour of one person's time as equivalent to another person's. In reality, labour value is more complex than that – a computer programmer has to spend hundreds of hours developing their craft before they can get to a point where they will be able to use that skill to help someone. Thus, while it may superficially appear that their hour requires the same amount of energy as someone who is offering to clear your back-yard for an hour, timebanking platforms often struggle to convince people to offer high-end skills that have taken many years to perfect. People thus normally use them to engage in activities outside their main line of work, or as a way to meet people and build community.

An important and often overlooked function of these alternative exchange systems is to get people to think about mainstream currency differently. Normal money lulls us into a complacent acquiescence, but the peculiarities of using an alternative force a deeper reflection on exchange, and with it, financial services. For example, as I muse about timebanking, I ask myself the question 'If money were measured in units of time, what would borrowing such money entail?' It seems the answer would be that borrowing time-units is the equivalent of a series of people coming to help you with something, which you reciprocally repay at a later date by helping them with something. This takes us back into the deep history of money, which according to David Graeber in his book *Debt: The First 5000 Years* (2011) did not develop to replace on-the-spot barter (as traditional economics insists), but rather developed from reciprocal mutual exchange processes. For example, imagine a friend makes you supper, and when you leave you say 'I owe you a supper in return.' Now imagine that was written down on a piece on paper. Now imagine it widened into a general statement saying 'I owe you general goods and services' and etched into a piece of pretty metal or paper. That's our current money. It abstracts a single trust relationship into a generalised trust relationship which is prone to appearing as an abstract thing-in-itself as we use it in everyday on-the-spot transactions. Thinking back in time from this point, we often imagine a lost age of 'barter', without much proof that it ever existed in any pure form.

AUTO-DISRUPTION: ESTABLISHING FEEDBACK LOOPS

This sense that we are seeing growing networks of co-ordinated yet decentralised production and consumption is beginning to get recognised by management thinkers such as Don Tapscott and Anthony Williams, who co-wrote *Wikinomics: How Mass Collaboration Changes Everything* (2006), and Yochai Benkler, who writes about commons-based peer production. There are management gurus who advocate 'sociocracy', company structures working on consent-based decision-making among informed individuals in inter-linked semi-autonomous circles, inspired by cybernetic theory.

An open-source economic movement requires an open-source finance movement that moves beyond the old concepts of co-operative finance such as mutual building societies and credit unions. For example, can we design systems for the freelance community – who struggle to access traditional financing – to tide each other over when things are tough? Or finance each other's projects, either in the form of money, or in the form of collaboration time? These are all open questions, and much like all open-source processes, answering them relies on simultaneous collaboration and dissent, constant challenge and re-testing. I may be able to design a new P2P financing platform, but I don't actually know whether it will achieve its aim of making the financial system more democratic and intuitive to people. Perhaps it initially works, but gradually ends up getting co-opted for negative ends. This outcome should be fed back as an input into communities of collaborators who can offer critical reflection, and use it as raw material for their own ongoing experimentation.

Over the last few years I've taken part in the Finance Innovation Lab, which was set up to act as a focal point for the alternative finance community, helping to collect information from a network of practitioners, relaying it back to them, and presenting it to the outside world. It thus serves, along with other similar initiatives around the world, as a feedback mechanism. If we dig deeper into the features of such a feedback system, three key principles stand out:

- *Feedback principle 1: Bring people together*. There are thousands of alternative finance projects scattered around the globe, but they still lack co-ordination, which means the partial knowledge they hold remains disconnected. For example, I may be unaware that someone is working on a community banking concept in Brazil, and only years later do I discover that it was a fantastic idea which lacked some element, in my possession, which it needed to continue. Partial, distributed, knowledge becomes more useful when combined with knowledge from others.
- *Feedback principle 2: Bring diverse people together*. Initiatives like the Finance Lab explicitly aim to bring a range of *different* people together. This differs from the traditional network, which is often built around people with common beliefs. A feedback network has to have inbuilt checks on groupthink, and the quickest way to rupture deep assumptions and transcend standard paradigms is to build in a diversity that encourages people to interact with others who think differently. What does

a pastor think about your idea, or an anthropologist? The Bloomsbury Group, which included figures like John Maynard Keynes, Virginia Woolf and Bertrand Russell, is a well-known example of a *multidisciplinary group* that met informally to debate and share ideas. Many more of these informal salons are needed.

- *Feedback principle 3: Disdain for hierarchy.* Finance is often a realm of experts, who may disagree on some levels, but who frequently display tacit agreement on basic precepts. A feedback system has to carry with it an inherent disdain for such stagnant hierarchy, moving away from expert panel discussions and towards free association between diverse participants. While it may be efficient to conduct a controlled university research programme into designing an electric car, attempts to alter large-scale interconnected systems are inherently more chaotic, requiring a mindset more like that of a jazz fusion improvisation.

Get Dancing! Beta-Testing the Future

Not everyone has the time to set about building alternatives to mainstream finance, but one thing anyone can do is to simply test out alternatives in their spare time. Using alternative finance platforms is a quick way to put your money where your mouth is, and allows one to speak from the heart about the alternatives available. In some radical circles, this concept of 'prefigurative politics' – sometimes described as 'being the change you want to see in the world' – is criticised as naive. Many revolutionary concepts though, begin with small groups of individuals acting a part to inspire others to join in, which then can feed on itself via *network effects*.

Facebook, for example, only exploded after a certain critical mass was reached. Likewise, a person may design a great mutual credit platform, but until it gains critical mass it will tend to languish in illiquidity, making transactions difficult because there are too few people. Acting as an early adopter of alternatives can help induce critical mass, allowing them to be activated or 'magnetised' via network effects. A useful activity for progressive justice organisations could simply be to encourage their membership bases to use alternative finance platforms and thus help build a small army of beta-testers. One fantastic example of this principle can be seen in a fun YouTube video called 'Guy starts dance party at Sasquatch Music Festival'. In it, an exuberant man dances by himself on a hill overlooking a concert while people watch him in bemused fashion. Then two others join him. Then a few more. Suddenly, waves of people are racing across the hill to join him, forming a huge high-spirited mass, sucking more in like a magnet.

Alternative Investment Management: Start a #FutureOfMoney Fund

One cheeky way to get dancing is to build a hedge fund specialising in truly alternative finance. Such a fund could help kickstart liquidity in alternative platforms and draw media attention. Here's how I would do it:

Phase 1: Draw up the asset allocation and decide what it will support. Mine will include:

- Long-term credit: Zopa loans, Abundance renewable energy debentures.
- Short-term credit: Invoice finance loans to small companies on MarketInvoice.
- Currency trading: P2P currency trading on CurrencyFair, and Bitcoin trading.
- Equity portfolio: Shares from Seedrs, and Brixton Energy community shares.

Phase 2: Raise money for the fund using a crowd-funding platform like Indiegogo. Aim to raise around £25,000. Those who contribute £20 get back-access into the website and forum. Those who donate £50 get to receive personalised financial reports. Those that donate £100 get to be part of the core investment advisory committee.

Phase 3: Launch a publicity campaign around the fund and start trading. Reinvest any profits back into artistic Kickstarter projects, or give them out as gifts via timebanks or sharing economy projects such as #punkmoney. Graffiti your financial reports in the side streets of Canary Wharf.

Building Viral Immunity: Becoming an Activist Enterprise

Many activist groups find themselves embroiled in battles to win grant financing from large foundations. It's inherently limiting and unhealthy, locking them into an 'NGO-Industrial complex' reliant on donations from wealthy firms and people. Why not use this as a spur to develop the financial system of the future, actively seeking new ways to create self-sustaining activist enterprises that don't rely on grants. Try out crowd-funding approaches, or design a community shares system to support your local projects. Start a mutual credit system between activist groups, or design an inter-group alternative currency as a simple means to demonstrate alternatives while simultaneously unlocking new resources. Create networks of hybrid organisations without labour contracts, built solely on equity financed principles. Radicalism doesn't go viral by relying on charitable foundations. Rather, like all good viruses, it goes viral by building an immunity to barriers.

Conclusion

In Yann Martel's book *Life of Pi*, a boy named Pi finds himself sharing a life-raft with an enormous Bengal tiger. Trying to push the tiger off the life-raft is not an option. Likewise with the financial system – it is part of our lives, and we need deeper frameworks in order to come to terms with it.

OCCUPY 7.0: A SEVEN-YEAR VISION FOR BUILDING A COMMUNITY OF HERETICS

A friend of mine who studies martial arts recently let me in on a catchy mantra used by various kung fu experts: 'You've got to go slow to go fast.' It struck me as a good way to see financial change. We often sense that the system needs to be changed *right now*. We may obsess about current leadership figures like Lloyd Blankfein of Goldman Sachs or Jamie Dimon of J.P. Morgan. Focusing too much on the present is part of the reason why, when the crisis hit, the opportunity to advance more profound structural reforms was largely missed: There simply weren't enough blueprints or examples for alternative models in the pipeline.

Ignoring short-term distractions is what creates speed. I believe that more energy should be focused on building schematics for policies and systems ahead of time, imagining how the future financial landscape might look, and how the vulnerabilities will have shifted. It doesn't need to be far into the future, perhaps five to seven years. In that time major financial centres could become the playgrounds of activist collectives built around the three central principles of exploring, jamming and building. This mixing of anthropology, the Hacker Ethos, and Do-it-Yourself culture has the potential to impact on capital flows across the world, and when financial crises present themselves, such collectives will have coherent and robust responses.

Calling all Policy Wonks

For people who have a taste for policy, there are opportunities to develop a battery of future policy proposals that can be released into the system. Chris Hewett of the Finance Innovation Lab's Disruptive Finance Policy Programme has developed a useful framework for thinking about this. For example, future policy initiatives are needed to:

- *Break down short-termism in markets*: This may include accounting reforms to account for long-term social and environmental costs embedded in short-term financial returns, and tax reforms to encourage long-term sustainable investment, or to encourage long-term equity holdings over debt.
- *Diversify away from banking monocultures*: This includes building policy frameworks that encourage local banking and new banks, developing appropriate and fair regulation for innovations such as peer-to-peer finance, and boosting green finance by making instruments like green bonds eligible for inclusion in pension plans.
- *Increase transparency, while reducing complexity and systemic risk*: This may include disclosure initiatives calling for transparency in bank loans and pension fund holdings. It includes combating 'too-big-to-fail' (TBTF) banks, reducing tax incentives that encourage excessive debt, and promoting new governance structures for banks. It also entails regulating the political lobbying power of large financial institutions, and increasing transparency in bodies like the City of London Corporation.

When considering policy, attention should also be given to financial professionals lower down the ranks, the ones who will displace the managers above them in the years to come. Perhaps less attention should be focused on the excesses of banks, and more on the quieter ecosystems of the young accountants, lawyers, insurers and credit raters who enable their operations. The mindset of the 2013 vintage of graduates going into The Big Four accounting firms right now could have profound consequences for business behaviour across the world in 2018. My conversation with Joe from KPMG at a 2013 house party may manifest in Joe slamming down the phone on a bolshy oil executive in 2025, refusing to sign off on a damaging project.

Explore the Darkness

Exploring the apparent darkness of finance is liberating: Constant exploration explodes overly complex abstractions, allowing you to zoom out and see the bigger picture, and zoom in to see the deep code. Walking freely within financial systems involves personal reflection. It can be as simple as spending an hour in the City, reflecting on what money is, and how it flows. It helps to bring hidden fears to the surface and to immunise one's mind against the various pieces of mental spam that download themselves as you interact via financial structures. Like Parkour enthusiasts, who spend their time running and jumping over walls, the idea is to *displace* yourself, such that walls no longer appear as 'walls', but rather as opportunities.

Ride the Tiger

Experiential learning, gonzo journalism and culture-hacking are highly underutilised tools of subversion and I really encourage people to help develop these techniques. Even simple exercises like buying a share, or playing poker to understand probabilities, can dissolve the abstract crystalline rigidity of much macroeconomics, or dispel the vague imprecision of popular theories. Blurring the 'self-other divide' enables access to otherwise daunting systems and allows one to detect the deeper cultural principles within them. It helps one understand how money flows might be diverted, or how financial instruments might be used to protect those with less power.

Be the Tiger

If we reflect deeply on the *Life of Pi* scenario though, we see that it's not only the life of Pi that matters. The tiger is a living creature too. Above all, *Life of Pi* sketches a portrait of the deep commonality of plight among all creatures. We can see it in our own lives every lunchtime when every single creature goes and does the same thing, regardless of who they are, and at night, when everyone sleeps. In one sense, there is only one creature in the boat, trying to come to terms with itself. Finance should not be thought of as something out there, run by other people. Sure, there's an entrenched power structure, but even Lords of Finance like Jamie Dimon have secret hopes and fears, just like anyone else.

Perhaps it's like the closing scene in *Fight Club*, where Edward Norton's character suddenly realises that he's not fighting Dyler Durden at all, but rather a darker element of himself. The financial dark ages are collectively reinforced and amplified in people's heads, and we remain deferential to its established boundaries, lacking a sense of personal engagement. We refer to mainstream finance workers, normatively, as 'financial professionals', but such individuals happen to be doing but one style of finance. Furthermore, a trader will not be engaged by being told that they're bad. They will be engaged by seeing a radical buzz, camaraderie, creativity and intellectual challenge that they're missing out on. Rather than snarling at the devout iconography in the gallery of mainstream finance, we should be iconoclasts, defacing the rich-old-dude portraits with rebellious Banksy-style installations.

The Moby Dick Economy

Writing this book has helped me organise my own ideas, and I thank you for taking the time to read it. I look forward to further seedbombing, circuitbending, culture-hacking and general shit-stirring, hopefully with you. I was asked to write a 'further resources' section too. Most further resources are found in one's natural environment, but the following are also useful:

- If you can get your hands on *The Oxford Book of Money* by Kevin Jackson it provides hundreds of fascinating excerpts from literature, letters and poetry, tracing people's perceptions of finance through the ages. In reading these, you can identify facets of your own thinking on these issues.

- If you'd like a conventional, but good, account of financial markets, try the *Financial Times Guide to Financial Markets*.
- If you want to get seriously hardcore, I thoroughly recommend downloading Aswath Damodaran's free corporate finance courses from his website (Damodaran Online). He basically wrote the manual on corporate finance that many investment banks use, and he has an entertaining, irreverent style of teaching. Getting your head around his courses is a good step towards decommissioning Goldman Sachs.
- A good free downloadable resource is *The Campaigner's Guide to Financial Markets* by Nick Hildyard and Mark Mansley. It's from 2001, so is slightly out of date, but has 200 pages worth of detailed tips and extensive resources for shareholder activism and financial lobbying. It can be found at www.thecornerhouse.org.uk

My favourite book on finance though, is called *Moby Dick*. It traces the story of Ishmael, who joins up with a motley crew of undiversified equity investors, full of energy, on a mad search for a white whale. They're not even sure if the whale exists, or whether it's just a projection of their imagination. If you only read one chapter, read the one called 'Fast-Fish and Loose-Fish'. It focuses on ownership claims. Whoever expends energy throwing their harpoon into the whale can claim it. If they hit, it's a Fast-fish. If they miss, it's a Loose-fish. It ends with the line 'And what are you, reader, but a Loose-fish and a Fast-fish too?' Different people read different things into that, but maybe that's the point. Finance is a set of tools, techniques and interconnected relationships waiting to be hacked. As Erich Fromm said, 'creativity requires the courage to let go of certainties', so get out on the high seas, Ishmael, and just do it.

Further Resources

My blog www.suitpossum.blogspot.com has extensive lists of resources on financial activism, alternative finance and economic anthropology. My YouTube channel (Suitpossum) also has useful video playlists covering a wide range of areas, from financial basics, to debates around high-frequency trading and speculation, to alternative currencies and sharing economy innovations.

OpenCourseWare Resources

iTunes University and YouTube EDU are great resources for finding free online courses (opencourseware) from top universities. There are many good courses in finance and economics, but I recommend the following:

- Prof. Robert Shiller's Yale Econ 252 course on financial markets: http://oyc.yale.edu/economics/econ-252-11
- Prof John Geanakoplos Yale Econ 251 course on financial theory: http://oyc.yale.edu/economics/econ-251
- Aswath Damodaran's website contains video and audio of his NYU Stern business school courses on corporate finance and valuation. Very technical and yet very manageable: http://pages.stern.nyu.edu/~adamodar
- The Khan Academy has great sections on finance: www.khanacademy.org

Financial Activism Resources and Financial Campaigns

There have been many interesting campaigns on the financial sector over the years, and resources built to help people in financial activism. Here is a selection to consider:

- Nick Hildyard and Mark Mansley's free e-book, *The Campaigners' Guide to Financial Markets* is available at www.thecornerhouse.org.uk/resource/campaigners%E2%80%99-guide-financial-markets
- FairPensions, for shareholder activism resources: www.fairpensions.org.uk
- BankTrack, for information on bank financing of destructive projects: www.banktrack.org

- Finance Watch, for financial policy initiatives: www.finance-watch. org
- Platform London, for information on fossil fuel finance: http:// platformlondon.org/oil-the-arts/fossil-fuel-finance
- Corporate Europe Observatory, for information on financial lobbying: http://corporateeurope.org/financial-lobby
- The Tax Justice Network, for information on tax havens: http:// www.taxjustice.net
- The Global Witness banking campaign, for information on financing of dictators: www.globalwitness.org/campaigns/banks
- 350.org's fossil fuel divestment campaign: http://gofossilfree.org
- The Rainforest Action Network's campaign against Bank of America's coal financing: http://ran.org/bank-america
- The Robin Hood Tax campaign: http://robinhoodtax.org.uk
- The World Development Movement's food speculation campaign: www.wdm.org.uk/food-speculation
- The Berne Declaration's work on commodities trading: http:// www.evb.ch/en/p19492.html
- Sandbag's work on climate change and emissions trading: www. sandbag.org.uk

Alternative Finance Resources

There are too many alternative finance projects to list here, but check out the following sites for a start:

- MoveYourMoney UK, for information on ethical banking alternatives: www.moveyourmoney.org.uk
- The Finance Innovation Lab, for alternative finance events and resources: www.thefinancelab.org
- The New Economics Foundation, for alternative banking research: http://www.neweconomics.org/programmes/finance-business
- The P2P Foundation, for peer-to-peer innovations: http:// p2pfoundation.net
- The UK Sustainable Investment and Finance Association, for responsible investment information: http://uksif.org
- The Global Impact Investing Network, for resources on social finance: www.thegiin.org/cgi-bin/iowa/investing/index.html
- London New Finance, for fintech events and reports: http://www. london.newfinance.org

Index